Songquest

Great Lakes Books

*A complete listing of the books in this series
can be found online at http://wsupress.wayne.edu*

SONGQUEST

THE *Journals* OF *Great Lakes Folklorist* *Ivan H. Walton*

EDITED BY

JOE GRIMM

Introduction by Laurie Kay Sommers

WAYNE STATE UNIVERSITY PRESS   DETROIT

Library of Congress Cataloging-in-Publication Data

Songquest : the journals of Great Lakes folklorist Ivan H. Walton / edited by Joe Grimm ;
introduction by Laurie Kay Sommers.
p. cm. — (Great Lakes books)
Includes bibliographical references and index.
ISBN 0-8143-3234-X (pbk. : alk. paper)
1. Sea songs—Great Lakes—History and criticism. 2. Folk music—Great Lakes—
History and criticism. 3. Walton, Ivan. I. Walton, Ivan. II. Grimm, Joe. III. Series.
ML3551.7.G74S65 2005
782.42162'130774—dc22
2004022771

Published with the assistance of a fund established by Thelma Gray James
of Wayne State University for the publication of folklore and English studies.

CONTENTS

PREFACE

The Great Depression, Prohibition, and "red-hot" socialism took center stage in America in the 1930s as the drama of an earlier age quietly closed. That bygone drama was the birth of industrialization, the rise of capitalism, and mechanical mastery of nature. As the curtain fell, one man was there to record the final lines of the actors who had played out that drama on the Great Lakes. He was Ivan H. Walton, and he was on a quest. His quest was to save the songs of the vanished days of sail.

That the songs were saved at all is remarkable; that Walton was the man who did it is incredible. Walton was not a sailor, he did not grow up near the Great Lakes, and he was not born until steamships had put sailboats on the run. Walton was born in 1893 to a farming family in Rosebush, as far away as one could get from a Great Lake in his part of Michigan's Lower Peninsula. But Walton did not take to farming. His 1913 college yearbook bore a photo of "Walt" with the notation, "Blessed is agriculture, if one does not have too much of it." Walton earned a teaching certificate at Central State Normal School, later renamed Central Michigan University. In the years after he left Mount Pleasant, Walton taught, coached, tried his hand at newspaper reporting, and spent nineteen months in the United States Air Services. He settled down at the University of Michigan, where he earned bachelor's and master's degrees in English and met Mildred D. Hallett, who would become his wife. In 1919 he joined the faculty of the English Department in the College of Engineering at the University of Michigan and taught until his retirement in 1963. There, he initially began compiling an anthology of Great Lakes literature, but voices from his youth steered him onto a new course. He remembered a cousin who had visited the farm at Rosebush and entertained his family with songs and stories from the woods and water. He remembered hearing sailors singing in a waterfront saloon in the fruit-packing port town of Muskegon, Michigan, during his first years of teaching. He suddenly realized that there was a potentially more valuable and fragile body of material to be collected: the songs and stories of the working man.

Walton set out in the summer of 1932 to gather into a book the songs that had been sung by working men in the age of sail, songs that steamboats had stilled more than thirty years earlier. Walton expected obstacles. People had warned him that age, drink, and death had silenced many of the songs. They were right. They had not, however, prepared him for the riches he would find, even in tattered remnants, of the lost age of sail. Nor had they prepared him for the people he would meet. There were men—and a few women—who had sailed, as he had expected, but there also were captains of tugs and steamboats, tenders of locks and canals, and keepers of boardinghouses and lighthouses. Each group had its own traditions. The sheer volume and variety of it all nearly drowned Walton. The songbook? He never finished it. After his death in 1968, a friend explained that Walton's unwritten book was a sign that he had simply seen and heard too much to fit between covers. Walton discovered not just songs but stories, beliefs, and traditions. The people he had met were not just sources but flesh-and-blood people with real lives built—or broken—on the inland seas.

Walton, part professor, part journalist and part folklorist, unearthed a variety of material within his specialty. We are fortunate that he left such extensive and detailed notes. His song notes became *Windjammers: Songs of the Great Lakes Sailors* (Wayne State University Press, 2002). His field notes became this book. Walton longhanded his way across hundreds of pages in the summers of 1932, 1933, 1934, and 1938. He wrote about the men and traditions of the past, the Depression and Prohibition of the present, and his own longings and frustrations.

The people Walton met told how the steamboat, with its promise of reliable schedules and cheaper rates, pushed the Great Lakes schooner under. Schooner owners countered by trimming crews and wages. They introduced animals and then machines to do the heavy work. Finally, they stripped away the sticks and sails and had tugs tow the once-proud schooners around by their noses. Captain William R. Dunn of Cleveland reflected typical sailor pride when he told Walton, "Life aboard the old schooners was a dog's life. In fact, no one now would make a dog live in the quarters we had, nor eat the food we ate. And often we had only snatches of sleep day after day during bad weather. But, by God, I'd do it again if I had the chance! A vessel under canvas is alive—you'd feel it, an' how we'd drive 'em! But them damn steamboats are just lifeless machines with no personality."

As the sailors' livelihood faded, so did their reading of weather signs, their stories, and their songs. The specialized knowledge that had once made them feel superior to landsmen had become as anachronistic and irrelevant as the vessels it helped them sail. They stopped talking about this material and, by the time Walton reached them, many said they had not thought about it for thirty years or more. Walton walked the crumbly edge between memory and history, saving what he could. Several people he had interviewed in 1934 were dead by the time he came back to see them in 1938. Others couldn't "fetch up" the material or had false memories. Some lied and others died before he ever got to them. The gauzy material he sought changed with every telling.

Walton developed a whole bag of memory aids including flattery, feigned ignorance, persistence, and old photos to prime and pump his contacts. Cigars, cigarettes, whiskey, and beer worked even better with some. His sources were, overall, vulnerable, weakened by the loss of their livelihood and hardened by the deprivations of the Great Depression. Their time running out, down on their luck, hobbled by hard lives on ships and in saloons, they faced ends as bleak as those of their dead vessels. In Milwaukee in 1932 Walton noted, "Back downtown, I learned at the mission that Mr. House had been at the company 'alms house' for a year. There were about a hundred men—certainly a forlorn looking group—awaiting a handout. A tragedy here in big numbers. Had a small lunch. Gave my eats money and some more to an old fellow who appears about at the bottom."

Walton took minutely detailed notes, not just on the songs but on his informants. He occasionally missed a first name—and some of his informants were vague on those—but he rarely omitted a guess at the informant's age and often included a physical description. In his early journals, Walton reconstructed interviews, line by line, showing his tacks and tracks as a researcher. He seldom judged the people he met, though he sometimes described them with an objectivity they would find unflattering. He almost always called them "Captain" or "Mister," even though he came to believe that being a Great Lakes captain was much like being a Southern Colonel. He would rather go for a long ride in the country with a loudmouth he knew would spoil his search that day than ask the person to stay behind. He couldn't bring himself to ask interfering people to leave the room, preferring to return the next day. Sometimes, he copied down a whole song he had already recorded, just to demonstrate interest. Still, there were times. One evening he wrote in exasperation, "[T]he assistant librarian was a young girl who seemed to have a great vacancy where some knowledge should be." After another frustrating, dead-end day he wrote, "I never felt so much like choking anyone before in a long time. It takes him ages to tell an incident, and when he gets to the point—there isn't any."

Walton's most frequent complaint was that "[n]obody is where they should be." He didn't seem to recognize that he fit that description, too. He was, after all, an English professor who taught in a college of engineering. A self-described dry-land sailor, Walton was asking mariners about their ways and what-fors forty years after those practices had become obsolete. With his neatly trimmed mustache and notebook, Walton was as out of place as a professor at a pier. He once noted, "One should wear old clothes and a couple days' beard when about the waterfront. Summer clothes cause suspicion." A few days later, having approached some men working on a vessel, he wrote, "They eyed me suspiciously. I should have had on old clothes." His personal taste in music had Walton ducking into churches and theaters for lofty music such as Leoncavallo's opera Pagliacci or Paderewski's *Moonlight Sonata*. Sunsets made Walton think of Wagner. About his business, though, Walton teased doggerel out of "Gasoline" George, "Foghorn," "Mountain Dew," and Bob "Brokenback" Collen.

It seems that Walton, "Mountain Dew," "Brokenback," and all the rest got to know and respect each other. Although Walton knew that these men had worked aboard leaky vessels, ate weevily food, and had nothing to sleep on but wet, lice-infested straw, he found their lives romantic. On a Lake Michigan crossing he wrote, "I think I would find a sailor's life quite to my liking." Another time, he put down, "I've decided that in my next life I'll spend most of it on water." He admired these men. Recalling his interview with one captain, Walton wrote, "His life-saving experience makes a landsman feel rather small and useless."

Walton's greatest burden was the solitude. He fell into pits of loneliness during his summertime sojourns. He dearly loved his wife, Mildred, whom he affectionately called "Peter," and their son, Lynn, yet he chose to spend week after week away from them. Late one night in his first summer out he wrote, "Just returned from a four-hour midnight walk—that or off the deep end. Sunday night and no mail until tomorrow—if then and God, oh God, it's lonesome." In later summers, he arranged for his wife and son to visit him or he visited home.

With his feet firmly planted in two places at once, Walton was just the sort of person for the job. He was able to get far enough into the world he was examining to understand it but stayed distant enough to keep his focus.

A few notes on the editing of these journals are in order. First of all, these are interviews with sailors, not saints. Some used blue or racist language. The journals have been edited but not steam-cleaned. That would be dishonest and portray life on the Lakes as more genteel than it was. Raw language seldom added anything to a story, but Walton kept it as an inherent part of the storyteller. For several speakers, Walton tried to record their stories in dialect. That has been preserved, too, though editing has brought some consistency to those passages.

This volume contains less than half of Walton's journals. After his travels, he marked parts of them—perhaps one-fourth—to be typed. Those excerpts, apparently chosen and polished by Walton himself, are in here. The editor added a like amount of similar material but used more of the personal reflections than Walton had included. What is not here? Walton and the editor omitted many dead-ends, disappointments, and duplications. Addresses for the leads he was pursuing are left out for privacy, and references to university colleagues and graduates he encountered are limited. Some passages about local history that did not relate to the Lakes have been cut, and some of his descriptions of scenery have been omitted.

As much as he wrote in his journals each day, they do not include everything Walton saw or heard. Walton also kept separate notes on song lyrics and the sources for that material. Comparisons of his score notations and these journals show that a person he credits with giving him a song might not show up in the journal at all. It seems he felt he had already covered the informant in the score notes and did not have to also include them in the journals. In several places, the editor has incorporated lyrics from Walton's song notes into the proper places in this book to give the reader a fuller sense of Walton's experiences and the songs that he found.

As you follow the journals, you will see that Walton's quarry changed. He started after songs but became interested in weather signs and beliefs. You'll see him investigate a new subject, dig in, and then ease off when repetition tells him he has uncovered most of it. The index will help you find the weather lore and beliefs scattered throughout the journals.

Brackets indicate additions made in the editing.

We must first recognize Ivan Walton's wife, Mildred, and son, Lynn, who weathered long separations from Walton as he went song-gathering. In later years, after Lynn had grown and married, Lynn's wife, Sue, dedicated hundreds of hours to helping Walton compile and transcribe parts of his field notes. They come to us from the careful hands of archivists at the University of Michigan's Bentley Historical Library. Similar care at the Historical Collections of the Great Lakes preserved the artwork of Loudon Wilson, whose work was donated by his sons Craig, Alan, Gary, and Thomas.

Several individuals with an interest in the lore of the Lakes were essential to imbuing the journals with the context that gives them meaning and texture. First among them is Dr. Laurie Kay Sommers, whose writing describes the significance of Walton's work to the world of folklore. Besides having a deep understanding of folklore, she has unique knowledge of Walton's work and Beaver Island, having followed his trail across many of the places he visited and the pages he wrote.

A small, ad hoc confederation of historians read early drafts, suggested improvements, and offered leads to answers and artwork. They are John Polacsek, a marine curator who knows seemingly unknowable things about Great Lakes maritime history; Lee Murdock, whose guiding star is, "What would Professor Walton do?"; and Gordon Olson, formerly the Grand Rapids city historian, who has an editor's eye.

Thanks to F. S. Fluker, a talented graphic artist at the *Detroit Free Press,* for the maps. Thanks, also, to Elizabeth B. Sherman, for support and for sharing some of her research for her book, *Beyond the Windswept Dunes: The Story of Maritime Muskegon* (Wayne State University Press, 2003). Former *Ann Arbor News* editor Arthur Gallagher, whose grandmother, Rose, was one of the first people Walton met, contributed a photograph and his warm support of the project.

Professional stewards of history, thanks to Arthur Woodford and Cynthia Biniek of the St. Clair Shores Library; Carol Clausen and Elizabeth Tunis at the National Library of Medicine's History of Medicine Division; and Matthew Barton at the Alan Lomax Archives in New York.

I am grateful for the support, mild threats, and help I received from Jane Hoehner, director of Wayne State University Press, and for the assistance of her whole staff, especially those who worked most closely on this book: Danielle DeLucia Burgess and Jennifer Backer.

Finally and most intensely, a long overdue thanks to the scores of men and women who gave these journals their content and color by plumbing their memories for the stories, song, and lore of a vanishing way of life.

INTRODUCTION

Ivan H. Walton and American Folklore

Laurie Kay Sommers

In the summer of 1932, folklorist Ivan Walton began his first collecting trip in search of the vanishing songs of Great Lakes sailors. On June 23, he packed a temperamental folding bed into an old Dodge and drove to the Lake Michigan shore at South Haven. On this trip, he wrote the first of four field logs that are excerpted in *Songquest*. As an academic folklorist, Walton understood the research value of keeping detailed records of his travels. These logs provide rare insight into the methods, experiences, personality, and findings of the pioneering collector of nineteenth-century Great Lakes sailor lore. Walton ultimately assembled one of the great occupational folklore collections in the United States.

In a 1939 letter to an acquaintance, Walton described the focus and importance of his work as follows:

> I have had the good fortune of being able to spend a number of my vacation periods on and about the Great Lakes and have taken advantage of this opportunity to assemble all that I could of the extant lore that is associated with these lakes. I have visited all the ports on both the American and Canadian sides and have talked to scores of old sailors, and from them I have assembled a considerable body of yarns, legends, superstitions, weather sayings, shanties, amusement songs, and other such material that grew out of commercial navigation. I have been particularly interested in sailor life and the lore that came out of it during the last half of the last century when the bulk of commerce between the lake ports was carried in sailing vessels. Life aboard these old schooners, barques, fore-'n-afters, and even sailing barges had a quality that was especially conducive to the growth of stories and songs. The material I have assembled, as far as I have been able to learn, is the only collection of its kind in existence. Some of it is a bit rough, as should be expected, but all of it is redolent of the devil-may-care, colorful, and often tragic life out of which it grew.

Walton's "assembled material" includes far more than the four field logs of the 1930s excerpted here. The Ivan Walton Collection also contains sound recordings made from 1938–60, tape transcripts, correspondence, published and unpublished manuscripts, student class materials, notes, clippings, 3 x 5 card files, and photos that cover an astonishing array of topics related to Great Lakes culture. Although each part of the collection has its own value, anyone who wishes to have a full understanding of Walton's findings and achievements should examine the collection in its entirety. The materials are housed at the Bentley Historical Library of the University of Michigan; partial copies are available at the Archive of Folk Culture at the Library of Congress and the Traditional Arts Research Collection at the Michigan State University Museum.

Ivan Walton was born too late to document the lore of the schoonermen as a living tradition. Already by the 1890s, large steam-powered freighters were supplanting the wooden sailing ships. In 1930, just two years before Walton penned his first field journal, the last Great Lakes schooner, the *Our Son*, was destroyed in a gale. Steamboats had ruled the Lakes for some thirty years. What Walton called "the golden era of Great Lakes sailing vessels" lasted from the 1860s through the 1880s. As he described it in "Songs of the Great Lakes Sailors," this was a period when "shipping of forest products, grains, and especially ores, increased at an astonishing rate, and sailing vessels, because of their economy and adaptability to the traffic and to the shallow harbors connecting river channels, increased in number from a few score to over 1,800. They were individually owned, ranged in size to approximately 600 tons, and were mostly schooner rigged in contrast to the square rig of ocean vessels. Their trips ranged from over night to others lasting from one to several weeks, depending on weather conditions."

Great Lakes schooners once were so commonplace that most nineteenth-century Midwesterners took them for granted. Few observers or actual sailors thought to write about traditions associated with "the great white wings" of the Lakes. This scarcity of information made Walton's tireless efforts to document the personal side of sailor life that much more significant. As a folklorist, Walton was not looking for the official versions of Great Lakes commerce told in government documents or published histories that focused on facts, figures, and events. Rather, he was looking for the lore which, as he put it, "was the common property of the Lakes sailor." The professional sailors of this golden age imported, adapted, and created a body of folklore—stories, songs, beliefs, customs, terminology, values, and attitudes—learned informally and passed on through oral transmission, which strongly reflected their life experience.

Walton came to folklore through the study of American literature in his position as an English professor. In the mid-1930s, he did graduate work in folklore at both the University of Chicago and the University of Illinois. In 1938 he helped found the Michigan Folklore Group, which, in 1940, became the Michigan Folkore Society. Walton served as the society's first president.

During the formative years of Walton's career, folklore scholarship in the United States was divided between literary folklorists who culled written and oral sources for different versions or variants of oral literary texts, and anthropologists who studied folklore in the context of living cultures and looked to its function in society. Walton drew on both approaches. "My interest in the Great Lakes dates back to within a few years of the beginning of my career," he wrote Cleveland author Marie Gilchrist in April 1932, "but only within the last few years have I done much about it when I have, as spare time permitted, been making a bibliography of all the literary material I can find that is expressive of what humans have experienced on and about the Lakes. I am not much interested in historical events, but rather in the human side of these and other phases of Lakes life as it has become crystallized in story and song and in what may in general be called lore. My bibliography now contains over three thousand items and is still far from complete. I have a publisher waiting for it as soon as I get it in shape." This exhaustive search of printed sources was typical of a literary folklorist. So, too, was his focus on oral traditions, beliefs, and customs, as opposed to material culture (which in Walton's day was more the domain of anthropologists) such as crafts, architecture, boat building, food, and the work tools of a sailor's trade. The anthropological influence is most evident in Walton's interest in what sailors' lore revealed about their everyday life. Early on, for example, he categorized sailor songs by their function: work songs, such as the chanteys used to help coordinate tasks onboard ship, and amusement songs sung on watch or in waterfront saloons.

Despite his extensive bibliographic search, Walton found little actual folklore in the printed record. The few exceptions, mostly memoirs of aging lakesmen, proved so tantalizing that Walton abruptly changed his approach. Bolstered by funding through a research grant from the University of Michigan, he postponed his book on Great Lakes literature in anticipation of new material gathered directly from the surviving lakesmen who actually experienced the age of sail. By June 23, 1932, he was on the road, making his first entry into his field log. This journey "into the field" was a momentous step for Walton. He changed from an armchair scholar who relied on published and archival sources to a fieldworker who went into communities where former sailors lived and obtained firsthand information through interviews.

Most collectors of the period kept records of their experiences in the field. Such logs were not written for publication; rather, they were highly personal research tools that recorded the collector's daily activities, moods, and reflections on his or her work. They reveal as much about how a collector worked as they do about what he found. We follow Walton into the seedy sections of old waterfront districts and into private homes and maritime businesses. We feel the heartbreak of an old sailor at the end of his rope or the thrill of a gripping reminiscence, hear similar stories repeated over and over, find that yet another aging sailor had died or was away from home, and then suddenly discover some exciting new lead or information.

The logs contain few descriptions of actual singing, since, as he put it in a 1936 letter to John A. Lomax, "My informants were all old men and mostly beyond the age of melody." The notable exception was on Beaver Island, which Walton visited in 1932, 1938, 1940, and then periodically until his retirement in 1963. The island was Walton's mother lode of folk music. Its predominantly Irish residents had a rich musical culture that drew on Irish roots and the traditions of sailors and lumberjacks whose experiences gave rise to the two great occupational folksong traditions of the nineteenth-century Upper Midwest. As Francie Roddy, born on Beaver Island of Irish parents, told Walton in 1932, "A good Irishman can make up a song if he can't get any any other way." In 1932 Walton first met two Islanders who would become his most recorded informants: fiddler and ballad singer Pat Bonner and ballad singer Johnny Green, both former lakesmen. In 1938, Walton returned to Beaver Island with Alan Lomax, who brought a sound recording machine from the Library of Congress. Lomax, continuing the work of his father, John, had become one of the premier collectors and popularizers of American folk music. Alan Lomax, in describing Green, wrote that he was "one of the most amazing ballad singers who has turned up in America, recorded over a hundred come-all-ye ballads—forecastle, lumberjack, lake sailor, Irish, popular, etc. Since that time he has written that he has recalled a hundred and fifty more."

Before 1938 and his first experience with portable recording machines, Walton used dictation, a technique typical of the period. Some long reminiscences appear in the logs verbatim along with a few song texts. In general, however, song texts and tunes rarely appear in the field logs. Walton usually copied these down separately. His encounter with Beaver Islander Pat Bonner on July 22, 1932, illustrates this process: "I took down from his singing a line at a time 'When First I Went to Sea' and a poem 5 1/2 pages—called 'the Stowaway.' He leaned over my notebook and beat time and pointed with his forefinger and sang a line at a time, and while I was trying to keep up with him he'd explain just what was going on according to the narrative."

While the logs reveal how Walton operated in the field, they do not explain why he collected certain items and omitted others. Walton's approach to folklore was shaped by the intellectual climate of his time. As a scholar interested in a distinctly American genre—the songs of Great Lakes sailors—Walton was part of a growing movement of American folklorists who were challenging the established canons within literary folklore of the late nineteenth and early twentieth centuries. The prevailing view, shaped in large part by influential Harvard ballad scholar Francis James Child and his students, had been that the only authentic, pure, and aesthetically pleasing oral literature in the United States originated in Europe before inferior printed genres polluted oral tradition. These survivals of an earlier time existed only in remote rural regions where time had passed the people by. Child's groundbreaking multivolume work, *The English and Scottish Popular Ballads, 1882–1898*, identified a corpus of 305 classic ballads, referred to as the "Child canon," which met his criteria of age, British origin, and authenticity. These classic Child ballads, as they were called, became the touchstone for much subsequent folksong collection in the United States. Numerous collectors of Walton's early career sought examples of Child ballads rather than material of American origin that reflected a distinctively American experience.

In the wake of World War I, however, American-born collectors like Walton increasingly sought examples of homegrown material that distinguished

American culture from its European roots. The country as a whole finally realized that it had a folklore of its own that could be a source of national pride and identity. Regional folksong collections flourished during this period, as did a growing number of publications about the songs of occupational groups. These included John A. Lomax and Alan Lomax's *Cowboy Songs and Other Frontier Ballads* (1910), Franz Rickaby's *Ballads and Songs of the Shanty-Boy* (1926), which included a few sailor songs, and Earl Clifton Beck's *Songs of the Michigan Lumberjacks* (1941). Some collectors focused on songs of salt-water sailors, with a particular emphasis on chanteys or work songs, but few before Walton collected songs of the inland seas. The notable exception was Rickaby's informant, Michael Cassius (M. C.) Dean, a former sailor and shanty boy from Minnesota, who published texts to several well-known Great Lakes sailor ballads in his collection, *The Flying Cloud* (1922).

Although collectors of Walton's generation broke away from the search for European survivals, they still drew on European concepts of romantic nationalism in their quest for authentic American folklore. Romantic nationalists in Europe believed that the wellspring of true national culture and identity was the oral literature of the European peasantry. Folklore historian Jerrold Hirsch suggests that collectors in the United States viewed isolated groups of Americans, who lived on the edges of society and preserved the lore of America's preindustrial past, as functional equivalents of European peasantry. For John A. Lomax, it was the cowboy. For Ivan Walton, it was the Great Lakes schoonerman. As Walton wrote in a graduate school paper titled "On Ballad Scholarship," Great Lakes schoonermen were a homogeneous group of "unlettered folk, if that term means unsophisticated and unacquainted with book knowledge." Walton and many of his peers were engaged in a race against time to collect the remnants of vanishing oral cultures before they succumbed to progress, industrialization, and rapid change. He focused on the songs and lore of the schoonermen because his academic training led him to believe that theirs was the only authentic Great Lakes marine lore. Progress and modernity, in Walton's worldview, were antithetical to the creation of folklore.

This aspect of Walton's worldview is particularly evident in his treatment of the steamboat, which replaced the old sailing ships and dominated Great Lakes commerce in Walton's time. As Walton wrote in "Types of Great Lakes Sailor Lore," a paper presented to the Michigan Academy in 1938, "Sailor lore seemingly the world over is associated primarily with sailing vessels and not with steamships. A vessel under canvas has a will of its own and therefore a personality that must be reckoned with, whereas a steamboat is pretty largely a machine and has relatively little appeal to the imagination." Like most folklorists of his day, Walton believed that machines and folklore did not mix. The schoonermen shared Walton's views of steamboat crews, albeit for different reasons. For Walton's aging sailors, the steamships ended a way of life most of them loved, despite the obvious dangers and hardship. For Walton, steamships ended the era of Great Lakes folklore as he understood it. Folklorists today define the field more broadly, finding folklore in rural, urban, and industrial settings, among all occupational groups and in all social classes.

As the steamboat example illustrates, hindsight allows us to put Walton's field logs into perspective not possible in his day. Walton missed an opportunity to compare and contrast the folklore of the two dominant forces on the Lakes—steamboats and sailboats—as they vied for supremacy. What else did Walton *not* collect? We can never fully know the answer, of course, but a few obvious examples deserve mention. Walton interviewed comparatively few women about their actual experiences, despite the fact that, according to Loyola history professor Theodore Karamanski, as many as 30 percent of all ships' cooks were women. As a literary folklorist, Walton had little interest in material culture. And with the exception of the Beaver Island Irish and a few examples of dialect songs, he did not explore themes of diversity and cross-cultural interaction that surely characterized the sailors' experiences.

A majority of Lakes sailors during the nineteenth century were foreign born, with especially large numbers of Irish and Scandinavians. Undoubtedly an important corpus of ethnic and immigrant sailor lore in languages other than English has been lost. In his field logs, Walton did note the nationality of most people he encountered and, where appropriate, attempted to record dialect. For example, when Walton asked Swedish-born sailor Andrew Peterson if he could recall any songs, Peterson's response was unintelligible. When Walton asked him to repeat it, the former sailor laughed and said, "Ay forgat. Dat was Swedish, an' Ay ain't t'ought on dat in fifty year." By Walton's day, most interviewees spoke English, which ultimately became the lingua franca onboard ship. But except for the few dialect songs, Walton collected little English-language material that addressed issues of ethnic difference, adaptation, or conflict.

Walton's own lack of foreign-language skills and the fading memories of the sailors themselves would have hindered any efforts to collect foreign-language lore. Yet, in an occupation filled with men from a diversity of European origins, there must have been a rich repertoire, in English, of ethnic jokes, nicknames, stereotypes, and anecdotes born of negotiations across and within ethnic boundaries. Even the ship's cook must have catered to the tastes of different ethnicities or suffered the wrath of the crew. In overlooking such material, Walton again was a product of his time. During the 1930s, the melting pot ideology reigned. Not surprisingly, the picture painted by Walton was of a homogeneous group bound by occupation, not one also characterized by ethnic diversity. Perhaps even more powerful is what folklorist Jim Leary has called "the xenophobic ruts of received scholarship." The Anglocentric canon of Francis James Child and his disciples was so pervasive that several generations of folklorists, including Walton's, had little use for European Americans and recent immigrants who were not Anglo-Protestants.

It is easy to critique in hindsight. By the standards of his time, however, Walton's collection was appropriately selective. He rapidly gained a well-deserved reputation as the preeminent scholar of Great Lakes sailor lore, fielding queries and correspondence from around the country and overseas. He began his fieldwork with a particular focus on schoonermen songs but eventually developed a more catholic approach to traditional material, including lakesmen terminology, slang, nicknames, weather lore, superstitions and beliefs, use of musical instruments, ghost stories, stories about greenhorns (especially the ship's boy), and legends of ghost ships. He explored subcultures in different Lake environments: schooners, canal boats, tugs, timber rafts, even (in spite of himself) a fleeting reference to Ward steamships out of Detroit whose black deckhands sang work songs and for their own amusement. His descriptions of the stereotypical attitudes schoonermen held about steamboat men, landlubbers, farmers, African Americans, and women are especially revealing of the values and social interactions of the period. His documentation of nicknames and anecdotes born of rivalry between salt-water and Lakes sailors show how folklore marked the boundaries between two distinct subgroups as they vied for bragging rights and jobs on the inland seas.

As a male researcher exploring a predominantly male subculture, Walton was able to document the seedier side of life, including saloons, boardinghouses, and brothels. Although folklorists as a rule ignored popular culture products of the mass media, Walton's logs give descriptions of port city variety shows (what sailors called "free and easy shows") and the advertising song sheets of Dave and Mose, two Jewish merchants from Buffalo, which Walton tried unsuccessfully to locate. As early as 1933 he also inquired about bawdy songs and parodies such as one might expect in a male-dominant occupational group. Although some collectors of the period—notably John A. Lomax with his African American blues and work songs and Vance Randolph in the Ozarks—also recorded ribald lore, little appeared in print. People who knew such material often were reluctant to share it with unfamiliar collectors. Even if bawdy lore was collected, moral codes of the period meant that it often remained out of the public eye in unpublished ethnographic collections such as Walton's.

A final word must be said about the Beaver Island material, which in many ways is in a league of its own. Walton shared this view. As he wrote Patrick Bonner in 1933, "My visit to Beaver Island was about the most interesting part of my trip last summer." He formed close friendships, which continued throughout his career, and he returned more frequently to Beaver Island than to any other place. A majority of his field recordings, which span the period 1938–60, and a significant portion of both the 1932 and 1938 field logs focus on time spent on Beaver Island. Walton found on Beaver his richest source of sailor song, but the sheer scope of Beaver Island's musical life prompted a separate article, "Folk Singing on Beaver Island" (1952). Unfortunately, the editing and omissions of *Songquest* fail to do justice to the breadth of the Beaver Island material; the 1932 and 1938 field logs paint a vivid sense of place that is available only in Walton's original.

Even with these omissions, however, *Songquest* is a welcome and long overdue compilation of Walton's 1930s field logs. The logs, combined with Walton's copious correspondence, give rare and valuable insights into his work as a folklorist. The logs, along with his sound recordings and transcripts, form the heart of his groundbreaking collection of schoonermen lore. Perhaps because Walton never finished his intended book his work has not received the exposure and acclaim that it deserves. We are fortunate that Joe Grimm and Wayne State University Press have collaborated to bring much of Walton's unpublished material to a larger audience. First with *Windjammers: Songs of the Great Lakes Sailors* (2002) and now with *Songquest,* the life's work of the premier collector of Great Lakes sailor lore is widely accessible for the first time.

A bibliography of Walton's published work appears at the end of this book. Special thanks to Yvonne Lockwood, Jim Leary, and Rebecca Clark for their assistance.

EDITOR'S NOTE: THE ESSENCE OF IT ALL

Men speak hundreds and thousands of words, but only a few sparkle with veracity and universality. The gems from Ivan Walton's journals are presented here. You'll get 90 percent of the book's lessons in less than 10 percent of the time. We appreciate that you bought the whole book, but you don't have to read it all. We provide this as a service to time-starved readers. They probably are the same people who would rather ride on powerboats than sailboats.

On Folk Songs

> Them damn songs are never twice alike.
> HARRIS CHRISTANSON, 1932

Well, that's the point of folk songs. They are made up, reinvented, twisted to suit the occasion or singer, and rarely written down. Walton came as close as he could to authentic versions of songs, mindful that a song might be different with each singing.

> Dose songs, dey drop through my memory.
> HANS O. NELSON, 1932

Old sailors' memories, like old boats, can be leaky. Walton encountered many men who swore that they knew every song sung up and down the Great Lakes—but who remembered none. At the time they sang them, few sailors thought they had anything worth holding onto. They let the notes drift off on the wind and the words drift out of their minds.

> They were just anything—nothing to remember.
> ALEX "PAT" GALLARNEAU, 1933

Precisely. Because they were sung to accompany the most mundane of tasks—raising an anchor or pumping out the bilge—they seemed unremarkable and were forgotten. The songs were made up on the spot and, for work songs especially, making a rhythmic sound was more important than making sense.

On Schooner Life

There ain't a goddamn thing on this earth as pretty as a ship carryin' all
'er canvas before a good breeze!
A. M. Conkey, 1933

Men felt real affection for the Great Lakes schooners and seemed to regard them
as living things that responded to the wind, the waves, and the actions of the men
who sailed them. Though their sails might be patched and dirty, schooners stirred
up such longing in some men that they left their wives and sweethearts for a full
sail and a running sea.

On Ocean Sailors vs. Lakesmen

Yes sir, lakesmen was a hell-'f-a-lot better sailors than ocean men at
everything but mendin' lines, an sails, an riggin'. Them shellbacks would
be scared damn near to death in a blow if there was a lee shore in sight.
They wanted lots of sea room. We got along all right together, but we'd
both knock hell out of a landsman who wanted a fight.
A. M. Conkey, 1933

Great Lakes sailors were sensitive about the size of their "ponds" when contrasted
with the vastness of the oceans, and they never missed a chance to proclaim their
superiority over the salt-water shellbacks who had come in from deep water for the
higher wages and shorter trips. Salt-water men came to the Lakes in great
numbers in the early lumber-shipping days. They got from one to five dollars a day
on the Lakes, up to ten times what they earned on salt water. Ocean men were not
willing to concede anything to freshwater men, so there were endless debates about
which breed was better.

Yes, you could hear them shellbacks sing halfway across the ocean when
putting on heavy canvas.
John McCauley, 1934

While there was strong partisanship as to which was the superior sailor, it was
largely conceded that the best singers—and most of the songs—came from salt
water.

Many sailors came up from salt water, but they was too slow for us, and
didn't stay long. They couldn't do anything without singing and that was
too slow for the lumber boats.
Al Corey, 1932

As we see, even singing ability could become a liability.

On Schooners vs. Steamboats

> Ah, those cinder-eaters weren't sailors and none of them could sing a
> chantey.
>
> GEORGE ROBERTSON, 1932

Most sailors would not associate with steamboat men and would not allow the
"cinder-eaters" to call themselves sailors. Boardinghouses that catered to sailors
would not admit steamboat men. In Chicago, Walton heard of one neighborhood
where schoonermen boarded on one side of the street, steamboat men on the other.
Steamboat men were not admitted to the Seamen's Union until the old schooners
had pretty well disappeared. The mutual disdain often led to fights.

> Hell, anybody who can drive a horse can drive one of them steamboats
> up and down here.
>
> CHARLES LEACH, 1933

Many sailors were more at home on water than on land. It followed, then, that
they would be disdainful of land-bound men, and who is more rooted to land than
a farmer? Sailors might call any greenhorn a farmer and delighted in saying that a
farmer at sea thought that one plowed the water as he would a field—in straight
furrows—even when that led to certain disaster.

> We always had a small crew and the men was always too tired and sleepy
> to sing, an' then, you don't feel like singin' on a tug or steamboat.
>
> FRANK MAHAFFEY, 1933

Many men said they just didn't get the urge to sing on mechanical contrivances
that needed no human effort to heave, haul, or pump. Such vessels seemed to be
soulless and undeserving of song. Logistically speaking, mechanized boats did not
require the unified human effort that a good work chantey could coordinate or the
large crews that could provide call and response around a chanteyman's
improvisations. Steam ended the days of sail and it also ended the singing.

On Weather Lore and Beliefs

> It took several years to learn to sail. You had to know about weather.
> There were hundreds of weather signs that a sailor had to know: "First
> the wind and then the rain, set your topsails out again."
>
> DAN MCDONALD, 1934

Misfits on land but at home on water, sailors boasted fiercely of their prowess with
lines and tackle. They may not have had much in the way of material possessions,
but their knowledge of seacraft and weather lore made them kings under canvas.

There are enough horseshoes on the bottom of the Lakes to shoe the
whole British cavalry.

JOHN MCCONNELL, 1934

The fact that the floors of the Great Lakes were littered with lucky horseshoes—still nailed to masts and pilothouses—indicates that they didn't, in every case, bring good fortune. There were probably as many signs, lucky ones and unlucky, as there are horseshoes on the bottom of the Great Lakes.

CHAPTER 1

1932: Lake Michigan

Lake Michigan is long and wide,
Lake Michigan is deep,
And gallant sailors man her ships,
Their friends for some do weep.
"The Schooner *Thomas Hume*"

Gusts of urgency blew Ivan H. Walton to and around the rim of Lake Michigan in 1932. He had come to understand that the ways and songs of the sailor were vanishing, and he meant to save what he could. He did not know how many stories and songs there had been. He did not know how many remained. He knew only that time was running out.

Walton's consciousness had been raised when the schooner *Our Son* went down in 1930. On February 29, 1932, he wrote to Milwaukee's Herman Runge: "I understand that the master of the *Our Son* was past seventy at the time his boat went down, and that he had spent most of his life on Lakes sailing vessels. I should like very much to locate him if possible, and to have a visit with him. Men whose active experience reaches back to the time when sail dominated the Lakes are rapidly disappearing, and with them most of the intimate knowledge of the human side of a very important phase of Great Lakes shipping."

In another letter he wrote that day, Walton told Captain James McCannel of Port McNicol, Ontario: "I just read a hundred-page account of some of Captain Nels Palmer's experiences on Great Lakes schooners and in the Coast Guard Service. It is very unfortunate that many more of the lakesmen who were on the Lakes when commercial sailing boats were still plentiful do not write out accounts of how they lived and what they did. Knowledge of that whole phase of life on the Lakes is fast disappearing with the men who lived it." (Palmer's reminiscences had been printed by the *Ludington Daily News* in the fall of 1930.)

Walton and his wife, Mildred, had made a trip on the Canada Steamship Lines in the summer of 1931, and the following winter he decided to go after the songs and lore. On the last day of March 1932, he wrote to John W. Stram of Ludington, Michigan, "I believe I wrote you before that I have been collecting for a number of years all of the literary material I can find that is expressive of human experience on and about the Lakes and I now have several thousand items. That which I am most anxious to get, however—

Professor Ivan Walton, ready to go to
work at the University of Michigan
(Courtesy Lynn and Sue Walton)

authentic accounts of sailing episodes and of the daily life aboard ship, sailor customs and superstitions, rivalries, legends, and especially sailor songs—is almost impossible to locate."

Now, he decided, he would trade arm's-length solicitations for firsthand interviews. His previous explorations had largely been by mail. Librarians, editors, and shipping company figures had been among his main sources. He would now go straight to the people he hoped would have direct memories of schooner days on the Great Lakes. This summer, Walton would find his sea legs as a field collector.

Frank Egleston Robbins, assistant to the president at the University of Michigan, launched Walton's search on June 15 with a letter. It said, "[T]he Committee on the Faculty Research Fund this afternoon appropriated $500 for field expenses this summer while collecting sailor songs and other lore connected with the Great Lakes." That was a lot of money in Depression-deflated 1932, when 13 million U.S. workers were unemployed and average income had shrunk to $843 a year.

Initially Walton relied on the same people he had interrogated by mail: librarians, lighthouse keepers, and others with mailing addresses. With experience, he soon turned to his instincts, scouring waterfronts and barrooms rather than libraries and offices. Taking the measure of a man's age and the cut of his jib, Walton began asking questions.

He probed narrowly, at first. He wanted to find songs, he wanted to know when and how they were used, and he wanted to know how they had migrated from the oceans

Map by F. S. Fluker

to the Lakes. He was not as concerned with "land sailors" or people who shipped aboard steamers, where singing was rare.

From the outset, Walton planned to publish a book of songs. The longer he collected, though, the broader his inquiry. As Walton became satisfied with his reconstruction of a song, he moved on to others, and then to stories and beliefs and customs. He began examining the rivalry among different breeds of men: deepwater sailors and lakers; steamboat men and sailors. And every good informant was a story himself. Each interview complicated rather than clarified. The book was pushed back.

Despite lousy leads and loneliness, Walton was remarkably lucky in 1932. Several people along his counter-clockwise sojourn around Lake Michigan directed him to Beaver Island and to the marine hospital and union hall of Chicago. All proved to be time capsules of song, story, and lore. On Beaver Island, the encyclopedic John Green tantalized Walton with weather signs in addition to songs, so he went after those, too. Others on the island intrigued him so with ghost stories that in later summers these became much larger parts of his search.

In his nightly notes, Walton recounted not just others' memories but also his own observations about his present-day world. He wrote about the sunsets, people's attitudes about Prohibition, and Franklin Delano Roosevelt's run for the White House. He took down the stuff of daily life: car repairs, hungering for a morsel of mail, a small-town baseball rhubarb, and a stomach swollen with stolen cherries. These details add a charming personal dimension to Walton's quest for song, just as his portrayals of his informants color their stories.

South Haven, Michigan, June 23, 1932

Not a very auspicious first day, and may the man who invented automobile folding beds be condemned to an eternity of setting one of them up in a car loaded for a summer's trip. Now for a needed change of occupation, before struggling with this contraption drives out of my head what little of the day's events are in it.

An automobile running board is not the most comfortable of seats, but overhead the night is glorious and from the westward across the city park comes the sound of Lake breakers. Had a two-hour walk on the beach—and what a beach South Haven has! And I had it all to myself. Any poetry in one's soul must be stirred by such a scene, but one shouldn't attempt to set up an automobile bed directly afterward. I hope to get this thing set up before daylight.

Left Ann Arbor about 10 a.m. with a car that had just spent two days in a garage: $32.80 worth. It is surprising how many things a garage man can find in a car that just must be repaired before it would be at all safe to start out for a summer's trip! And twenty-five miles an hour for the first hundred miles and not much faster for the next and all the "What's-the-matter-with-you" looks of passing cars somewhat subtract from the full June day.

Well, I'm here and have started my search for Great Lakes sailor songs and lore. Arrived about 4:30 p.m. and drove through the city to the lakeshore. Lively breakers were rolling in. Off the breakwater at the harbor entrance, rebounding waves dashed against them causing a loud roar and column of spray, which was beautiful in the bright sunlight.

No boats in sight on the lake. Drove back up town and stopped at a gas station to inquire about the location of the city library and found I had parked directly in front of it.

Miss Mabel Barnes, librarian, was afraid there wasn't much of the material I'm seeking in this town as "the people here are not much interested in such things," and as, "this isn't much of an historic place."

After dinner, I called on Mrs. Ira Smith, a lady about fifty and daughter of Captain John Perne, who died last year and who had spent a lifetime sailing on oceans and Lakes. Mrs. Smith informed me that last summer a man had called to see her father about the same subject. She did not know his name nor anything about him other than someone at Benton Harbor had sent him. She knew no Lakes songs herself, but could remember being a little girl on one of her father's boats and hearing the sailors sing as they worked the capstan. [While the inland sailors of the Great Lakes say their "frog ponds" can be as treacherous as any ocean, they call their vessels boats, not ships, even the great 1,000–footers.] The song had a slow, marked rhythm, but she could not remember any of the words nor the time. Her mother said she had often heard the sailors "yo-he-yo," but hadn't paid much attention to it. Mrs. Smith added that her father liked music and singing very much, but was no singer himself, and doubted very much if he could sing me any of the Lakes songs used, even if he were still alive.

She said I should ask Mrs. Arthur [Rose] Gallagher, daughter of Captain Charles Allers, about her father's whereabouts, as he would be a valuable man to see. He is now about eighty, but still on the Lakes. She said I should also see Mr. E. S. Dykeman, whose father lived here many years, was a fruit merchant and quite a literary character. He wrote many newspaper articles and speeches.

Now for another struggle with this damn bed. I would like to get onto it in time to get up early tomorrow.

Nite, Pete & Lynn.

South Haven, Michigan, June 24, 1932

7:30 a.m.: I did it, and now must take this thing down. It looks as though most of my summer would be occupied with setting up and taking down this bed. Wakened with sun shining in my face. More later.

10:30 p.m.: Called again, about 1 p.m., at the residence of E. S. Dykeman to examine his father's poem on the wreck of the *Harmonia*. He had been unable to locate it. He showed me more of his father's notebooks and then went with me to see Captain John Langland, keeper of the South Haven light. He's a big, "sandy" complexioned man with burnt gray hair and a stained mustache that curls out over his mouth. How can he eat? But by his size, he does. We sat out on a seat beside his home overlooking the harbor and channel, which is the dredged-out Black River.

"Yes, I've been tending the light here for thirteen years, and for twenty years before that the Portage Lake light just north of Manistee, and helped at others before that. No, it doesn't seem so long, but I'll soon be all through, retiring

The view of South Haven Harbor in the early or mid-1890s. Locally built in 1893, the *City of Kalamazoo* was 162 feet long. Two men ride a horse and buggy in the foreground, and a swing bridge stands in the back. The smaller vessel just beyond the *City of Kalamazoo* is the *Lorain L.*, a sister ship also built at South Haven by H. W. Williams to run fruit from South Haven across Lake Michigan to Chicago. A fruit-packing company warehouse is at right foreground. (Courtesy Dossin Great Lakes Museum)

the first day of July. Served my time. Yes, I sailed the Lakes some, but not much. I'm a land sailor and have seen lots of sailors and sailboats in my time. Lumber barges and schooners and scows so thick at times they couldn't find anchoring ground and a blow would come up and they'd all go out to sea to ride it out. They were a hard lot, those early sailors, mostly big Scandinavians. Yes, they were singing most of the time."

"Do you know any of the songs?"

"No, I never paid much attention to them. They were mostly yo-hee-o-ing. Oh, yes, they always sang when they worked together. The land men didn't have much to do with the men off the boats. Sometimes, one man would sing a line and then they'd all join in."

"Were the songs about Lake events, or women, or something else?"

"Oh, bless you, I couldn't tell. I don't think they were much. I never paid much attention to them."

"Did you hear many sailor yarns when the Lakes schooners were still numerous?"

"Oh, yes. They were always talking. You couldn't believe them at all. No, I don't remember what they'd talk about."

"You're retiring next month?"

"Yes, I'll be all through in a few days, now."

"Don't suppose you're sorry?"

"No, I've had enough. And then they're building up that warehouse down there and shutting off all the view of the harbor."

We then went over to the Coast Guard station and called on Captain Fisher. Sailboat days were over before his time. He showed us the first volume of the South Haven station log. It was for the year 1887 and contains many accounts of wrecks of varying degrees of seriousness to sailboats. He said each station keeps a copy of the record of all its life-saving activities and sends another copy to the district commissioner and one to "headquarters." He said I might read all I wanted of them.

Then went to see Mr. Lancaster "Lank" Ludwig, sixty-five to seventy years of age, who has spent practically all his summers and some winters on the Lakes since he was big enough to work on a boat. He has master's papers, but never commanded a boat. He has heard sailor singing—and used to sing a lot himself. There was "Blow the Man Down" and a great many others, but he couldn't remember any of them. There was a lot of "yo-ho-ing" in them, he said. His brother, Mr. Van Ludwig or "Soub," would know them—he used to sing them. He lives about fifteen miles away at Paw Paw Lake.

Out of courtesy, I asked Mr. Dykeman to go along, and he did, even though the backseat of the car was filled and the three of us had to ride in the front seat and he's about a yard "abeam." I knew this audience would spoil any chance of getting anything, as Mr. Dykeman had a strong tendency toward talking.

We found "Soub"—or Van, as he was called—a short, gray, nervous man about seventy-five to eighty, but good for another forty years, always puffing at a pipe. He sailed the Lakes for over forty years, mostly on lumber barges.

Mr. Dykeman: "Soub, this gentleman comes from the Michigan University at Ann Arbor—that's where my son went, you know, he knew my son there—lived in the same house—well, he wants you to sing some of the old marine songs."

Soub: "What old marine songs? I don't know any."

Walton: "Mr. Ludwig, I'm trying to collect what I can of the songs that were sung on the Great Lakes when the sailboats were still here, those used by the sailors when they worked together."

Soub: "Oh, I never paid much attention to them."

Mr. Dykeman: "Yes, you did, Van. We used to sing them. You know lots of them."

Soub: "Have forgotten them all."

Lank: "Come on, Soub, sing some for the gentleman. We've brought him all the way out here."

Soub: "Don't know any."

Walton: "I don't expect you to sing, but I would like very much to get the words to some of the songs that were song on the sailboats."

Mr. Dykeman: "You used to know them, Soub. I've heard you sing lots of them. Come on and sing for us. You still play the piano, don't you?"

Soub: "Yes, yes, I can play."

Mr. Dykeman: "Well, then do it."

Soub: "I'll sing you one."

He went to the piano and hummed a while at an air that had a good, slow rhythm, and then, "I went to see my Susan Jane, She met me at the door . . ."

I tried various ways to get him away from his audience of his wife, Lank, and Mr. Dykeman, but couldn't.

We returned to South Haven, dinner, and I called at the residence of Mrs. Rose Gallagher, about forty, daughter of Captain Charles Allers of Beaver Island. She was born on the island and lived there until she married. She had heard sailor songs from her brother and others all her life.

"Can you recall them now?"

"No, no, I've forgotten them all."

"Can you remember the titles of any?"

"'Bury Me Not in the Deep Blue Sea,' and 'Rolling Home,' and another about the *Alpena* and 'Song and Sigh.' A Benton Harbor man wrote that one about the *Chicora* when she went down. There was one more called the 'Jujubaju.'"

"Was that by any chance about a boat called the *Bigerlow*?"

"Yes, that was it."

"Did you ever hear the sailors singing as they worked a capstan?"

"Yes, many times."

"Can you tell me the titles or words of any of those songs?"

"No, I don't believe I ever knew any. No one could tell what they were singing, but my father, Captain Allers, will know them if anybody does. He ran away from Germany when he was fourteen so that he wouldn't have to serve in the army—that was in Bismarck's time—and he sailed all over the oceans and for years and years sailed the Lakes. He lives at St. James on Beaver Island. He'll talk enough to you. How he likes to talk to people who'll listen to him! He was here a week or so ago. Celebrated his eighty-fourth birthday. You'll find him on the island. Anybody can tell you where he lives."

Now to bed—think I'll sleep out.

Night, Pete & Lynn.

SOUTH HAVEN, MICHIGAN, JUNE 25, 1932

Got my face washed in bed this morning. Set the bed up last night beside the car in the city park and saw lightning to the north. About 11:30 p.m., the last I remember, the stars were dimming. About 6 o'clock this morning, I awakened in a rain—not so good. Weather is clearing now.

I forgot to mention last night Mr. Arthur Gallagher, the talkative Irish husband of Mrs. Gallagher. Born and raised on Beaver Island—a fisherman there. He worked in mills here but is now fishing: "right back where I was twenty-five years ago, but I get along. Yes, Mister, the Beaver Irishmen were all lakesmen and were always singing."

"Do you recall what they sang?"

"Oh, bless you, everything."

"What kind of boats did they sail?"

"Schooners, two- and three-masters, lumber barges, but mostly fishing boats."

"Did you ever hear the schoonermen singing as they made sail, or hauled anchor?"

"Yes, yes, many's a time."

"Do you recall what they sang?"

"Well, now, I ought to—by golly, I can't. Rose ought to know them. Say, you write to the Sears & Roebuck radio station, WLS. They sing lots of old-time songs. They ought to have some. I'll tell you another place. Do you know the *Sturgeon Bay Advocate*? It was a good weekly along about 1912 and is probably going yet. It used to have a page just devoted to Lakes songs and poems and stories. I used to like it. Another one is the *Charlevoix Sentinel*. It's good on marine stuff, too."

Now ready for eats and then off to Saugatuck.

Holland State Park, Michigan, June 25, 1932

It's now about 10 p.m. I'm writing in the car and considering much the close of the day and to take a swim or not to take a swim. The "not" seems to be in the majority. All around are campers in cars, tents, and otherwise. Just took a walk a mile or two up the beach. No boats in sight and the lake very quiet.

Now, the day's affairs:

Called on Mr. Newnham, justice of the peace, about eighty, a bristly Englishman from London. Crossed the ocean in the winter of 1866–67, ten weeks in an ocean schooner. He came to the Lakes as steam was beginning and took up steamboating for forty-three years. He has been an engineer and chief engineer on Lakes steamers and now has an engineer's license good anywhere in the United States. During the war was chief on a dredge in New York Harbor.

"You've seen the Lakes shipping change from sail to steam."

"Yes, yes, I saw it all. There wasn't much steam when I first came, and then for a while there were both, but steam won out."

"I suppose you've been pretty well all over the Lakes."

"On all of them from Chicago to Duluth to Montreal."

"In all seasons and weather."

"Just about."

"When you crossed the ocean, I suppose there were at times quite a lot of making, changing, and lowering sails."

"Yes, in ten weeks of winter I guess we hit about all kinds of weather and wind there is and we had to shift for all of it."

"Was there much chanteying?"

"Oh, yes, my sakes, yes. Salt sailors couldn't do anything without chanteying."

[Chanteys, pronounced "shanties," were sung to unify men in work, typically hauling or heaving. They were simpler than songs sung for amusement.]

"Was a song called, 'Blow the Man Down' sung much?"

"It was 'Blow the Moon Down,' wasn't it? Yes, that was a good one, and 'Pull on the Bo'line' was another, and one about 'Shenandoah' and one that was about 'The Banks of Sacramento.'"

"Have you ever heard any of those on the Lakes?"

"Well, no, not much. They don't sing much on steamboats, and I never had much to do with sailboats. Sometimes when a schooner would be making sail when leaving a harbor we'd hear them, but we didn't pay much attention to the sailboat men."

"Can you recall any of the choruses where the men would all sing together?"

"No, I think those Lakes sailors sang most anything to make a noise so they could pull together."

Captain R. W. Sewers, eighty-four, is a little, dried-up Dutchman weighing about ninety pounds. He sailed the Lakes for many years and has fished for fifty-three. His son is now in the fishing business. Mr. Sewers was playing cards with a crony when I called, and was not very talkative.

"I guess I've been around Saugatuck as long as most of 'em. Yep, I've used about all kinds of fishing boats there is, in close to shore and out 'most across to the other side—mostly lake trout. Sold pretty largely in Chicago."

"Were there many schooners along here in the 1890s?"

"Many? Well, I should say so! I've seen as many as fifty becalmed right out in front of the harbor here at one time, and then a little breeze'd come up and they'd all move off together."

"Did the sailors sing much when making sail or working about the ship?"

"Yes, you could hear them 'most anytime."

"Do you remember any of the songs they sang?"

"Nope, I think they just made 'em up."

"Do you know the names of any of them?"

"Nope."

Next called on Joshua Brown, a retired eighty-year-old former lakesman, a big 230-pounder, red-faced, good-natured, and quite active. He built the Coast Guard station at Ludington and was in charge for about five years and before that sailed on lumber barges. "I sailed about sixty years ago, carried lumber from mills about upper Michigan to Chicago and other ports. That was a hell of a life at Escanaba. The man who owned the boat owned the mills. A bar kept us out over a mile and we had to run a line in and raft the lumber out and then hand it up on deck a board at a time. The cold water'd run back on us. We were stripped to the waist and wore leather aprons. When we started to load a ship we never stopped until it was finished if it took us two days."

"Did you pull to a song while taking the rafts out?"

"No, those damn mill hands who helped us didn't know anything."

"Did you onboard while working the ship?"

"Yes, and the men who yelled louder pulled least."

"Do you recall the words to any of them?"

"There was one about the cook," and he began, "There was," and finished by humming a tune to la la . . ." I can't get it, but almost." He tried several times.

"Did you ever sing any around quarters?"

"Yes, at times."

"What did you sing?"

"Well, now, that's strange, but I can't recall any of them."

Captain Wilson was a younger man, about seventy-five, but looked nearer fifty, slender and very active. Was on the Lakes for about forty years. "Oh, sure, we used to sing 'em. A sailor couldn't work without singing. I've seen one man alone pulling a rope to a song. Those old shellbacks [salt-water sailors] who came to the Lakes always had to sing."

"Did you ever hear 'Rolling Home'?"

"Yes, and one about going round the Horn."

"And 'Blow the Man Down'?"

"Yes."

"Did you hear any work songs like those that were about Lakes subjects?"

"They were about 'most anything."

"Can you recall any of them?"

"Here's one we used to sing after," and he sang and hummed a verse of "The *Bigler.*"

"And that brings me another:

All around Presque Isle, my boys,
The seagulls they do roar,
And they all join in the chorus

Then there was something about the *Persian*'s crew, "lost on Lake Huron's shore."

"When were songs like those sung?"

"Oh, 'most any time when a group of men were sitting around and not working."

"Can you repeat any of those songs when the men were working?"

"Well, now, I thought I could. . . . There were a lot of 'yo-ho's' in 'em. If somebody would just start one, I could." A half hour's tries couldn't bring them.

He said they had a song that somebody in Muskegon wrote at the time of a big strike there, that everybody sang for a while. He said it was written to the tune of "The Longshoreman."

I had a fish dinner and came on to Holland. I had a beautiful drive as the lowering sun fringed the dune tops all the way.

I found Mr. B. G. Mulder, editor of the *Holland City News,* at his home. A fat Dutchman who likes to talk, he said the people of Holland are mostly Dutch and were more for agriculture and business than marine matters. He said a number of schooners carried lumber out of here in the early days, but the Dutch didn't go in much for singing. He said they were rather a solemn, industrious lot. The *Alpena* was wrecked off Holland's shore and wreckage came in here. He said I should see Captain A. C. Anderson of the steamer *South American.*

I called upon Captain Anderson, who said he'd been on steamboats all his life. He could remember hearing schoonermen singing at the capstan, etc., but never knew any of their songs. He invited me to come aboard the *South American* tomorrow and said he'd show me all of it.

HOLLAND, MICHIGAN, JUNE 26, 1932

A fine night. I slept parallel to the Milky Way on a sand pile behind a poplar tree. Counted most of the stars in the Milky Way, but lost count after the nine millionth. The night was cool and I was tired. I was awakened by a bright sun in my face this morning. I took a long walk up the beach, and planned to go swimming, but was too lazy. Will this afternoon. I am in the Warm Friend Tavern in Holland now. I called at the *South American* for Captain Anderson just after noon, but he had returned to his residence and I saw him there on the way back up town.

The *South American* and sister ship, the *North American,* are tied up at their wintering dock about a mile down the harbor at Black Lake. They are two beauties of ships, all freshly painted and ready for the opening day of the 1932 season, which is next Wednesday. They run from here to Mackinac Island, then Parry Sound, Detroit, Cleveland, and Buffalo, and return to Chicago each week.

Captain Anderson invited me to look him up at Mackinac Island in case I'm there when his boat comes in. He suggested I might profitably talk with Mr. Frank Vanry, ex–fire chief of Holland, who was on the Lakes a great many years, and also Captain Laidlaw at Whitehall, Michigan.

Visited Mr. Vanry, about seventy, who sailed the Lakes some time ago in lumber hookers. [Hookers were smaller vessels that moved, in harbor, by having sailors row out with a small anchor, drop it, and have men aboard the hooker draw in the line to haul the boat up over the anchor. This was repeated until the vessel had "hooked" its way to where it could tie up or get under sail. The small anchor was called a kedge and the process was called kedging. There were stone hookers and lumber hookers, depending on the cargo.] Vanry had heard sailors sing, but was quite indefinite as to what or when. He could not recall any of the songs. He has a copy of a song about the loss of the *Alpena.*

"I was the last living man ashore to speak to the captain," he said. "I was in a small lumber boat laying alongside the *Alpena* when she left her dock. I heard the lightkeeper tell him that the barometer was going down fast and a bad night was coming, but the captain said he'd make it and he went out and headed direct for Chicago."

"How near did he get?"

"Within about thirty-five miles. Had he gone direct to Milwaukee, he'd have made it. I remember the boat leaving and the night and all, as though it were but yesterday, and I can give you a lot of Holland history—I know about all of it— but I don't remember any of those old songs. Never tried to, and that was a long time ago."

"Do you recall just when the songs were used? In what kind of work?"

"Whenever a group of men had to work together."

"Did they all sing?"

"Usually if any one was too bad, the others would sometimes tell him to keep still, but usually they'd all join."

Mr. Gerritt Doesburg is an old man of nearly ninety. A short time ago, he fell and cut his scalp so that he had to go to the hospital. Mrs. Doesburg says it has affected seriously both his hearing and his memory. I couldn't make him understand what I wanted, or possibly he couldn't keep his mind on the subject long enough to answer. Mrs. Doesburg said that a few years ago he could have entertained me for hours. She added that before the Civil War, Mr. Doesburg went on Lakes boats for the adventure of it. His father "learned" him the printer's trade, but he liked sailing too much for that. "Liked the singing, the water and all." When he came back from the war, he took up sailing again for a business. "He had a good voice and liked to sing, and the men liked to hear him."

"Did you go out on the boats any, Mrs. Doesburg?"

"Yes, I used to go on my father's boat some."

"You've heard some of the songs, then, those that the men sang when they worked together hoisting canvas, or other work?"

"Yes, the work seemed easier when they sang."

"Did the mate order the men 'to heave and chantey'?"

"No, he just told them what to do and they'd sing themselves as they worked. I remember that they would always sing if they had to put up the canvas to straighten it out after it had been taken down in a hurry in a storm. It would be wet and heavy and they didn't like to do it, so they'd sing and it wouldn't be so hard. If they didn't sing, they'd swear—sometimes they did anyhow—and they could swear pretty bad."

"Can you remember any of the songs they sang?"

"I've just been trying to, but I can't remember. If I'd be on a ship and they'd start, I could tell the rest of it, but those days are over! My, but there used to be so many, and now all gone, and there's only two or three men left in Holland who used to sail."

"Did the songs tell stories?"

"Yes, the crew would make up new stories for some of the old tunes—some of them were pretty bad."

"Did the men ever sing about events on the boats, wrecks, storms, or things like that when they were not working?"

"Yes, they did. On my father's boat they had some. Each crew had some, I think, about the boat they were on—that is, when they were on it a long time. My father's boat was the *Three Bells* and the men had a song:

The *Three Bells* and her jolly crew
of hardy men and a captain true
They—

"I can't just remember the rest of it. They were in a bad storm and nearly got wrecked and the song tells about it. I think Peter Skoon over by the high school could give you some of those old songs."

So, I called at Peter's house and found him on his front porch with his pipe and a book that looked like a Bible. I explained to him what I wanted and how I happened to come to him. He said it was nearly forty years ago that he was on sailboats. He said he could not recall ever having heard any real chanteys on any boats he was on. "Somebody would sing out a sort of a 'yo-hee-o' to keep the men together, but you couldn't call that singing."

"Did you have any other songs?"

"Yes, we had the popular music-hall songs from Chicago and other places. I once wrote some parodies for our ship on some of them."

"Do you still have any of them?"

"No, they've been gone for years."

"Were there many salt-water men on Lakes boats?"

"Yes, the shellbacks were pretty thick sometimes."

"How did they feel toward the lakesmen?"

"Oh, they thought they were better than we were."

"How did you fellows feel toward the steamboat men when they began to appear?"

"Well, we didn't have much to do with them. I guess that was because they took away our business."

It's now an hour past midnight and I'm about to set up a bunk for the rest of the night. This Grand Haven State Park has been pretty thickly populated since I arrived. A fog has come up during the last hour and the foghorns of the three boats that left here during that time are sounding at regular intervals—a passenger boat and two car ferries—also the Grand Haven foghorn. Those horn sounds out of the blackness give me a strange feeling. When I drove into Grand Haven this evening, a big bald sand dune on the point at the end of the main street and across the harbor was outlined against a crimson sky—very beautiful.

Start Grand Haven for better luck tomorrow.

Mail in the morning.

Nite, Peter and Lynn.

GRAND HAVEN, MICHIGAN, JUNE 27, 1932

The next U.S. Constitutional amendment should prohibit the manufacture, selling, giving away, transporting, and using of automobile beds, and may he who invented this one spend eternity setting the damn thing up and taking it down on damp rainy nights in a car loaded for a summer's trip.

A thick fog settled about 10 last night and shut out the world from a few feet past the car windows. Alone, alone, now much alone. Only the lake surf and the answering foghorns of three boats out on the lake, each growing dimmer and dimmer, three blasts and three and three.

With the morning, a bright sun and clear, the sky a new day and new zest and hope. Work should be planned in the morning.

First mail today. Went down early for it: a photo-stat page from the Burton Library, a refusal of transportation from the boat company, forwarded letter from Elgie—is coming about July 10—and one and another short from Pete. After reading my mail and writing some, I visited the city library to learn what Miss DeYoung, librarian, had assembled, but she had nothing. Then called at office of *Grand Haven Daily Tribune* to talk with Mr. Almon W. McCall, editor, about thirty. He took me across street to see a Mr. Kiel who "knows everybody in town." He said I should see Mr. H. P. Mulligan, U.S. boiler inspector with an office in the Post Office Building.

Mr. Mulligan was in his office, engaged with another man, but he came out anyway. He is a big, husky, dark-complexioned Irishman about sixty-five. He said he'd spent most of his sailing days in the engine end of steamers, but had heard many of the older Lakes songs and liked them.

I asked him about a song mentioned by Mr. Kiel about the *Robert E. Emmet*. Mulligan said he didn't think he knew it. Then I mentioned many of the old ocean chanteys and he said he'd heard them all in different Lake ports and boats. He added that Captain William Preston would know more than he did and that I should see him.

I drove to the Coast Guard station out around the harbor and dunes. Looked about the grounds a while and watched the work being done on replacing the old pier by a new concrete one and suddenly found Captain Preston standing nearby looking at me. I spent the next four or five hours with him and feel quite bewildered now trying to recall what he said about Lakes songs.

He's about sixty, hale and husky and good for another hundred. He left Norway with his family when he was six. He was on his father's boat on the Lakes as a boy, and it was tied up in the river at Bay City at the time of the great lumberyard fire there. He saw it started by a couple of boys smoking between two lumber piles on the river's edge after a swim. In 1891, Preston went east and skippered on ocean boats and sailed the oceans for seven years, going twice around the world. He showed me a picture of the four-masted barkentine *John Ena,* in which he rounded Africa and South America. He came back to the Lakes and sailed here again and then entered the Coast Guard Reserves where he has been for twenty-nine years. He has been at many stations: Port Huron, the Straits of Mackinac, Beaver Island, Milwaukee, and Chicago. He was at Chicago at the time of the *Eastland* disaster and saved twenty-two people from drowning. He took out 165 bodies trapped twelve feet under water. [The 275–foot excursion steamer *Eastland* rolled over in Chicago Harbor in 1915 killing 835 in the deadliest Great Lakes disaster ever.] Preston was awarded the government's *Eastland* Medal for his actions. A few years ago, he was in flood-relief work in Mississippi and took one of the Grand Haven station boats and part of its crew with him. He is proud of his men—a real character. His life-saving experience makes a landsman feel rather small and useless.

He has heard chanteys, great numbers of them, on the Lakes.

"Were there salt-water chanteys, or different ones?"

"Both. Salt-water men came to the Lakes in great numbers in the early lumber-shipping days. They go from one to five dollars a day here and that looked like big money to an ocean sailor who never got more than fifteen or eighteen dollars a month. Half of the members of the crews were deep-water men when I first began."

"Did they do much singing when working on the boats?"

"Oh, yes, they couldn't work without singing."

"What ocean chanteys were used?"

"I couldn't begin to remember them. There was 'Blow the Moon Down,' 'Blow, Boys, Blow,' 'Old Rio,' 'Cali-for-ni,' 'Shenandoah,' and no end of them."

"Was that first one, 'Blow the Moon Down,' or 'Blow the Man Down'?"

"We always sang it 'moon.'"

"What does it mean?"

"Well, you know the moon has a lot to do with the weather. You never get a good blow when the moon is up."

"You mean the full moon."

"Yes, you get your blow and storms, too, when the moon's down. It could be said either way—that the wind blows the moon down or that the moon, when it's down, comes the blows. When the sailors wanted a good wind, they'd sing this chantey."

"Can you recall any of the others—those that were sung on the Lakes alone?"

"I really didn't know those so well, and then some of those deep-water songs got changed so they told about some things that happened on the Lakes."

"Can you recall any of the titles or subjects?"

"There was one about Fayette Brown and his nigger crew. Old Brown wouldn't pay the wages and hired a scab crew, and the song talks about it. He was from Chicago. [Actually, *Fayette Brown* was the name of the vessel. The captain, Joseph Moffett, was the target of the sailors' scorn and is in the song, too.] There was another about the *Manistee*. She was a lumber hooker. I'll think of the words pretty soon. There was a good one called 'The Silver Wake.' That's the moon shining on the wake of the boat. We had one about what men had to eat. That was a good one, too."

After visiting a while, he thought of some songs he'd cut out of newspapers many years ago and he fished out a roll of them and gave them to me on my promise to return them.

He also found an ocean song, "Wreck of the *Atlantic*," written in pencil, and passed it to me.

GRAND HAVEN, MICHIGAN, JUNE 28, 1932

Don't know what I've done with all of this day. Mail this morning. Another boat company says no ride—ruling of the Interstate Commerce Commission will not permit it. Will have to have something done with that outfit. Another letter from

Pete—good one but no word from Lynn boy. Wrote Burton Library in Detroit, Lynn, and Elgie. Also ordered Joanna Colcord's book, *Roll and Go* from Wahr's in Ann Arbor. Rambled about the harbor a while, picked up conversation with some likely appearing characters, but got nothing. One should wear old clothes and a couple days' beard when about the waterfront. Summer clothes cause suspicion.

Visited Captain George Robertson, eighty-four. He's Scotch and much of his memory and balance are gone. He was on deep water for seven years where he sailed the *Marco Polo* and other schooners. One trip carried a cargo of coal from England to the Mediterranean island of Malta. He never was a singer. Began sailing in 1869. Heard many old chanteys when on the ocean and some of them on the Lakes. Salt-water men came to the Lakes because wages, quarters, and treatment were all better and they brought ocean songs with them. They added verses to them and changed them. At times, a crew on a long trip, like from Lake Michigan to Buffalo, would make up a song on an ocean tune talking of the trip. If they didn't like the captain or mate, they'd make up "blackguard" songs about them. Robertson never tried to remember any of them.

"About when did their work songs begin to disappear?"

"The steamboats took the trade away from the old schooners and much of their profits, so they cut down on their crews and worked their men harder. Men have to have some time to themselves to make songs and to sing. When the crews got down from twelve to fifteen men to three to six, there wasn't much singing. But I have heard one man out on lookout sing and sing."

"I've been told that the deep-water men were better singers than the inland sailors—"

"They were, and better sailors, too."

"How did they compare with the steamboat men?"

"Ah, those cinder-eaters weren't sailors and none of them could sing a chantey."

"Do you remember any of the work songs you heard along in the 1870s and 1880s?"

"No, they soon leave you when you don't hear them for a while. There's no singing onboard anymore. The sailboats are all gone and the men that go on the steamboats now have had too much school to make good songs."

The *City of Grand Rapids* and *Missouri* were both at their piers and are going out soon.

They are now just disappearing over the horizon.

Very sleepy.

Nite.

GRAND HAVEN, MICHIGAN, JUNE 29, 1932

Awakened this morning to a blow and rain. Lines of white water all along the shore. Watched *City of Grand Rapids* and *Missouri* come in—each rolling quite noticeably. Called at Mr. Mulligan's office and he had written out for me:

> It was on a Sunday morning
> About the hour of ten
> When the tug *Robert Emmet*
> Pulled us out on Lake Michigan.

> Chorus: Watch her, catch her . . .

> Another: We were loaded down with barley

> Also: So, heave her, me bullies

Went aboard the *City of Grand Rapids*. Captain Delatre is about forty and the schooner days were long before his time, but his father had been an old-time Lakes skipper and was "full of chanteys." He has heard often the song about:

> We sailed to Escanaba
> We worked our fingers sore

He couldn't recall the rest.

"Was that song called 'Red Iron Ore'?"

"Yes, that was it."

He showed me a picture of the old schooner *Our Son*, which went down in the fall of 1930. [The vessel was named after the first owner's son, who died shortly before the schooner was launched.] She's an "old timer" with a three-cornered tops'l high above all others. "Have you any old deep-water men aboard?"

"Yes, there's Al, 'Foghorn Al,' as they call him, and old Gus, Gus Nelson."

I found both working on the freight deck. They eyed me suspiciously. I should have had on old clothes. Al was the busiest man on the ship and it was to leave in about an hour. The boat is not here nights, so I could not wait and talk with them when off duty.

Al was stubby, a lot of roll to his walk, and he had on a couple of weeks' beard. He was dressed in blue denims. He had been four years on all the oceans and twenty-five on the Lakes.

"Ever hear any chanteys?"

"Sure I have, hundreds of times. How could the men pull together with no chanteys?"

"Ever hear 'Blow the Moon Down'?"

"Yes, and 'Blow Man, Blow,' an' 'Hooray for the Rio Grande,' an' I knowed lots of 'em in those days. [The Rio Grande typically referred to in this song is the river in South America.]

"Did you sing these songs on the early Lakes schooners?"

"Some at first, but it took all the deep-water men to chantey."

"Do you know any of them now?"

"Nope, they're all gone. There ain't no real sailors anymore. I got some work to do," and he began to draw away. "Sailors have to have two or three drinks 'fore they can sing, and no good places anymore." And he was gone.

I found Gus repairing a big box. He is seventy or possibly more, from Norway, went to sea as a boy, and has been on the Lakes near thirty years. He is somewhat thinner than Al and more meditative. He also wore blue denim work clothes and a sailor cap.

"How many times have you been around the Horn [Cape Horn, the stormy southern tip of South America]?"

"Many times, many times."

"Pretty rough weather there."

"That's where you get weather and it takes a good ship to make it."

"You went 'round in a schooner?"

"Yes, I've been in China, Australia, Africa 'n'—"

"How did you happen to come to the Lakes?"

"They paid good money here when I first came."

"Were you on any of the old lumber boats?"

"Yes, many of them. I was on the last one around here."

"The *Our Son?*"

"Yes, that's the one. We were four men in the fo'c'sle and aft, the skipper, mate and cook."

"Not many for hoisting canvas, was it?"

"Not enough."

"How many men on ocean schooners?"

"Oh, from ten to twenty."

"They'd make quite a noise on a good chantey, wouldn't they?"

"You're darn right. And they could haul. In those days, they was sailors. The fellows around here ain't sailors."

"Did you chantey much on the Lakes schooners when you first came up?"

"Yes, yes, sure, when there were enough men."

"Did you sing the same songs that you did on the ocean?"

"Sometimes."

"Did you ever sing one like this?" I whistled "Blow the Man/Moon Down."

"Oh, yes, many times."

"And this one: 'Watch her, catch her, jump up on her juberju.'"

"Yes, I heard that one."

"Can you recall any others?"

"Nope. I forgot all of 'em. Sailors don't sing anymore, just out for the money they can make. They ain't no real sailors anymore."

He then was reminded of his work and said he had to get it finished. I suspect that a few bottles of beer would greatly refresh his memory.

Went aboard the car ferry *City of Milwaukee,* and first officer Captain C. H. McCauley called me—or rather invited me—to his stateroom. He was just getting up. He is about seventy, a former salt-water sailor and has had some years in Lakes schooners. He said that in the 1880s and 1890s, a great many deep-water men came to the Lakes and brought their chanteys with them. He had heard some songs with tunes from the ocean and words about Lake events and boats. He said the words changed much from crew to crew and that the old schooner chanteys often came back to him as he was in the quiet of the night watch, especially when he happened to be thinking of his sailboat trips.

I had a similar talk with Captain Cavanaugh. He, too, is from a family of sailors. He has been on the Lakes over forty years and often heard early sailboat chanteys. He added that the songs that grew up on the Lakes showed much more spirit than those on deep water. He said a deep-water sailor was treated much like a dog, but the lakesmen received good wages, good quarters, and food. They were used like men, and their songs showed it.

I called on Captain James K. Young, now about eighty-four, who retired twelve years ago. He was on sailboats in the 1880s and was master of the steamer *Sandsucker* for a number of years. "Yes, the old schooner crews would chantey and bawl at all work on the ropes or capstan. They would always sing on a hard pull and when they had to kedge the old schooner into Chicago harbor, and also Buffalo harbor—that is, carry a line out with a small anchor, drop it and haul up to it and then carry it out again."

I then went to see Captain William Rosie, about sixty and master of the *Sandsucker*, which works in this region. He has always been a steamboat man and has heard a few chanteys, especially in saloons when he was beginning his career. He said the sailors and steamboat men alike would gather at sailor holdouts when in port at night, but he never knew any of them.

I spent 6:30–8:30 p.m. with John Kelly, commander of the Coast Guard District. He is a big, friendly Irishman in his sixties and likes to talk. He has had considerable salt-water experience, but no Lakes experience until a few years ago, when he acquired his present job. He has twenty or more marine views and paintings of ocean sailboats about his house. He showed me them all and explained each, with the histories of the boats and locations of the scenes. He has some beauties. Among them the *Flying Cloud*. I told him of the song I have about that one and promised to send him a copy. We had some refreshments, talked politics, the Depression, Prohibition, and even back to sea chanteys. He told of capstan chanteys, hoisting chanteys, "homeward bound" chanteys and hummed and sang a number he particularly liked. He is very much interested in this work.

Another day.

Night, Peter and Lynn boy.

GRAND HAVEN, MICHIGAN, JUNE 30, 1932

Began the day with mail—a fine letter from Lynn boy—the first one—and one from mother. Wrote Pete and Lynn a card, ordered some more calling cards from Wahr's. Will need them before summer is out.

Went around the harbor docks, picked up conversation with a half dozen likely looking characters, but only one had been on Lakes and he on recent steamboats. Went aboard the *Grand Rapids* but found no one familiar with the period concerned.

Shortly after lunchtime, I went out to see Captain Preston at the Coast Guard station again. He said he'd been able to recall one little rhyme about "Escanaba and the Red Iron Ore":

Some took a shovel,
And some took a spade,
I took a wheelbarrow,
Every man to his trade.

He says there's more to the song and that it describes loading a boat with iron ore at Escanaba, Michigan, and taking it down the Lakes. ["Up" and "down" the Lakes often had little to do with north or south. Often it meant sailing ore and wood from points of origin such as Chicago, Milwaukee, and Duluth "down" to destinations such as Cleveland and Buffalo.] He gave me the names of some prospects at Milwaukee and Chicago. Then he settled the weather, Prohibition and the Democratic convention and then I came on to Muskegon. It was a pleasant ride most of way.

Dinner and a movie—both pretty bad.

Grand Haven and Muskegon, Michigan, July 1, 1932

Visited Louis Coleman, watchman in Brinen Lumber Yards. He was on the Lakes in the late 1870s. He was in Muskegon at the time of the big strike of 1881–82, but doesn't know the "Muskegon Strike Song." Lakes sailors sang much when he first sailed, he said, but in the late 1880s, crews were cut down to three to five men and then there was little or no more singing. Trips on lumber schooners from around here were short. They would load during the day, sail at night, unload in Chicago as soon as they arrived, and then head back for another load. The men on those vessels were pretty tired. He was no singer himself and remembers little or none of the songs. He heard much "e-ho-ing" in songs. He remembers "Blow, Man, Blow," and "Pull on the Bowline," but not any of the words. He remembers no songs about Lakes events or subjects.

Martin Oleson sailed from Norway in 1870 when a boy. He was on oceans for eleven years and sailed around the world several times in English boats: London to Sydney, Australia to New Zealand, then to China and on around, first in a four-master and then in clipper ships. Ocean crews of twenty to forty men would always sing when working, Oleson said. The "chanteyman would sit on the capstan and lead and others would all join in. Pulling is not hard work that way." He remembers "Sally Brown," "Heave Away to Sacramento," "Heave Away to Rio," and "Rolling Home," and added that they had "songs for everything." Oleson came to the Lakes in 1882. The wages were much better than on the ocean, crews were smaller, and there were bonuses. Boats were also smaller and trips short. Many ocean men were on the Lakes boats. They sang many of the ocean songs while hoisting canvas when he first came to the Lakes, but reduced crews soon put an end to it. He retired from sailing several years ago as a master. He spends time in his "sailor's garden," which he took much pride in showing me.

In the early evening, I called at the home of Captain Tom Robinson, retired lighthouse keeper. I found him to be very ill, unable to see anyone. His wife and the families of his three daughters are very interested in this subject and insisted on my staying a while. Captain Robinson was the oldest man in the service when he retired a few years ago, they said. His daughter Joan, who did most of talking, said the captain would like nothing better than to talk of such a subject. She said he had associated all his life with Lakes sailors and his father before him had been an ocean sailor. He knows many songs, rhymes, and stories, and when he's able to talk, she shall write down as many as she can and send them to me. She remembers hearing a song about the *Maple Leaf* and the *Bigler*, which tells about the *Bigler* ramming the *Maple Leaf.* She recalled another, "Rosie Dear," about a ship's cook, a dialect song. [This likely was the French dialect scow song "The *Julie Plante*," often set near Detroit.]

Working together, the daughters wrote out a song their father often sang, "Building Castles in the Air." He had told them lakesmen often sang it in more sober moments, but there was not much Lakes atmosphere or association in it.

They mentioned a song about "Lost on the *London*," which tells of an English ship going down in the Bay of Biscay [between the western coast of France and the northern coast of Spain]. They also wrote out "The Sailor's Grave," and took it up to their father's room and read it to him for corrections. It described a burial at sea; however, I have never heard of any burial from a ship on the Great Lakes. Also, the words were quite sophisticated.

Am sitting in the front seat of the car now, writing on a board on my lap. Darkness has settled and it's raining and cold, and a gale is blowing from the northwest. Was out on the south breakwater a short time ago and watched big waves coming in. They rolled gloriously and rain and spray soaked everything, and the wind—how she howled. Two boys came out. One, about eighteen, was blown off his feet and nearly off the breakwater, so we all came back in. My old raincoat acted more like a sail than protection. Came back to the car and watched two passenger boats and a car ferry go out. All did some pretty good pitching as they cleared the breakwater gap and then began to roll as the ferry headed northwest for Milwaukee and the passenger boats southwest for Chicago. I would like to be on one of them.

Muskegon, Michigan, July 2, 1932

Pretty cool last night. Breakfast and mail. Nice letter from Pete and one from her and Lynn. Wrote several letters and sent Pete and Lynn a couple of cards. Looked up usual addresses at the library. Had lunch with Paul Elliott, marine reporter for the *Muskegon Chronicle.* He gave me a copy of a story about the sinking of the *Our Son* when bound for Muskegon with load of pulpwood. He had little or no material that I didn't already have.

An "extra" issue early in the day stated that Franklin D. Roosevelt has been nominated at the Democratic Convention for the presidency, so I suppose

America's great vaudeville show is over for 1932. [The convention was held at Chicago Stadium from June 27 to July 2 and resulted in the nomination of Roosevelt with John Nance Garner of Texas as his running mate.]

Called on Captain William J. Drumm, in his late eighties, of Muskegon Heights. He has been on tugboats since 1882 and for ten years before that on lumber schooners.

"No work for tugs anymore," he said. He recognized names of a number of deep-water chanteys. He had heard them in his early days, but knew no words and none about the Lakes. He said they used to sing when hoisting sail when he was a boy. The last year he was on schooners he was mate and had an old Irish crew who "would always rather sing than work," but he paid no attention "to their damn noise." I repeated some lines from "The *Bigler*": "Watch her, catch her, jump on her juberju," and he smiled and said they used to sing that in saloons at night after a few whiskeys. "You could hear them a mile."

He said lakesmen were always opposed to beginning a season's work on Friday. Some thought a woman aboard brought bad luck and the same for cats. He said that there was often racing when two boats happened to be on the same course. Few captains would go out of their way to race another boat. Much of the sailing was at night. Competition was getting pretty keen between tugs even in the 1890s. He has known Chicago River tugs to go as far as the Sturgeon Bay canal in looking for tows, even though they get paid only for the pull in the river. He said Detroit River tugs would go up Lake Huron all the way to the north end to get tows from each other.

"It used to be so a man could tell something about the weather—when the wind backed up against the sun, you could look for a blow, or when there was a wet moon—but you can't tell much about it anymore. Before the woods was all cut down, a sailboat could about always get a breeze to go around and then get a slant for Chicago at night from the land breeze from the Wisconsin shore. You can't do that anymore. The forests are pretty well gone, now.

"Yes, they're hauling pulpwood in here now by truck—little stuff that shouldn't be cut at all—it's a damn shame—wasted millions of it right here and now the woods are all gone and the boats, too. A damn shame—and what are we coming to?"

Mr. Alex Sutherland, almost sixty-five and not well, said his stepfather had come up from deep water, and he had heard him talk about chanteys used on ocean sailboats, but never heard any himself and doubted if there were any on the Lakes. He took some trips with his stepfather across Lake Michigan and to Chicago in the 1890s. The vessels had small crews and there was no singing. Men would "yo-hee" when they pulled. He remembers being becalmed on the Lake one night in a schooner loaded with lumber, all canvas set, and a "cat's paw," a gust of wind, came long and nearly capsized them. He is not very familiar with schooner life. The two-masted *Lyman Davis* was one of the fastest boats of her day, he had heard.

Mr. James Smith, in his late sixties, is editor of the *Muskegon Observer*, and seemingly a general source of information on anything relating to Muskegon. He can remember when there were thirty-six lumber mills on Muskegon Lake and lumbermen around by the hundreds. The town was pretty wild then. He has also seen Muskegon Lake about covered with lumber schooners. He knows no songs or lore of any kind but was much interested in my work and wanted to know all about it. He thinks it is well worth doing, but it may be too late. He referred me to Mr. Irwin Ludwig, a nephew of the South Haven Ludwigs.

I found Mr. Louis H. Conger at his company's fuel dock at the foot of Fourth Street. He graduated from the University of Michigan in 1904 and is active still in alumni affairs. He has been around here most of his life and is closely associated with the Lakes. Schooner days were much earlier than his time. He knows "The *Lady Elgin*" and "*Julie Plante*," but no lore nor any other songs. He phoned a number of people who might know some and gave me several names of people to call upon. Mrs. Conger came with a car for him while we were in his office. She, too, is interested. We had a pleasant visit until about 10:30 p.m. He expected a boatload of coal in about midnight. It would unload on the dock they were just building and start back for Port Huron at once. "Can't pay them ten dollars an hour to lay over the Fourth here," he said.

MUSKEGON, MICHIGAN, JULY 3, 1932

No more days like this one, please. One more and I'll be all finished. Cold and rainy this morning, rainy and cold at noon, and twice as much now—plus the foghorn! And alone. Went downtown for some coffee to warm up on. Drove to a half dozen places to consult people whose names I have, but could find only one, Bob Sargent, about twenty-five, who lives at the city armory as watchman. Is somewhat of an entertainer, but knows no Lakes material. He said his father, George Sargent of Ravenna, Michigan, had a book with a great many songs in it and some about the Lakes. I might write him.

Dinner and a movie: Greta Garbo in *As You Desire Me*, based on a Pirandello play. Well done, but I suspect Pirandello's ending is quite different from that in the film.

The Lake is quite loud tonight.

MUSKEGON, MICHIGAN, JULY 4, 1932

Another holiday will about ruin me for the summer. On Saturday afternoon, few that I wanted to see were where they should be. On Sunday, there was only one and today is not much better. Should have had this day at Ludington and gone fishing.

Called on Captain Garfield at the Coast Guard station this morning and caught him just as he was getting ready to leave for the day. He has been sick and in the marine hospital in Chicago. He heard much singing among convalescing old sailors. He suggested that would be a very good place for me to be around for a while. One old man called Mountain Dew and another called Foghorn and a third named John Ken sang quite a lot. He said they sang old-time chanteys. He said he was expecting to go back there in a week or two and would get all of them he

The Muskegon Coast Guard station. (From postcard)

could for me and send them along. He has heard Lake sailor songs, but remembers none.

I finally found Peter Cardinal, deputy sheriff some twenty years ago and then in the Coast Guard for years. When I asked him about "Rosie Dear," he said it was in William Henry Drummond's "La Habitant" and the real name was "*Julie La Plante.*" I think I already have it. He remembered hearing another French-Canadian dialect song about "a little red canoe." He said it told the story of a couple of Frenchmen in a canoe on the Detroit River where they hook a big fish, which takes them out around the river. They go between a barge and its tow and cut the line, etc.

I found Hans O. Nelson in a little dirty shack on a point of land on the opposite corner of Muskegon Lake. He is in his nineties, a Norwegian who has sailed all his life. He was dressed up, but the shack looked pretty bad. I think he was somewhat embarrassed at my calling at his home. He was pretty close-mouthed at first. He told me he was on deep water for seven years, came to the Lakes in 1882 and has worked on Lakes boats ever since. He has been on many of them and in all parts of the Lakes. He was working as the cook on the *Our Son* the season before it went down. "We nearly lost her then—part of her deckload was lost in a bad storm on a trip that season." Two years ago, he was working on a raft barge when it was wrecked on Lake Huron. A tow was pulling two barges to Duluth and all were pretty old. A blow came and, after trying for hours to make harbor, the tow cut the barges loose, headed in, and sank a half mile from shore.

The oval at Pere Marquette Park, Muskegon, Michigan. (From postcard)

The Coast Guard got all the men off except the cook, who was lost. The Coast Guard saved the men off both barges. [The U.S. Coast Guard was created in 1915 as the result of reorganization intended to cut down government bureaucracy. Several agencies were combined to create the Coast Guard, including the Lighthouse Service, the Revenue Cutter Service, the Steamboat Inspection Service, and the U.S. Lifesaving Service. The Lifesaving Service dated back to 1848 when, after a series of shipwrecks, Congress created the service to maintain stations and small boats along the coastlines to help mariners in distress. The Lifesaving Service maintained rescue stations along the oceans and the Great Lakes.]

Mr. Nelson said there was much singing on the oceans and some on the Lakes when he first came. In 1929, there were four deep-water men on the *Our Son* and they sang "dose songs, dey drop through my memory." He can sometimes recall them when working about, but has had no steady work for over a year. He spends much of his time whittling out ships and can build a ship in a bottle. He has made many that way. He says the Sailors Union in Chicago is the last place to hear sailor songs.

I had lunch at Frank Pascoe's fish place. The cook does know how to prepare fish. Three perch, soft drink and crackers: 30 cents. The only silver on the table was a knife; "forks not allowed."

Drove back to the "oval" and parked facing the lake as usual and wrote this. There are seemingly hundreds of people here, many in bathing suits yet, but few are in the water. I tried swimming this morning, but the water seemed to be on the point of freezing. Am going down to the boat docks again.

Midnight: Went aboard *City of Grand Rapids,* the *Virginia* and the *Missouri.* The first is bound for Chicago and is a pretty nice boat. Was on it at Grand Haven. The *Virginia* came in from Ludington while I was there. There were no old heads aboard and the officers were not familiar with old lore. On the freight deck, where many men were working, they had a radio crooner making a sickly pretense at singing. The *Missouri* came in late and I met Captain Frank Richardson on the dock. He seemed pretty gruff and not interested at first and walked off, but came back in a few minutes and was quite friendly. He had heard many old songs and had been on the Lakes "for years, my boy." I told him I was going across with him in a week or two. He promised to note down all he could recall and have them ready for me when I came back. [In June, Walton had received a letter from the Wisconsin & Michigan Transportation Company, granting his request for passage on a Lakes vessel.]

Now, to bed.

Muskegon and Montague, Michigan, July 5, 1932

Called at the home of Mr. William H. Wilson, but he was not up yet at 9:30 a.m. I waited. His wife appeared first—and can she talk. Mr. Wilson hasn't had much experience on the Lakes himself, but his family has owned schooners and steamboats as long as he can remember. He can remember sailors singing on his father's boats when he was a boy, but can't remember what they sang. He told some episodes of "Rough-Weather Pete," one of his father's captains. He brought a schooner from Georgian Bay with the rudder shoe gone and various other difficulties, and when questioned by his father about the risk of losing the ship and men replied, "I knew the old tub would know her way home." Mr. Wilson said few sailors could or ever did much swimming. They didn't like to go in the water.

I believe I neglected to tell about my drunken friend late last night. While watching the *Missouri* leave Muskegon harbor, I was approached by a man about sixty who was quite disheveled and with the aroma of earlier activities strongly about him. He explained that he was out of a job and money and hadn't had any food for several days, and could I kindly loan him just twenty-five cents? He said he was a sailor, "'n' a damn good one, too. Knew more about ships than that damn mate who wouldn't give me a job."

"How long have you been sailing?"

"Longer 'n anybody on that damn ship, an' I'm a better sailor, too!"

"Did you ever work on any of the old sailing vessels on the Lakes?"

"Sure, all of 'em."

"Do you know any of the chanteys the sailors sang while making sail or doing other work aboard ship?"

"Oh, hell, yes! Every damn one any sailor ever sang."

"Well, I'll give you twenty-five cents for every one you can sing for me."

He cleared his throat a few times and assumed a dramatic pose with his face turned up toward the sky, and began a song about an octave lower than he could possibly sing, telling of Irish Pat's visit to a dentist's office. He bogged down after a few lines.

"Do you know any others?"

"Sure, lots of 'em." And he began the same one again.

"No. Sing me a capstan chantey—any one you can recall."

"All right." After a pause, he began the same one a third time.

I decided that he wasn't a very good prospect, gave him his 25 cents and watched him go up to two other men and, I suppose, ask them for the loan of "just a quarter" to buy some much needed food.

Came on to Montague. Inquired at the corner drugstore and was referred to the hotel across street. Found four old heads gossiping there. Gave them cigars and asked about Lakes sailors and led up to what I wanted. Mr. J. G. Farrell, son-in-law of the owner, gave me the following:

Here sails a fast packet,
She's a packet of fame
She belongs to White Lake
And the *Swallow's* her name

Bound away on Lake Michigan
Where the howling winds blow,
Bound away on the *Swallow*
To Chicago we go.

I think this song is a parody on the ocean song "The *Dreadnaught*."

MONTAGUE, PENTWATER, MICHIGAN, JULY 6, 1932

I went out to Murray's Inn on the south side of the channel between White Lake and the big lake, a very attractive drive. I found William Murray, the proprietor, a man about sixty or more, who has lived near this location all his life. He is a fat, friendly Irishman.

He says he has heard many more but is unable to recall them. He said if he could get a line or tune, he could soon recall more. I asked him about some titles and subjects I'd obtained, but he knew only one, a slightly different version of "The *Bigler*" chorus:

Watch her, catch her
Jump on her old jib-boom
Give her the sheet to the windward
We is the boys to shove her through;

And you ought to hear them howling
When the wind was blowing free
On our trip down to Buffalo
Past Skill-a-bu-drip-I-dee.

I got a boat from the inn and rowed across the end of the lake and down the channel to the White River Coast Guard Station. Captain Smith had not been at that station long, but about the Lakes all his life. He is now near retiring age. As a young man, he had worked in lumber woods winters and sailed summers. He said a great many men did that and recalled songs sung both in lumber camps and on boats and in shore saloons: "Harry Bail," "The Foreman Young Monroe," "The Little Brown Bulls," "Fair Fanny Moore," "Creole Girl of Lake Pontchartrain," "Indian's Lament." He said there were a great many more. Chanteys are hard to remember, as they were more to work by than for singing. He remembered hearing a song about Louis Sands of Manistee who, in paying his men, deducted and abstracted, etc., until his men had no wages left.

He recalled that near the Sailors' Union in Chicago was the usual rooming house district of the sailors between cruises. As steamboats grew in number, the steamboat men would all room on one side of the street and sailboat men on other—they did not mix. Schoonermen considered themselves more the real sailors. There were not infrequent fights when they met in saloons. Steamboat men had no songs.

I called at the home of Captain Fred Stahl and found him listening to a radio report of a baseball game. I asked him again about songs that accompanied making sail.

"Yes, I used to hear that damn noise some, but I wouldn't call it singing. When I was a kid around here, the lumber schooners used to come into Pentwater Lake to await good weather, dozens of 'em at a time. And then, when the seas went down some, they'd tow out and make a hell of a noise getting up canvas so they'd catch the wind as soon as they'd get out."

"When was that?"

"Oh, that was near sixty years ago."

"Do you remember any of the words the men sang together as they pulled?"

"No, they just said anything."

Pentwater and Ludington, Michigan, July 8, 1932

I went to Captain Al Corey's home. Found him hoeing beans in a small field behind his farm home. He went on the Lakes in the early 1870s as a ship's "boy" when 13 and was on every season until he retired a few years ago. At one time, there were hundreds of lumber schooners on Lake Michigan. "Yes, many sailors came up from salt water, but they was too slow for us, and didn't stay long. They couldn't do anything without singing and that was too slow for the lumber boats. The mate would come around and 'goddamn' 'em and 'Christ almighty, get them sails up.' Singing made it too slow. One or two trips was enough for most of those shellbacks and they didn't stay long."

"Didn't you like to sing when you pulled?"

"No. I never could sing when we got loaded. We wanted to be out and going. First ones to Chicago got the best places to tie up and wait for buyers."

Walton after a successful fishing trip at
Pigeon River, Michigan, in 1930.
(Courtesy Lynn and Sue Walton)

"The salt-water men were pretty good sailors, weren't they?"

"Well, not any better than the ones from around here."

"Didn't they sing quite a bit on some boats?"

"Oh, yes, on some of them they did, but it was too slow for us."

"How about when you were ashore?"

"Oh, we had some good ones then," and then he went into a long
description of "the gang" that were the life of Pentwater in the old days, especially
in winter, their "Pall Bearers' Union." One wouldn't go to a funeral unless they all
did, and one time when carrying the coffin of "an old fellow who died out a couple
miles from town," we were all as wobbly as "a galley full of gull shit."

I got him back to the Lakes, but he insisted on telling me about the
exploits of "the gang." I pulled him back several times and fed him two cigars, but
concluded there wasn't much poetry in the soul of Captain Corey.

I came on to Ludington. I picked up a boy from Chelsea, Michigan, who
was going up into cherry country to pick cherries during season, but he could get
only 1/4 cent a pound and was quite discouraged. I had dinner and then called at
the city library. The librarian was away on a vacation, and the assistant librarian
was a young girl who seemed to have a great vacancy where some knowledge
should be. She found an early local history, but it practically ignored the Lake.

Then I went out to the lakeshore, and so ended the day.

LUDINGTON, MICHIGAN, JULY 9, 1932

No Lakes work today—FISHING.

While going to the bank where he works, John Stram introduced me to Dr. Hoffman, the University of Michigan, 1890, upon my inquiring about someone who might want to go fishing. Dr. Hoffman closed up his office and said fishing was more important than tending ladies' ailments. We drove back to his house and got his outfit, including a pair of waders for me, and drove out to the middle branch of the Pere Marquette River, a very beautiful stream, and went fishing. I had dinner with Dr. Hoffman upon returning to Ludington. Trout. Lots of them. Stram came over after me and I spent the night at his home. This day and past night and prospects of this one have been worth a million. Have been getting pretty lonesome.

LUDINGTON, MICHIGAN, JULY 10, 1932

Am parked on a bluff overlooking Lake Michigan as the sun sets and a bright half moon lights the western sky. The waves are making their usual crash, crash, crash on the shore out in front and from me to the horizon a widening silvered way. On the left edge of it blinks the white and red breakwater lights. The skyline to the northwest is a deep indigo, which shades off to near darkness on the other end. Peter, you should be here.

Repacked at Stram's Hotel this morning and once more in the evening. Made another trip about the harbor, but no results, then called at the home of Captain Duncan Milligan, an eighty-two-year-old Scotchman who is still good for a half century. He came to the Lakes in 1872 after being on ocean sailboats for six years. Recalled chanteying on the ocean, but said there was nothing of the kind on the Lakes or any of the boats he was on. He said lakesmen called out "yo-ho," "yo-hie," or "all pull" and would pull on the last syllable instead of singing. When told of what other lakesmen had said about this, he said there may have been some, but not like on ocean boats. He said living conditions on Lakes boats were much better than on ocean sailboats, but men had to work faster and harder. He added that there was considerable singing ashore, but he never knew the songs they sang. He recognized the chorus for "The *Bigler*," saying he'd heard it many times. He didn't seem to be familiar with lore of any kind, at least none that I could get at through questions. He said the men with deep-water training made the best Lake sailors, and that a master of a sailing craft had to know much more than the master of a steamboat.

Night, Pete and Lynn.

LUDINGTON, MICHIGAN, JULY 11, 1932

I had some difficulty today in locating the farm home of Andrew Peterson, a native of Sweden, for twelve years a salt-water sailor, then a lakesman and for the past four decades a farmer. The farming area northeast of Ludington, Michigan, is

Sunset on Lake Michigan. (From *Picturesque America*)

well populated with Petersons—Lars, Jon, Ole, Peter, Chris, Gus, Andy, and seemingly a score of others, and practically all were, at some time in their lives, sailors. They all answered my inquiry in their Swedish-accented friendly way: "Ya, my name is Pay-der-so-on."

I finally found Andrew's farm, and the sprightly eighty-two-year-old was out by his frame barn, selling a fat cow to a butcher. That was a real stage show with much gesticulating, shrugging of shoulders and short walks from the scene as if the deal were all off. They finally settled on a price of thirty dollars. When the money was proffered, Andrew took a large roll of bills out of his sagging hip pocket, added the new bills to it and returned the enlarged roll to its original place. Then, with a friendly invitation to visit him again "ven out dis vey," he handed the butcher the light rope with which the cow was tied.

That business over, he looked at me questioningly until I asked him about sailing. He then brightened up with a "ya, ya, ya, ay sail long ago. I sail over de vhol vorld twelve year, den ay kom to Lakes." Two hours later, he was still far ranging.

He worked his way from New York to Buffalo on an Erie Canal boat about 1880, and then shipped on a grain schooner to Chicago. There was no chanteying on that vessel when they made sail or did other group work. The mate called out "yo-ho" and "yo-he" as the crew hauled on the lines, and he continually exhorted them to work faster. Later, Andrew shipped on many other Lakes vessels, and he added that whenever there were any deep-water men aboard they did all the hard work to the rhythm of chanteys. Local sailors usually joined in gladly. "Vork ain't so hard dat vay."

When asked if he could recall any of the songs they used, he thought a minute and then lined out a few lines in a high voice and in a deeper tone gave the crew's responses as he went through all the motions of hauling on a line. As I couldn't make out any of his words, I asked him to repeat. He laughed and said, "Ay forgat. Dat was Swedish, an' Ay ain't t'ought on dat in fifty year." In response to a question about the subjects of the chanteys, his reply was, "Oh, dem chanteymen, dey sing about anyt'ing, a' sailors, dey sing vor dose vimmin dat kom out on dock ven sailboat kom in to Buffalo." He added, "Ay sorry ay forgat dem ole song. Der vas alvays some fellows aboard who knew dem."

After a long talk about sailor life and ways, he mentioned quite casually that he was onboard the schooner *Anna Cook* and approaching the Chicago harbor when they were caught in a bad northerner. No tug answered their signal, and they drifted in closer and closer to the old Chicago breakwater and almost crashed into it when a big sea hit them and carried them entirely over into safe water.

When I was about to leave him, he took me by the arm and said, "Ay t'ink on von ole chantey song, vot English sailormen sing ven der vessel make sail by American boat," and then, with all the motions of hauling on a line, he sang:

A Yankee ship kom down the reever,
    Blow boys, blow boys, blow!
Her tops'ls set and all a-sheever

Blow, my bully boys, blow!

An vat you t'ink dey have for dinner?
    Blow boys, blow boys, blow!
Donkey's heart and monkey's leever,
    Blow, my bully boys, blow!

MANISTEE, MICHIGAN, JULY 12, 1932

I spent much of yesterday waiting. The morning is not a very good time to visit people on this quest. Had valves on car adjusted and speedometer treated to a going-over so as to make it operate.

Mr. W. H. Hall, keeper of the Manistee light, said he'd been aboard the Lakes forty some years. When at St. Helen's Island light at the Straits in the late 1890s, he had often seen twenty or more sailboats tied up awaiting favorable winds or weather. When they were preparing to leave—weighing anchor and making sail—there would be lots of chanteying. I asked specifically if it were just "yo-ho-ing," or real chanteying where one of them would sing a line or two and then all would join in, and he said there was both. He said he liked to hear them and used to watch and listen to them when he could.

U. OF MICHIGAN FISHERIES RESEARCH CAMP, BEAR LAKE, MANISTEE, MICHIGAN, JULY 13, 1932

Captain Nels Thompson, retired Lakes captain, was very much interested in this collecting. He said it was a shame it wasn't done twenty years ago when there were a great many songs telling of the careers of ships, wrecks, races, and some of the well-known characters of the Lakes.

He began sailing in Lakes schooners in 1878 and was out every season until this present season, and now shipping is so dead that there are few boats running. He changed to steamboating about twenty years ago, but would much rather be on schooners. He did nearly all of his sailing on grain boats between Chicago and Erie ports, mostly Buffalo. Had both salt- and freshwater sailors in his crews. He thinks the freshwater men were just as good sailors as those from the oceans. Sailors on the "lumber hookers" on the short runs to Chicago from the other Lake Michigan ports practically never sang when working on the boats. They were always in too much of a hurry and men had to work almost night and day. But on the longer trips on "the down-lakers" where it took them from one to three weeks to go one way, the men often worked to chanteys: "Early in the Morning," "Blow, Boys, Blow," "Poor Old Joe," "Haul on the Bowline," "Homeward Bound," and many others he couldn't recall. He said there was always some fellow in the crew who could make up verses, and he'd sing them and all the men would join in on the chorus. They'd often "roast" the cook, particularly if he wasn't a very good one, and at times the mate or captain.

Sometimes the songs would tell about the trip and they were often about women. He never took them seriously and no one tried to remember them. They changed from one singing to the next. The men would practically always chantey when pulling up to the Buffalo piers by a line, which they did at times to save tow bills and at other times when tugs were not available "and how them men could roar—they had good lungs in them days."

He said there wasn't much chanteying on the sailboats after the 1880s. Steamboats were getting quite plentiful then and were fast taking the trade away from the sailboats. Competition got very fierce and there was much "bad blood" between the sail and steamboat men. Steamboats could guarantee delivery of their cargoes at a certain time and could practically always make much better time than a schooner, even when it had favorable winds. The sailors served a losing fight and took it out on the steamboat men. They called the steamboat men "bums," "cinder-eaters" and "many other names we don't repeat." They wouldn't permit the steamboat men to call themselves "sailors" and wouldn't permit them in the some rooming houses or in the saloons. The sailors always regarded themselves as much superior to the steamboat men. This feeling died down in the 1890s when the steamboats came to equal or outnumber the schooners, and many of the former sailboat men had to ship on steamboats in order to get jobs. Many of the old schoonermen refused to do this and went into shore work and got scattered all over the country. He had many songs "that tell stories" which the men would sometimes sing in the fo'c'sle or when ashore, but they, too, are gone now.

Captain Harry Nelson was at home, a little cool at first, but a cigar and praise of the old salt-water sailors thawed him out and he became the most willing and enthusiastic man so far this summer. We talked for about three hours. He explained different kinds of sailing ships, how they are operated, trips he had taken during the twenty or so years he had sailed the oceans, the last few of which he made second mate and then first mate. He was wrecked several times, picked up once after drifting several days in a lifeboat, deserted ship once with another man in port in Transvaal, South Africa, when the rush to the new mines was there. After hiding in bushes for three days, they were found by police who were scouring the country to find them to get the rewards that were offered—and taken out of the fugitives' pay—and returned to his ship. He was "around the Horn" many times in all kinds of weather when most of the course was by "dead reckoning"— guesswork.

He liked the old life on the sea and ran away from home as a boy to go. All his family was sailors, and most were lost at sea. "It was a hard life and a man never knew when he shipped out that he'd get back."

And chanteys! "Yes, I should say so. Lots of them. Salt-water sailors always worked to chanteys." And then in answer to my questions, he explained the different kinds used on ocean schooners, how they were used, the similarity of them in all languages and how they took the drudgery out of work. A good chanteyman was a favored man in a crew. On boats with big crews, he usually didn't have to work—just lead the singing. He often sat on the capstan as men walked around it pushing on the bars. The chanteyman made up verses as he went along about the boat, the officers, crew, sweethearts, events, etc. When they had a long pull, he'd have to keep going till they got through. The men would all come in on the chorus. "You could hear them halfway 'cross the ocean." On some ships, the chanteyman would play a fiddle or an accordion. "I used to be a sort of a chanteyman myself when there was not any good ones aboard." He recognized all the ocean chantey titles that I could mention. He said that no Lakes schooner he was ever on used them at all regularly. He came to the Lakes in 1892. At rare intervals, some sailor— usually a salt-water man—would start up one and the other men would join in, but this was very rarely. He used to start them himself when he first came to the Lakes and "was before the mast." [Sailors slept in the bow of the ship—in front of the mast—and stayed at that end of the vessel unless working or summoned aft by the captain or mate.] He soon came to be a mate and then a master. He said he had heard men who had been on the Lakes many years before he came tell about some "Lake chanteys" which told about Lakes events, but he never knew any. Lakes sailors in the 1890s would at times sing chanteys in the fo'c'sle and ashore for amusement, but very seldom while working. He tried repeatedly, but couldn't recall any.

He feels quite bitter because he can't get a job on a boat anymore. "They take the young fellows who don't know a damn thing about sailing and think I'm too old." He said the ocean sailors were much superior to the freshwater men. "On the ocean, you took years to learn it. Had to learn it all, too, by God, so you could do anything about a ship. These fellows think they're sailors after a couple of trips in a stokehole."

I made several trips before finding Captain Harold Hill in his office in the Hill Bros. Automotive shop. He is a younger man who began his Lakes career in 1903 on sailboats. He had heard some songs that men sang for amusement, but never wrote them down. "If you did that, the other men would think there was something wrong with you—that you weren't a real sailor. You were supposed to know them and say nothing about them."

Tom Ellefson is a Norwegian about seventy-five to eighty, who had about eight years on the ocean and came to the Lakes in the early 1880s. Three brothers also came. His family as far back as he knows was all sailors and fishermen. He remembers seeing as many as fifty full-rigged schooners awaiting the opening of ice in spring to set out for ports all over the world. He first went to sea when about twelve. He said there was much chanteying on all ocean sailboats then. There was some on Lakes schooners when he first came, but not as regularly as on the ocean boats. Crews were smaller and the longest trips were "only down to Buffalo." Sailors would often sing chanteys in show saloons. They had many songs they'd sing about trips, wrecks, and other events and experiences. He remembers there was one about the career of the schooner *Julia B. Merrill* and another about the schooner *Monsoon*, which went down under full sail. "The crew were all pretty drunk, I heard. She probably waterlogged. Yes, all hands were lost—the song tells about it." He couldn't recall where he'd heard it. One would hear such songs anywhere sailors got together and had nothing to do.

There were a "couple of 'gospel boats' around for quite a time. The *Glad*

Tidings and the *Patowac*." The captains and crews on them were all missionaries and held religious meetings whenever they were in any port.

NORTH OF FRANKFORT, MICHIGAN, JULY 15, 1932

Came on to Arcadia and called on Olaf Hanson, "Pierport Ole," about eighty, somewhat deaf and in slow recovery from a two-month illness. His memory is quite impaired. He was on the ocean for fourteen years, and made four trips to Australia and one around the world. "We had real sailors and sailing on the ocean," he said. They sang chanteys for all good work. One time, when pulling into an Atlantic harbor against the current of a stream, they worked for five hours and chanteyed all the time. In 1880, he came to the Lakes and they sang chanteys on some of the Lakes schooners, but not regularly. In the 1890s, big schooners were cut down and made into tow barges. Before this, they had crews of eight to twelve men and they'd use chanteys when a number of deep-water sailors were aboard— especially when the shore audience contained women. He remembered singing many songs, especially when in shore saloons, but could not recall any chanteys about Lakes subjects. He didn't think he had ever heard any Lakes stories or legends or superstitions comparable to those on the ocean. "Brace the main sheet" meant to take a drink of whiskey.

Captain John Neilson, Scandinavian, is about eighty, straight, dignified, with white hair and a mustache. He is now living alone in a large home just east of the village. He, too, began on the ocean. He much preferred ocean sailing to the Lakes for larger crews, larger ships, and longer trips. He had heard stories of the Sargasso Sea [this section of the north Atlantic is said to have strange creatures living amid its floating seaweed], the flying Dutchman [a ghostly ship doomed to sail for eternity], phantom ships, etc., but nothing like this on the Lakes. Wages and living were better on the Lakes, however. He liked to work to chanteys. Men could pull harder and not know they were working. He came to the Lakes about 1884. Lumber schooners were always in too much of a hurry to get to Chicago. The men's chief aim was to find time for sleep. On "lower lakers," conditions were better. They sang on some of them. The chanteys were not very definite. When big schooners disappeared as steamboats took over, chanteying also went except when men would sing for pleasure and something to do.

I found John McKinnon, retired lightkeeper, at his home. He took me across the street to the home of the family of Captain Miller, who died last year. His daughter, Mrs. Gates, knew no material of this kind and referred me to her cousin, Captain Manus J. Bonner of Charlevoix. He's a former Beaver Islander and sailed the Lakes for many years.

SUTTONS BAY, MICHIGAN, JULY 16, 1932

I began the day by visiting the Point Betsie Light, located in a very picturesque place between the lake and the high ridge of dunes that divide Lake Michigan and Crystal Lake. The keeper was about to go to the cherry festival at Traverse City, somewhat against his will but with the insistence of his family. He showed me the light, including the very elaborate and expensive lens and clockwork that controls its revolving, and the foghorn and radio signal mechanism. He had it all shined up to the last degree.

"Do you always keep the station shined up like this?"

"Well, not all the time. We're expecting the inspector along tomorrow."

"Does he let you know when he's coming?"

"No, he doesn't, but we know."

"How?"

"He's quite a yachtsman, and very interested in the races from Chicago, where he lives, to Mackinac Island. [The Chicago-to-Mackinac sailboat race, first run in 1898, is the world's oldest and longest freshwater sailboat race.] I noticed in the newspaper the other day that the race this summer started yesterday. He'll follow along the shore and ought to get here about tomorrow. He gets up to Mackinac when they do and helps them drink their champagne."

"Hank" LaFreniere of Frankfort, the assistant keeper, is about fifty-five, a Frenchman and former Beaver Islander, and said he had heard many times a song about the tug *Seven Brothers*. The song tells of its trip from Chicago past the various lights and finally rounding the island to the harbor. He said the Irish on Beaver Island were great singers and a large number of the old sailors are still there. He gave me the names of a number of them.

I went back around the end of Crystal Lake and on to Empire, a very beautiful drive. The only possibility I could find in Empire was Captain Kent, a former Coast Guard captain at Muskegon for thirty years and at Manitou Island. He returned about fifteen years ago. He was somewhat surly and told me at least twenty times that there is no such material as I'm searching for and never was. Men on Lakes boats had to work too hard, too few of them were on each boat, and they were not together long enough because the custom on the Lakes was to pay them off at the end of every trip and so there were continually new crews. Well! Not so good.

The big sand dunes of Sleeping Bear and the sudden burst of the lake as one cuts through the dunes into the village are sights not often found. Inquired for cottages there: fifteen to forty dollars a week. I went on around to Leland on the strip of land between Lake Leelanau and Lake Michigan. The afternoon sun hung over the Manitou Islands. Wooded sand hills all about. What a place to live!

I had a wonderful moonlit drive east to Suttons Bay, mostly without car lights. There were big hills on either side of the winding road and a bright, full moon that touched the landscape with magic. I parked the car and walked across a field and up a big hill. Except for two busy whip-poor-wills, the world was all quiet and thoughtful.

The village was closed and retired for the night when I arrived. The most inviting place I could find to stay for the remainder of the night was a cherry orchard just back of a church, and here I am. The tree is loaded with sweet cherries and I'm relieving it of as many as my capacity will permit—no one being around to count.

Night, Peter and Lynn. You would have enjoyed the night.

Suttons Bay, Michigan, July 17, 1932

My parking place and the cherries were not as ideal as they seemed last night. The cherries gave me a bellyache about 4 a.m. and I just got to sleep again when a great clanging of bells began. This inoffensive appearing church turned out to be Catholic and seemingly all the natives in the countryside go to early mass. I couldn't dress until they got inside, and now must be off before they get loose again.

Mostly by accident, I met Mr. J. H. Kennedy, a former lumber camp singer and sometimes sailor. He offered to go with me to Northport to consult another ex-lumberman and singer, Mr. William M. Gill. This seemed to be a pretty good opportunity. We drove to Mr. Gill's house, about a half or three-quarters of a mile south of the village, but found Mr. Gill absent, attending a baseball game that afternoon between a Northport team and one from Traverse City. We went to the game and found Mr. Gill in the midst of a considerable crowd. The ninth inning was about half over and evidently a pretty hot one. The score stood 4–4 and, as the inning progressed, the Traverse City pitcher got himself into a pretty bad situation with the bases full and a count of three balls and two strikes on the Northport batter. The Northport crowd went pretty noisy at this point, and the Traverse City pitcher got pretty worried and called a conference. The decision was for him to continue. After a hesitation with all the Northporters on their feet and yelling, he threw a deep out, and the umpire called, "ball four," and walked the runner in from third base, making the final score 5–4 in favor of Northport.

The Traverse City catcher turned around and grabbed the umpire, and raised his fist to strike as some Northport players grabbed him. In not more than a few seconds, both teams were milling about the home plate and a good share of the audience as well. A grand free-for-all was in progress when two state police rushed in from nowhere with their sticks swinging to rescue the umpire. After tapping a number of enthusiasts with their sticks, they came out of the melee with the official in tow. I noticed that one was without his hat and was rubbing his jaw.

Eventually, Mr. Gill was asked many things, among them whether Michigan lumbermen actually told Paul Bunyan stories in camp. He smiled and asked if I knew how Paul made squared timber for shipment down the Lakes. [Loggers squared off the butt ends of felled trees to be able to pack more into a vessel. These squared-off logs were called waneys]. Of course, I didn't. It seems that the great lumberman would walk up to a pine, five feet wide or even wider, fasten a broad axe on the inside of each foot, then score and cut the branches off two sides as he climbed to the top. Then, he would hew these two sides as he slid down. Then, he'd treat the other two sides in the same way, and the squared timber was ready to be cut down and into the desired lengths for shipment.

Traverse City, Michigan, July 19, 1932

Captain Martin Johnson was sitting under a tree alone and was exceedingly glad when I arrived so he'd have someone to talk with. He's in his early eighties and in pretty bad physical condition. He ran away from his home in Saginaw when nine after receiving a beating from his mother. He went to Port Huron to get a job as a "boy" on a schooner and sailed from then until the failure of his eyes forced him to retire eleven years ago. He began on the Lakes during the Civil War and received his master's papers and a vessel when he was in his twenties. He sailed on big, four-masted grain and coal carriers, with crews of twelve to sixteen. They would at times use chanteys in hoisting the main canvas or anchor, and at other times pulled to someone "singing out." "That's when there were real men—they ain't none now—the men then used to be."

And the women! "I don't know what they're coming to. In my day, they had some pride and modesty, but now the less they can wear, the better they like it."

"Did the men on the boats sing much when you first began sailing on the Lakes?"

"Oh, yes, sailors always sing when a few get together. I used to go forward sometimes in evening dogwatches [4–6 p.m. and 6–8 p.m.] when they'd be singing and listen to them. It would just wring your heart sometimes—and they had some that were pretty bad."

"Do you know some of those that were sung very often on your boat?"

"I used to know fifty or more all about sailors, but I can't seem to remember 'em now. I used to could remember everything, but I can't anymore. Old Cap' Johnson isn't much good anymore."

"Did your men sing any work songs so they could all work together when pulling up the mainsails or anchor?"

"Sometimes they did."

"What were some of the songs about?"

"I can't remember at all."

"Do you recall that at any such times someone didn't 'sing out' instead of all the men singing?"

"Yes, sure. They did that sometime."

"What did they 'sing out' on such occasions?"

"Sometimes a man would just say, 'ho, ho, ho, ho.' And then there was some you won't find printed anywhere."

"What were they?"

"Well, different ones like, 'Bellies down . . . asses high' and anything they might think of."

"What kind of songs would they sing when ashore?"

"Some of those shore fellows were great singers."

"What kinds of songs would they sing?"

"I'm sorry I can't be of much help to you on that. Since my wife left me four years ago, and I've got this rheumatiz in my leg and can't get around, I tell you, I've about lost my mind and I can't remember things anymore. She lived with me forty-four years and then one morning she got up from breakfast, packed a satchel and left and I ain't seen her since. I often dream about her, though, and them's pleasant dreams, but I ain't never seen her since that morning she left me."

"Why did she leave?"

"Well, sir, I don't know, but if a woman can live with a man forty-four years, he can't be all bad, can he?"

He knew the juberju song ["The *E. C. Roberts*"]—parts:

[Chorus]
Watch her, catch her
Jump up on her juberju
Give her the sheet and let her go
We're the boys to push her through.
You ought to heard her howling
Her course was down the shore
She's bound down to Cleveland
With nine hundred tons of ore.

[Final verse]
Now we're in Cleveland,
Tied up 'longside the pier
And the boys are down on Main Street
A-drinking lager beer.

When I arrived back in camp, a group of cherry pickers were singing to a banjo, so I joined in and sang a flock of old sailor, cowboy, army, college, and popular songs until after 11 p.m.

Now it's past midnight again and to bed.

Night Peter, Lynn.

Charlevoix, Michigan, July 20, 1932

Sam Rose was in his barbershop beside a bridge over the channels, and is about seventy-nine. His father was lost in the Civil War and his mother married a Lakes sailor and she went as cook and he as "boy" at age nine. He was mate for his stepfather at sixteen and continued sailing for more than fifty years. He carried lumber from Muskegon and nearby ports to Chicago and later from more-distant ports. He heard much singing among sailors: "Skillagalee and Wobble Shanks," "It Was in the Year 1801," "Louis Sands," "Fair Fanny Moore," "Foreman Young Monroe," "*Law* and *Danforth*," "The *Lady of the Lakes*," "*Annie M. Peterson*." They had two Swedes in their crew for several years who sang sailor songs in broken English a great deal. Rose could not recall words of any of their songs. "I've been barbering for the last twenty years, and haven't thought of those old songs all that time. I used to like to hear them."

Found Captain Manus J. Bonner at his home. He's an Irishman, about eighty, slightly stooped and has very white hair and a mustache. He was very friendly and interested in this work and willing to help. He gave me names of several Beaver Islanders to see. He was born on the island. Both his parents are from Ireland and the same for Mrs. Bonner. He began sailing as a boy and followed the Lakes continuously, even making a few trips last year as substitute captain on boats out of Charlevoix.

He said men on his boats didn't do much regular chanteying. He had heard some, particularly on long, hard pulls on the main sheets [lines]. Much of their crews were from the island and they sang a great deal, especially when ashore evenings. I asked him if he had heard a song about "The *Lady of the Lakes*" and he at once said:

> Farewell unto my Eliza Gray
> For I know her heart will break
> When she gets news that I am drowned
> On the *Lady of the Lakes*.

Said he'd "get" the rest pretty soon. He had heard a song about Louis Sands, but couldn't recall it well. He wasn't sure about "The *Annie M. Peterson*," but knew the boat well. "She was a smart sailing boat in a fair wind. Could outsail most of 'em, but she was over-yarded and carried too much canvas for a blow or to beat against strong headwinds." He asked if I knew "The Sailor's Alphabet" and, as I didn't, he gave it to me with, "I hadn't thought of that for twenty-five years."

> A is the anchor of our gallant ship,
> B is the bowsprit that in the seas dip,
> C is the capstan so merrily goes 'round, and
> D is the davits to which our boat's bound.
>
> So merry, so merry, so merry are we,
> No mortals on earth are as happy as we;
> Hi derry, ho derry, hi derry down,
> Give sailor boys rum and there's nothing goes wrong!
>
> E is the ensign at our masthead,
> F is the fo'c'sle where is our bed,
> G is the gun'l, against it seas splash,
> H is the hawser that holds the ship fast.
>
> I is the iron, without it we're lost,
> J is the jolly boat that rows us acrost
> K is the keelson as I have been told, and
> L is the lany'rd that keeps a good hold.
>
> M is the mainmast so stout and so tall,
> N is the nettings that hangs our hammocks all.
> O is the oars we often do row, and
> P is the pennant so lightly does flow.

Q is the quarterdeck on which our good captain stood,
R is the riggin' so stout and so good.
S is the steward that weighs our beef, and
T is the tops'ls we oft have to reef.

U is the union to which our troubles pass,
V is the vang that holds steady the gaff.
W is the wheel by which we do steer, and
X, Y and Z are the rest of the gear.

He asked if I had a song about "The Drunken Captain" and then gave me it—all thirteen stanzas. Said he didn't "drank" himself nor "smoked." Had seen too much of what drinking does to sailors. Has on many occasions left Chicago and other ports trying to use a fresh breeze that was blowing, and found his men so drunk that half of them had d.t.'s [delirium tremens] and the other half were not able to do any work. He had to send them all below and he and the mate did the best they could to manage the boat. "I've always rooted for Prohibition, but don't think I'll do it again—not after seeing what it's doing to young boys and girls."

Unfortunately, this remark led to politics and I discerned that Mr. Bonner was a rabid anti-Hoover. Venting his feelings on Hoover led to Europe and the war debt and the England-Ireland conflict. We should have stayed out of the war and let Germany wipe England off the face of the Earth, and then he enumerated Ireland's grievances, told events his mother and father had described that happened before they left Ireland. There were no more songs after this.

He insisted that I come back and see him after I got back from island. His brother Pat is over there and was a great man to sing and even made up songs. Mrs. Bonner earlier in evening told of her brother, the captain of the car ferry *Pere Marquette 18,* being lost as the boat foundered on Lake Michigan with *No. 17* standing by. She gave me a copy of a song written about it by Frank McCauley beginning, "From Ludington one dark September day." I promised to copy it off and return it to her. Also, *"Julia Dean."* She also mentioned a song about the *Clifton* written by Captain Bonner's brother Pat.

Beaver Island, Michigan, July 21, 1932

Came over from Charlevoix on the *Ossian Bedell.* Left about 9:15 a.m. and arrived about 12:30 p.m. at St. James, à la King Strang, a tumble-down sleepy place with fishermen's nets all around. [James Jesse Strang led a Mormon sect that came to dominate Beaver Island. Strang had himself coronated as a king and ruled the island until some of his followers attacked him in 1856, wounding him fatally. Mainlanders, many of them displaced Irish people, ran the others off the island.] On the dock were Irish of all descriptions—big, little, dark-haired, red-haired and whatnot, and at one end of the dock a collection of Indians.

Had a long talk with Captain Gallagher, formerly of the island, on the way over. He has many relatives here. On the dock, he introduced me to a cousin,

Colorful Captain Charlie C. Allers at St. James, Beaver Island. (Courtesy Arthur Gallagher)

Frank Gallagher, who he said would start me out, so I had dinner and we were off. Drove about six miles southwest and came out on the west side of Beaver Island opposite High Island, which looks a half mile away, but is over four. It and Garden Island beyond are inhabited by Indians.

I visited the home of three bachelor uncles of Captain Gallagher—three Irishmen about five foot four and in age from sixty to seventy named O'Donnell. They talk in high voices with lots of Irish in them. They live on a farm on a small inland lake. Then we came to the home of a retired native of Chicago that Frank couldn't get past without going in after some beer. That over, we found the home of Pat Bonner, but he was working out in the fields, so we drove to the home of Frank "Francie" Roddy. He, too, was working in the hay field, but a heavy shower of rain ended that and he came home. He's a big fellow, heavy, red-faced, about six foot three or more and about sixty years old and Irish. He was born here and spent his life here except thirty years of sailing the Lakes. His father, Andrew, was also a sailor "and could sing all day without stopping—with a few drinks." Francie himself seemed much like his father.

He gave me a version of "The *Lady of the Lakes*" like the stanzas from Captain Bonner. He said it was well known among Lakes sailors. He also gave words to "The Steam Tug *Olson*," a few lines of "The Indian's Lament," and started on "Fair Fanny Moore" when some friends came along. He said he had to do his chores despite the rain, but to come back in the evening, which I did, but before he got to songs, again two more friends' cars came along for the evening and that ended our affairs again. He said to come back tomorrow.

We started for the home of Pat Bonner, but when we were inquiring at a farmhouse as to where he lived, he drove by with his family bound "for town" and that was that.

We then looked up the home of Captain Charlie C. Allers and found him and Mrs. Allers at home. He's perhaps the most romantic figure on the island. We didn't get to songs, that is, not seriously. He has some written down which he's going to dig out for tomorrow. He will try to recall others. He's a picturesque old lad, eighty-four years old, and according to his stories, has been all over the world in ocean sailboats—about frozen in Archangel, Russia, and cooked in Indian seas, mixed up with Chinese pirates, etc.,

Is a good talker and likes to. Has a royal hatred for "those damned bigoted Irish Catholics," yet one of his best friends was Father Jewell Gillespie, a priest who was here a few years ago. He's also a "hot" socialist. Sees the last war as the great attempt of capitalism to maintain itself. Russia is now the great leader of mankind. The new Russian regime is to revolutionize the world.

A nightcap and goodnight, captain. See you tomorrow.

Beaver Island, Michigan, July 22, 1932

Wakened this morning with about a dozen little Indians examining the car very closely, trying doors, wheels, etc. They ran off when I showed signs of life.

Made my first visit to the home of Pat Bonner, about five miles out from town. He was out in his fields with the Charlevoix County agent examining crops. He came up to the house about 11 a.m. and my day with Pat began.

He used to know a few songs, but had forgotten them all, "but did ya ever hear one about—" and we were off till dinner was ready and I had to join them—wife, brother, son John and orphan nephew living with them, and on until 4 p.m.

He had learned "The Steam Tug *Olson*" from Francie Roddy years ago, and went through it all without a stop. Made some corrections in Francie's version—inserted a stanza or two, etc.

He gave a couple stanzas of "The Banks of Newfoundland," "The *Cumberland*'s Crew," "The *Richards*," "The Black Prince," "The *Merrimac*," and "The *Hesperus*," all ocean songs he had learned on Lakes boats. The last turned out to be Longfellow's ballad, "The Schooner *Hesperus*." He also started on "The Buffalo Girls Are Coming Out Tonight," and after repeating that line three times went off on another which he said was an ocean song but a "damn good one." He sang "When First I Went to Sea," and an unending one—five and a half pages—called "The Stowaway." He leaned over my notebook and beat time with his forefinger and sang a line at a time. While I was trying to keep up with him, he'd explain just what was going on according to the narrative. I managed to get him back to the Lakes for a few stanzas of "The Gallagher Boys," but he got stuck on it and in rapid succession named about a dozen people on the island who ought to know it. It's the story of three island boys, two Gallaghers and Tommy Boyle—half the people in all events here are Gallaghers—who late in fall went over to Traverse City on the mainland for winter provisions. On the way back, they were hit by a bad storm, which raged for a couple days. Their small sailboat came ashore with the provisions near the south side of the island, but the boys were lost. "That was about thirty years ago or more when we was cut off entirely from the mainland in the winter. John Green knows that well, and many another as well."

Bonner then extracted from the wall or table or some other mysterious place an old broken fiddle box and took out a fiddle and handed it to me to "look over." It had e, a, and g strings aboard with the d broken at the bridge. It was pretty badly shopworn, chin worn, etc., but had a marvelous tone as I tried out an impromptu "melody in A" à la Walton. I took it to the window and looked inside, and behold! In somewhat faded letters: *Antonius Stradivarius Cremonentis, Faciebad Anno 1713.*

That gives one somewhat of a start, whether genuine or not.

Bonner said he got it from his brother-in-law, who had acquired it near Escanaba, Michigan, probably forty years ago from a fellow who was broke and came to the lumber camp where he was working. Says John tied the string together, reversed it so the knot was near the key and Pat tuned it up and couldn't keep from fiddling, and then came Irish reels, jigs, and whatnot for an hour or more.

"Don't you ever get tired?"

"No, I've played all night long for many a dance around here." And again he settled back, eyes closed, a grin on his face, hand up a third of the way on the bow, and sawed off a few more to the thumping of his foot on the floor. I got him back to "The Gallagher Boys," but he couldn't recall it.

Pat recalled that he had some hay out that should be put in, so he put a fresh chew in the starboard cheek, picked up his overflow can in the middle of the floor, and asked me if I'd ever heard "The Old Lutheran Breeches."

I then asked about "The Steamer *Clifton*," a song which his brother, Captain Manus Bonner, told me Pat had composed on the sinking of that steamer in Lake Huron in September 1924. He dug it up, or rather, Mrs. Bonner did, and gave it to me to copy. As he was edging over toward the door, "I used to know hundreds of them songs—my memory's getting bad now, but when I was on the boats we made up songs about the ship, and most everything that happened. Sometimes we were near two weeks on the way down to Chicago and that was all the amusement we had."

"Do you remember them yet?"

"No, we just made them up as we needed them. Yah know, a real Irishman can make up a song about anything" and he was gone to his hay for the rest of the evening, and to fiddle for a dance that night.

What a Pat! Age anywhere from fifty to a hundred years old, small, about five foot four, somewhat stooped, right eye cocked and blurred, teeth mostly gone, hair plentiful and slightly gray, lots of life and Irish all through.

Mrs. Bonner told me that he made up a song about the *Clifton* a week or so after the boat went down in Lake Huron with a number of Beaver Island boys on. She told me that "Salty" Gallagher, father of Emmett Gallagher, the captain of the boat, also had a song written by Frank E. McCauley, also of the island, who died last year.

About 5 p.m., accompanied by John Bonner, I started for the lighthouse at the south end of the island to see Tom Bonner and Dominick Gallagher, who is said to know many songs. We had a long drive on the road or old narrow-gauge railroad bed. For about fifteen miles, we found only two houses or shanties at what John called "camps" where woodcutters lived.

We overtook "Salty" Gallagher on the way to town and brought him in. He said he had a song about his son, who was captain of the *Clifton*, and would hand it up and let me copy it if I wished. He's about seventy-five and is called "Salty" because he made a couple of schooner trips on salt water and to distinguish him from the other 399 Gallaghers.

BEAVER ISLAND, MICHIGAN, JULY 23, 1932

Stopped in the post office to mail some letters and had a talk with postmaster William "Willie" Boyle, who is in his early sixties and who has lived on the island most of his life. He knew a few of the songs I have, but no new ones. He recalled hearing "Cruise of the *Annie M. Peterson*," "John Brown and His Noble Crew," "The Gospel Ship *Glad Tidings*," "Louis Sands of Manistee," and "Buffalo Girls."

When working in lumber woods north of Escanaba about thirty years ago, there was in the camp a Lakes sailor of about forty or more who, in the evenings, especially Saturday evenings, would sing sailor songs "by the hour." "He had one in particular that I always intended to write down. It was about the Lakes schooner *Winslow*, but I never did." He doesn't recall the man's name, nor where he came from, nor verses or any more of the song, not even the story it told.

In the evening, I drove out about four miles to John Green's, a farmer, around seventy, native, who has spent his life except the last few years on Lakes boats in the sailing season, and the lumber woods in winters. This was my fourth attempt to see him. He was sitting on his porch smoking and was not in a very friendly state of mind. I could get nothing out of him for some time until I intentionally misread the opening stanza of "The Gallagher Boys," which I had been told he knew well. He corrected me on it, and then I had him check the rest of it and a couple of others and after that he was quite agreeable. He knows most of the songs I now have and a large number of lumber camp songs. He got a letter from [lumber camp lore collector] Franz Rickaby about eight years ago wanting to see him, but "he didn't show up." Green said a large number of Lakes sailors worked in the woods in winter and sang sailor songs there and worked on boats in the summer and sang lumber camp songs aboard the schooners. Both sailors and "lumberjacks" were anxious to hear new songs. He said he usually could sing any song after he'd heard it twice. In the woods, men would often sit in a circle in the evening in the bunkhouse and each would sing a song in his turn. On schooners, that would sometimes be done in the fo'c'sle. Green used to be able to sing over a hundred songs. He said the following songs were sung as much on the Lakes boats as in the camps:

> The Foreman Young Monroe
> Jim Whalen
> The Lost Jimmy Whalen
> Johnny Murphy
> Save Your Money When You're Young
> Michigan-i-o or Canada-i-o
> The Shanty Boy and the Farmer's Son
> The Little Brown Bulls
> The Falling of the Pine
> The Lac San Pierre [Lake St. Clair]
> Harry Bail
> Silver Jack
> Bung Yer Eye
> Fair Charlotte
> James Bird
> The *Cumberland*'s Crew
> The *Flying Cloud*
> The *Persian*'s Crew
> The *Bigler*'s Crew
> The Dying Soldier

"Michigan-i-o" was sung practically the same as Rickaby had it except "Canada-i-o" was substituted for "Michigan-i-o."

Green mentioned the following as also being sung on Lakes boats: "The Black Shoe," the story of a boat lost at sea, food gone and men drew lots in a black shoe to determine which shall be eaten. "The *Nancy's* Brig," "The *Middlesex Flora*" the story of an English schooner. Doesn't know all of it, but Captain Owen Gallagher, back of the Catholic church does. "*Lady Leroy*," an ocean schooner song, tells of a sailor and girl eloping and father of the girl sails after them in another ship. "The *Vernon*" is the story of a Lakes schooner which went down in Lake Michigan, probably off Manitowoc.

All you true-feeling Christians, I hope you will draw near
And learn my doleful story, I'm sure you'll drop a tear,
Concerning our dear comrades who lately left our shore;
They left us to lament, who'll never see them more.

On October twenty-fifth the *Vernon* steamed away,
Onboard our six dear friends with spirits light and gay.
And little did they think as they bid their friends good-bye
That their fate would be so soon in watery graves to lie.

It was on a Friday evening they headed up the lake,
And no one thought that the *Vernon* would be lost before daybreak.
Their peaceful sleep was broken by cries that filled the air—
The steamer she was sinking, grim death at them did stare!

"Christmas Eve" tells of a small boy sitting on his mother's lap—she is in tears—because her husband is lost at sea and he is asking why father doesn't return. "The Stately *Southerner*," a story of John Paul Jones's sea fights.

He said he knew many more if he could just think of them. The talk drifted to weather and he gave the following as signs you can depend on:

A sun-dog [a rainbow or white band around the sun] in the morning,
    he'll bark before night.
And a dog in the evening is a sailor's delight.

Mackerel scales and mares' tails
Make lofty ships take in sails.

[A mackerel sky is one filled with cirrocumulus clouds, which are stretched thin by high winds, allowing patches of blue sky to show through, making them look like fish scales. Mares' tails are high cirrus clouds stretched into streaks with tufts at the end. Both formations can presage an approaching cold front with high winds. Ships with tall masts would take in their sails to save their rigging and masts.]

Smoke going low over water: bad weather.

Seagulls flying high over land: gale of wind.

Pigs carrying straw or other litter: bad storm.

Direction of head of "milkmaids' path" [the Milky Way] indicates direction of prevailing winds for following day.

White frost in morning indicates southerly winds during day.

Northern lights are a sign of colder weather.

The further north the new moon appears, the colder the weather.

When a hunter can't hang his horn on the moon [last quarter]—bad weather.

Good weather with "coming moon" and bad weather with the "going back" of the moon.

BEAVER ISLAND, MICHIGAN, JULY 24, 1932

Stopped at the home of Francie Roddy. He told of sailing with his father, Andrew, who could sing songs for a week and never repeat one. "He had no learning at all. Never went to school none. But he knew more songs than any man I ever saw." He told of his singing at the wheel all through his watch, good weather or bad. Most of all "me father's" men sang.

"What kind of songs did they sing?"

"Every kind. Any new one father'd hear, he'd soon know it and be singing it himself, songs about sailing, lumbering, love songs, songs from the Old Country and any kind, but most of 'em were about sailors."

"Lakes sailors?

"Well, no, about the ocean mostly, but some were about the Lakes."

"When would the men have time to sing?"

"Any time when they weren't asleep. Sometimes it took us two weeks to beat down to Chicago, and singing was the only amusement we had."

"Where did the men come from who were in your father's crew?"

"Most of 'em come from the island here."

"They were Irish, then?"

"Yes, nearly all of them. Sometimes, we'd pick up a Swede or Norwegian, but they didn't sing much. A good Irishman can make up a song if he can't get any, any other way. There are a number on the island now who make up some good ones every little while. The people around here don't sing near as much as they used to, though. The young people would rather listen to that stuff they get over the radio.

"There was a lady here a few years ago—a Mrs. Derry, who collected songs for a number of years all around the island. John Green and me sang her a lot of 'em one night. Her husband was in the fire department at Grand Rapids. They're both dead now, I hear."

Then Pat Bonner's son John and I got on the trail of "Charley Anthony" Gallagher, who has spent his forty to sixty years getting nowhere, but having a good time on the way. I found him at "Big Willie" Gallagher's. John went up to the house to inquire about Charley Anthony and was told he wasn't there, and then later was asked who I was and if I had a warrant for Charley Anthony. When assured that I was harmless, Charley Anthony appeared and I was called in. Charley Anthony "had a few drinks under his belt." The conversation drifted to experience and finally, ghost stories.

"Peter Rabbit" Gallagher, a husky man about thirty, asked if we'd ever heard of the ghost ship on Lake Michigan and told of the men on a Pere Marquette car ferry seeing the *Chicora* in the fall of the year. [The wooden schooner vanished on Lake Michigan in 1895.] "They often sight her late in the evening, steaming along a couple of miles off their bow and then suddenly lose her."

"What does she do?"

"Just sails along and then suddenly vanishes."

"Have you ever seen her?"

"Yes, a number of times. I've pointed her out to other fellows on the boat, and they've seen her, too. If you see any of the car-ferry men, just ask them."

"I'm not doubting your word at all, I've heard of them. What does it appear for, what does it mean?"

"Well, we always have a hell of a storm right after we see her."

"Big Willie" Gallagher then told of having heard that some boats have sighted LaSalle's *Griffin,* the first boat ever to sail on the Lakes. It has been said her crew mutinied and made off with her cargo. Different boats "have picked her up" and then "lost her."

Peter Rabbit was in the crew of the freighter *William Nelson,* which recovered the crew of the *Our Son* when she foundered in September of 1930. He told of maneuvering the *Nelson* until her bow was against that of the *Our Son.* They helped men from the *Our Son* to get aboard. The car ferry *Pere Marquette 22* was standing by, but her deck was up so high they could not get the men off.

Aboard the *Ossian Bedell,* July 25, 1932

She's rolling and twisting and squeaking at all joints and many places between.

Earlier in the day, I found "Salty" Gallagher on his front porch, so visited him again. Asked him about the steamer *Vernon,* and he said he knew her—lost a brother on her when she went down. His son was captain of the *Clifton* and was lost, too. It seems the island has lost heavily on the Lakes. A large percent of the older men were sailors.

This morning I found Dominick Gallagher, who is just about to retire from keeping the light at the south end of the island. He knows a great many old Irish songs that his father learned as a boy in Ireland. He could recall none abut ships that I don't already have. He said he once sailed on a "haunted ship" [the schooner *Augusta*], the one that sank the *Lady Elgin*. [The excursion steamer *Lady Elgin* sank in Lake Michigan in 1860 with the loss of 380 lives after being gored in the night by the lumber-laden schooner *Augusta*. A song, "The Loss of the *Lady Elgin*," became popular across the country and the *Augusta* was reviled as an unlucky ship.] Dominick Gallagher didn't know it was the same ship until after she left shore. After the collision, the *Augusta* was taken to the Lower Lakes, her name changed and she was taken to the Atlantic Ocean. About thirty years later, according to Dominick, she was brought back to the Lakes and "was haunted, or the devil was in her, for every time she lost at least one man overboard or some other way, and sailors got so they wouldn't sail aboard her."

Meantime, the *Ossian Bedell* wobbles on three hours to Charlevoix. I suppose that's straight going. This up and down and sideways will greatly increase her mileage.

Back again later.

No mail awaiting me at Charlevoix—none for a week. Will read a while, that may help.

CHARLEVOIX, MICHIGAN, JULY 26, 1932

Read until about 3 a.m. and woke up to a cold, misty morning. Repacked, shined up a little, typed some on a table on the front porch, and then came back to Charlevoix.

Met Captain Manus Bonner on the street and he had to know all about my findings on Beaver Island. We then went to his home and, in the course of our conversation and sandwiched in between his wife's interruptions, he gave me the song "Tommy Boyle," by Father Gallagher. Tommy was with "the Gallagher Boys" and lost on the trip told in the song of that name. I hope the good father was a better priest than he was a songwriter.

I spent most of the evening with Mr. Joseph Cooper. Born near Georgian Bay, he's a retired timber cruiser, over eighty, with a good memory and a liking for songs and stories. He is now writing about some of his experiences for "a fellow from a Detroit newspaper," who hasn't done anything about it for some time. He has cruised timber in Michigan, Wisconsin, Minnesota, and Ontario and had lumber mills of his own. The last ones were near Newberry, Michigan. He had many log drives down rivers and some experience on Lakes. When asked about songs, he remembered hearing a number of them. When I mentioned "Skillagalee," he at once said:

From Skillagalee to Waugoschance we made the water boil.

Then he recalled the following from an old song:

And when we passed the South Manitou
A gale was blowing on
The chief mate said to the man at the wheel

"How are you steering, John?"
"I'm steering north by northeast,
Down for Mackinaw Port."
"That's right," he says, "my hearty,
Keep her on that course."

The song mentions Sleeping Bear, White Shoals, and some other places. The ship goes ashore.

He also gave me a version of "The Shanty Man's Life" beginning "I was a roving young fellow," and another without a name beginning, "I is Joe Bowers." I don't remember that [lumber lore collector Franz] Rickaby has either. Must look them up.

East Jordan, Michigan, July 27, 1932

Charles Starrit, ex-lightkeeper and sailor of Charlevoix, is a small, bristly, talkative, and very active man in his early eighties. His gray hair formed a halo around his much-used sailor cap, and his unlaundered but ample shirt and trousers—with some necessary buttons missing—flapped in the breeze as he walked. His pipe took much of his attention, and gave him about one puff per match, and many opportunities to display the tattooed artistry on his forearms—a heart pierced by an arrow on one and on the other the front view of a well-favored nude woman.

He said that he left home at the age of nine and sailed as a "boy" on an ocean-sailing vessel and didn't see his family again until age twenty-one. He then served an enlistment in the U.S. Navy, and following this sailed on the Lakes and then served in the U.S. Lighthouse Service until he retired a few years back.

He implied that he knew many sailor songs and stories, both oceans and Lakes, but at that time he just couldn't recall a thing. He said that on ocean ships and on early Lakes vessels the crews worked to chanteys, but in the Navy everything was done on the bosun's pipe.

Chippewa Cove Woods, fourteen miles north of Harbor Springs, Michigan, July 30, 1932

About the middle of the afternoon, I left Harbor Springs, Michigan, for Mackinaw City by way of the scenic lakeshore drive, and stopped off at Chippewa Cove Woods to visit Ivan Swift, some of whose writings I had earlier enjoyed. His simple, timbered, and high-gabled summer home/studio, "The Lofts," with its great stone chimney fit its setting. As no response followed my use of the brass latch-string-knocker on the outer door, I spent an hour or so exploring the beautiful tree-covered area on the high shore of Lake Michigan. A return to the house brought from within a "Come on in," and I entered and found him leisurely smoking a pipe in a big easy chair by an oversized north window.

The airy spaciousness of the unpartitioned interior, the big stone fireplace, and the dominating loft at one end was most impressive, and for a greeting I said simply, "I like this." He answered, "So do I." With no further preliminaries, we

Ivan's much-missed "Pete" and their son, Lynn. (Courtesy Lynn and Sue Walton)

talked until midnight. He wanted to know all about the material I'm collecting and told of his own writing and painting, and of local Indian friends and some of the legends he has learned from them. He talked at length of other writers including George Sterling, Opie Read, and Robert Frost.

As the evening grew late, I made a gesture to leave, and he said I must see his hand press and book bindery. We ascended a rugged ladder to the loft and examined his shop, and he autographed and gave me a copy of his poems, *Faggots of Cedar,* which he had himself printed and bound. As I was leaving he called out, "By the way, what's your name?"

MACKINAW CITY, MICHIGAN, JULY 31, 1932

It's now near the hour for daylight to be reappearing. Just returned from a four-hour midnight walk—that or off the deep end. Sunday night and no mail until tomorrow—if then and God, oh God, it's lonesome and on they pile and pile and I walk.

MACKINAW CITY, MICHIGAN, AUGUST 1, 1932

Just returned from post office. Lots of mail: two letters and three cards from Pete, two from Lynn and Mother and a book and cards from Wahr's.

While I was lunching in a restaurant in Mackinaw City, a man in his late seventies with some coffee and a sandwich sat down at my table. I learned that he had many years ago been a schooner sailor on Lakes vessels, and had later spent many years in the U.S. Lighthouse Service at Cheboygan, Michigan, and other ports. I inquired if he could recall any songs that schoonermen used to sing either aboard ship or ashore, or any of the stories or sayings that he may have heard. He answered with some apparent disgust that he used to know "no end of that kind of stuff," but in 1893 he "had become converted to the Lord's way of life," and since then had "put all them worldly and sinful songs," out of his life forever! [Ironically, 1893 was the year of Walton's birth.]

In early evening, I called in to see the local lightkeeper. He said I should have come last year when his father was alive. He could sing "no end" of songs. He himself had never been able to sing at all and didn't care much about it then and had never learned any. He couldn't recall any of his father's songs. He took me up in the tower to start the light for the night.

Went to the Mackinaw City ferry docks and aboard the *Chief Wawatam*. Captain John Stoffelbeam was somewhat busy so I didn't talk with him long. He said that as a boy in the early 1880s he used to stand and listen by the hour in Chicago to sailors chanteying as they were towing out and making sail ready for a trip northward. He seems to know none himself.

MACKINAW CITY, MICHIGAN, AUGUST 2, 1932

This is a wonderful night to be some other place than where I am now. It's raining, quite cold, and foggy, and about ten rods away moans and groans the foghorn every twenty seconds. It's now 9:45 p.m. and I just got back from a day at Cheboygan.

Captain Charles I. Cay Ford was the best bet there. I had to wait until evening to see him. He is about sixty-five and began sailing the Lakes in 1887. He said he used to know some Lake songs, but couldn't recall them. He had not tried for thirty years, he said. He sang "The Dark-Eyed Sailor" and I took it down, also the tune, the best I could. Said he'd sung and heard that song all about the Lakes. He had also heard sailors sing "The Ship That Never Returned," "Fair Fanny Moore," "Creole Girl of Lake Pontchartrain," "The Prisoner's Song," "A Shadow Comes between My Love and Me," "Harry Bail," "Gerry's Rock," "Schooner *Hesperus*," "*Lady Elgin*," and many more. He was on the tug *Champion* for a number of years taking schooners from Lake St. Clair and the Detroit River.

MACKINAW CITY, MICHIGAN, AUGUST 3, 1932

Found Oscar Smith in old blacksmith shop next door to his home. He's a dirty old lad—hasn't had a bath since he last fell in the river as a boy and he's now seventy-two and about through with this world. He was born in Newaygo County, Michigan, and learned blacksmithing as a boy. He sailed the Lakes in the summers from 1876 to 1890 and spent winters in the lumber woods. He spent a couple of years in British Columbia, retired here and operated a saloon in the Stimpson House for fourteen years. He is a fiddler-singer and takes his fiddle wherever he goes. He is in pretty bad physical condition, near the end of his career, I think.

His son Howard said Oscar knew the song "From Skillagalee to Waugoschance," but it turned out to be "The *Bigler*'s Crew," which he knew entire, also "The *Persian*'s Crew." He thought he had heard "The *Annie M. Peterson*," "The *Vernon*," "A Wet Sheet and a Rolling Sea," "*Lady of the Lakes*," "The Gospel Ship *Glad Tidings*," "It Was in the Year 1801," "When We Reached the South Manitou," "*Sand Patch*," "The *Winslow*," and "Fanny Moore." He said he'd heard a dozen songs about "Louis Sands of Manistee." He also still remembers parts of a large number of other songs popular in his day such as "The Creole Girl," "Indian's Lament," "Just as the Sun Went Down," "Poor Little Joe"—I took this one down to humor him—and a number of lumber camp songs, practically all of which are in Rickaby.

I went over to Mackinac Island on the *Algomah*. Talked with the captain in the pilothouse most of the way over and on the return. Got some names from him. Found most people familiar with this material to be dead. "If you'd been here last year," or "two years ago when —— and —— were alive."

Called on "Mat" Baley, proprietor of the Park Drug Store. His father was an island "pioneer" who wrote a guide to the island. E. O. Wood used it in his two-volume work, *Historic Mackinac*. He knew no Lakes material himself. Found Mr. [Newton Jerome "Rome"] Murdick in his candy kitchen by the telegraph office. He is in very bad physical condition, but can recall when the "Straits were full of sailboats. Sailors were singing all the time."

I found Michael McNally, eighty-eight, at his home. He began sailing on the Lakes when he was nineteen and stayed with it as long as sailboats lasted. He was born on Mackinac Island and has had his home on the island all his life.

"When I first can remember, there were more than eight thousand Indians living here, and now there's only resorters and not a full-blood Indian on the island."

He can remember counting one hundred thirty, three- and four-masted schooners in the Straits at one time. They would often get beached, or windbound, or sometimes when they'd come up too early in the spring they couldn't get through for the ice until the wind would shift and then there'd be a merry time and a noisy one getting up anchor and sails. Many times the village authorities would go out and ask the captains to stop the singing and noise so the people could get some sleep. In the 1870s, the sailors were about half salt-water men. On some boats, whole crews would be ocean men and they'd always sing while working. "They couldn't put their hats on without singing."

"Did they sing those songs when making sail, or just sing out, 'yo-hee' and the like?"

"Both. They usually had songs, what sailors call chanteys. The ocean men would come up to the Lakes in the spring and go back to the Atlantic ports in the fall. Some got to going to the lumber woods in the winter. They never had any money and had to get winter work."

St. Ignace, Michigan, August 4, 1932

I left Mackinaw City this morning as soon as the mail came in. The day started fine: a card from Lynn and Mother. A good ride across the Straits. The air was cool and clear. Islands at either end of Straits show up well against the deep blue of the water.

When the ferry arrived, the *Chief Wawatam* was tied up at the dock. Went aboard and found Captain John Stoffelbeam and 2nd officer Allan Berdeau, the latter of St. Ignace, Michigan. Captain Stoffelbeam asked if I had a song with a chorus: "Watch her, catch her. . . ." It is "The *Bigler*'s Crew." He had heard many as a boy when first starting on the Lakes, but doesn't remember any of them.

Mr. Berdeau said he once knew a song about "The Schooner *Antelope*," which was lost in Lake Huron, he thinks in 1860. He has a great memory for Lakes boats, crews, events, and episodes. Has been on the Lakes for forty-plus years. He told of an old Irish captain who always took his fiddle with him. He got in a bad blow on Lake Michigan one evening and kept on fiddling below in his cabin. The mate eventually called down to him, but he kept on. Later, the wind and seas increased and the mate shouted down, "This boat'll go to hell if I don't get some more help up her damn quick!" The captain said, "B'God, if she do I'll be jumping off at Charlevoix as she goes by."

Someone, I think it was Captain F. A. Bailey, gave me this one:

Schooner *Antelope*

We left Chicago far behind
The wind was blowing fair
We reefed her down and made her snug
As the wind increased to a gale.

It made the water blue and red
Because of the clay and sand
It lined the beach for miles and miles
On the shores of Michigan.

Manistique, Michigan, August 6, 1932

No day like this before!

Found Captain Carey and his brother Captain Pat at home. They were quite talkative but knew no songs. They were tugging in Chicago at the time of the big tug strike. Schooners then changed to tow barges and tugging on the Lakes began to lose out and in a few years practically disappeared. They have seen over sixty ore schooners in the bay behind Sand Point—Escanaba—for ore. Tugs would come all the way to the harbor from Port Huron for them, take a number in tow all the way to Cleveland and return. Competition was very keen. He explained that the first Lakes captains and pilots union strike lost out because they high-hatted [acted superior to] the engineers and firemen and refused to allow them to join their union, so when they struck for higher wages, "after" men kept on working and scab crews forward took the boats. This led to "after" men being admitted.

At Tom Downing's shack on North Third Street, his brother Mike said he was out at his "rat farm" ten miles north of the city. Some men took him out yesterday, he thought to a party. "Tom's quite a singer." I went out U.S. 92 eight miles and then two miles on a winding sand road, then cut-over country to the "farm" and found six men and two women and most of them pretty drunk. [Michigan logging operations stripped the land so cleanly that the land was said to have been "cut over." Ensuing erosion carried away fertile soil and left the heavier, underlying sand behind creating a barren, stump-filled landscape.] A man called Red was seemingly in charge. He and one other, Tom, were not so far along. Tom was in his late sixties and pretty ragged and dirty, was about nine-tenths under. The women were trying to measure him for a grave they were about to dig for him and one of them rolled around on the ground with him, quite scantily clad. The men took me for a Prohibition officer. I explained what I wanted of Tom, but without much effect. One fellow, well built, hair thinning, and a slight accent, kept looking at me out of the corner of his eye and talking in riddles and finally asked if I'd ever "traveled in the East," and eyed me very closely. I thought he meant New England and then it dawned upon me that he was trying to put some signs on me and I told him I wasn't a moron, if that was what he was getting at.

He began talking again mysteriously in double meanings—we were a long way out of town—the lake was deep—I was alone, etc. He accidentally uncovered some empty .32- or .38-caliber cartridges with his foot and pointed to some more in a tree branch where I stood. I asked him what he was getting at and he answered, "I seen through yuh as soon's yuh come. Yuh ain't puttin' anything over on me, see? I'd just as soon bump you as look at you."

I told him he was all wrong and then, bluffing, as to act afraid would put me in a pretty bad place, I told him that if he was trying to scare me it wasn't succeeding very well. "And brother, I have two fists that ain't afraid of no man." The others were an interested audience.

He told me to stand right where I was and he took one of the men aside and they talked for a while as he kept watching me out of the corner of his eye. Tom came weaving over where I was and wanted to know if I was going to arrest him. I told him no, not if he'd sing me a song.

"I know a hundred damn good songs, and I'll sing every one for you, all the songs you want."

Mr. Cat's Eyes went into the house and come out with a bottle and came up to me and said, "Will you drink like a man?"

"Sure, a small one."

The iron ore loading docks at Escanaba, Michigan, in about 1886 with the city beyond the tracks that are atop the loading docks. The vessel in the foreground is not an ore boat but a "rabbit," the wooden *George A. Marsh,* built at Sandusky, Ohio, for hopping in and out of ports with cargoes of general freight. (Courtesy Dossin Great Lakes Museum)

So he poured out a couple of swallows, and I downed it and he took one and then he poured a half glass and offered it to me and I said I had plenty and he said, "You refuse to drink with me like a man?"

"Well, I've had enough. You can call it what you like."

He started something else, looking me straight in the eyes and I at him. At that time, Red told Tom to give us a good song. He looked up blankly and I asked him about a number that I'm looking for and he shook his head and then finally he got an idea and then, weaving between me and a tree, he started out on a song his words running all together. At the end of what probably were stanzas, I recognized the words to "The *Lady of the Lakes,*" a song of which I knew but one stanza. Before he'd gone far he got it mixed with one of those sung earlier. He sat down on the running board of a car and sang a yodel song, only he couldn't get the yodel and then got off on some pure smut again. He had consumed the drink poured out for me and it put him too far under to sit up straight enough to sing.

Red looked at me and then wandered over to my car and I followed. He said he knew I was all right, but didn't understand what I wanted. So, I explained, showed him some of the material I have, my driver's license and Army identification folder. That seemed to do the business. He said he served in the Navy. Mr. Cat's Eyes came over to hear what was being said and Red explained that I'd been in the Army and was "OK." He said that I'd heard that Tom had a lot of songs and wanted to get some of them. I told Red I'd like to at least get that one song from Tom and probably some others and he said to come back in the morning and he'd keep Tom sober until I came. Bill—or whatever his name was—also became friendlier then and assured me that Tom "knew a goddamned lot of 'em," and it would be worth my time to come back.

Escanaba, Michigan, August 7, 1932

There shouldn't be any Sundays when at this work. Nobody is where they should be.

Went back out to the "rat farm" to see Tom Downing. Found the place quiet, peaceful, and deserted. One man informed me that Tom's brother came after him last night and he was now back in town, so I drove back to the city and found him in "the morning-after" condition. Their house is a one-story, one-room contrivance and the dirtiest in the state—bad smell and flies by the millions. Tom was in bed and in a pretty bad way. No singing today. Got "The *Lady of the Lakes*" from him, but it wasn't what I expected. There must be two songs about it. His head was quite muddled and his memory not functioning. Mike said he didn't think Tom knew any songs about the Lakes.

Menominee, Michigan, August 8, 1932

Another day without results, but much wandering.

Decided I'd had enough of Escanaba and its continuous rain, so started south in direction of Menominee. Stopped at Cedar River, an old lumber town. The only man who had ever had anything to do with the Lakes was now home-brewing for a living—beer 10 cents per. Talked with him for some time, but no hopes, so on to Menominee.

Menominee, Michigan, August 9, 1932

Another day of much prospecting and no nuggets. Off for better territory in the morning.

Called at the library again and got names of a few prospects in Marinette, Wisconsin, and then went across the river. In the evening, called at home of Captain Orin Engwall. He was just preparing twelve boxes of fish for Chicago via truck. He crewed between Georgian Bay and Lake Michigan ports. He knows remnants of a few songs, but I could not get them from him. He saw the schooner *Annie M. Peterson,* and said she was about the best on the Lakes for speed. When coming out of Chicago, she would hoist the cabin broom up on her mainmast as a challenge to all others for a race. [This custom is said to have started with Englishman Sir Francis Drake, who "swept the seas" of the Spanish armada in the late sixteenth century.] At times, there would be ten to fifteen others laying outside the harbor, all set for a race, but in a few hours "she'd see them all over her stern." On one occasion, the *Oak Leaf* raced her to Green Bay and both came into Sturgeon Bay channel, all sails and even. Neither would lay to for the other. Yards

The schooner *City of Grand Haven,* built at that city, docked forever at the boneyard at Marinette, Wisconsin, in 1939. The 127-foot vessel was built in 1872 and abandoned in 1937. (Courtesy Dossin Great Lakes Museum)

became caught and broken in each and there was other damage. He said that a song tells the story but that it was not very decent. He would not give it to me.

STURGEON BAY, WISCONSIN, AUGUST 10, 1932

August Deluriche, about seventy-five, began on the Lakes as a boy of ten, and six or eight years later went to the ocean and stayed there for fourteen years and came back. He was a chanteyman on ocean sailboats and went nine times around the world. Knows parts of many ocean chanteys, but little or none of Lakes songs and I got nothing new from him. For the last six years, he has been sailing yachts. He was on Chicago ex-mayor William H. "Big Bill" Thompson's yacht and thinks him a big, ignorant "bag of wind."

Had my birthday dinner of an egg sandwich and coffee and then hunted up a place to stay the remainder of the night.

STURGEON BAY, WISCONSIN, AUGUST 11, 1932

In the evening, I drove out to the bachelor home of Guy L. "Irish Mac" McCracken, who I was told was a former sailor and a "character" and might know a lot of Lakes material. I found his one-room home, a large wheelhouse of a wrecked steamboat with outside port and starboard running lights. Inside "the Anchorage" was a large ship's wheel in its proper place and some household equipment including a combination heating and cooking stove, a table, bunk, and

Guy L. "Irish Mac" McCracken's home, "The Anchorage" at Sturgeon Bay, Wisconsin, in a photo given to Walton by Captain Edward Carus of nearby Manitowoc. The horseshoe hanging over the door is ends up so the luck won't run out. (Courtesy Ivan H. Walton Collection, Bentley Historical Library, University of Michigan)

on one side a shelf of carved ship models. He was probably in his late fifties, rather tall and thin with a good crop of graying, disheveled hair, several days' growth of beard, and clothing that had obviously been slept in. He was pretty drunk and telling a friend, who was in much the same condition, about an argument he had had, but he couldn't recall with whom nor what it was about. He had, however, told his adversary plenty, "and right to the dirty bastard's face."

In a lull between drinks and orations, I finally got his attention on Great Lakes sailing, and that set him off on another tack. Yes sir, he knew hundreds of songs—wrote 'em all himself, every goddamn one—and could sing 'em all, and if I'd just give him twenty-five dollars or get him another bottle of whiskey, he'd sing me all the goddamn songs I wanted.

"Well, how about trying one right now?"

"Oh, I can sing a hundred, maybe a thousand, can't I, Bill?"

"No, you're a damn liar, Mac. You never sang a song in your life."

"Yes, I can, and I'll show you, you goddamn, pig-headed Swede."

After a few false starts, he was able to recall only a few lines of a church hymn. The prospects here were not very good, so I departed as the two got into an argument over which one had owned the bottle of whiskey they'd just consumed.

I learned later that Mac had lost his home in a tax sale and the new owner was having much difficulty getting possession and that the argument Mac was trying to tell was probably with the new owner. I also learned that he had for some time made his living, such as it was, by carving model Lakes and ocean vessels under full sail out of pieces of cedar taken from a big log lying outside against his house. He was a highly skilled artist at it, but quite undependable as far as delivery was concerned. When sailing in his younger days, Mac had an accident that left him with one stiff and shortened leg, and on each of his models, he left his signature, a carved crew member with the same affliction.

In a long unused slip at the Sturgeon Bay harbor, the old schooner *Lucia A. Simpson* lay stern down with her after deck awash. She had settled in the sand with her mizzenmast blown out and her fore and mainmasts and yards askew as she came in from her last trip several years ago. Nearby looking at her stood Fred Nelson, probably in his late seventies. He was of medium size, rather gaunt, with pronounced blue eyes. He wore an old cap over his protruding gray hair, and a freshly laundered open shirt and bagging trousers.

Scandinavian born, he went to sea as a boy of fifteen on big, Atlantic square-riggers. He sailed wherever the ships took him over most of the world until the tall ships disappeared from salt water. Nelson came to the Great Lakes for the last years of sail. He was master of the schooner *Our Son* in her last few seasons and on her final trip when she foundered in a gale on Lake Michigan on Sept. 20, 1930. She was the last of all the commercial schooners that sailed the Great Lakes. [Two other vessels contend as the Great Lakes' last commercial sailing vessel, but they were built after the schooner days had ended. One is the *Helen MacLeod II,* launched at Bayfield, Ontario, in 1926. It was built along the lines of a Mackinac lumber hooker and was used as a fishing vessel until 1945. It was sold to two

Detroit historians in 1950, renamed *Anna S. Piggott,* and used as a yacht. The Detroit Historical Museum rebuilt the vessel in 1955 as a sea cadet training vessel. After several more changes of ownership, the vessel was purchased in 1996 by the Bayfield Historical Society and returned home. A second contender was the three-masted schooner *J. T. Wing,* launched in 1921 at Nova Scotia. After a career carrying Prohibition-era liquor, mahogany, pulpwood, and posts, the vessel wound up as a museum ship at Belle Isle, Michigan. The vessel was torched in 1956 to make room for Detroit's Dossin Great Lakes Museum, the source for some of the photos in this book.]

When asked why he didn't sail on steamships, Nelson's reply was a loud, "Bah! Dat ain't sailin'." He said he liked the big square-riggers with their crews of thirty or more men before the mast, "an how dey would sing when we pull up de hook! De chanteyman sit on caps'an head an' open his mouth a whole foot an' roar so dey can hear heem ten mile, and de crew, dey all sing louder an' him, an' Jesus Christ, how de canvas go up!"

He said that most Lakes vessels had crews of only from six to ten or twelve men forward, but if they had some deep-water men aboard and the mate would permit it, the men would sing chanteys while working. Some mates thought that chanteying made the work go too slowly—"but ten men singin' a lively chantey could outhaul twenty wid no song."

"What were the songs about?"

"Oh, dem chantey songs, dey vas about most anything. De chanteyman jus' sing what he remember or make up at de time about de captain, mate, de trip, an' always about de cook an' what happen ashore, an' dose women dey meet dere."

"Can you sing any now? Or perhaps just recite some lines?"

"No, nope, dey all gone, now. Ay don' hear any dem songs for twenty-five, thirty year, an' ay forget. Ay once wrote many chantey songs in a book, an' sailors, dey all like to see it, but ay lose heem one time in a bad blow. De Coast Guard, dey take us off de ship, but she break up an' go down wit all my t'ings. On de last trip on de *Our Son,* ay lose my gud compass an' everyt'ing. She was pretty ol' ship an' her seams dey open in de beeg seas an' she waterlog before de *Nelson* come along an' take us off. An' now no more sail on de Lakes; all change. Dere used to be damn gud sailormen dat go on ships, but now all steamboats, an' dey ship any harbor rat dat come along, an' leave de real sailormen widout any jobs. Wat you t'ink dis country's coming to?"

As we talked, portly, cigar-smoking "Big Bill" Thompson of Chicago came out to one of the repair docks where his palatial yacht was being overhauled and repainted.

"Look at heem—eat enough for six men, an' he own dat boat! T'ousands of dollars in her an' t'ousands of men around wid no jobs or money. You t'ink der be a revolution, maybe?" Nelson walked away slowly, and I watched him go aboard the lumber barge *Mueller,* where he had a temporary job as a watchman.

The schooner *G. J. Boyce,* built at Manitowoc, Wisconsin, in 1884, in a photograph given to Walton by Captain Edward Carus. (Courtesy Ivan H. Walton Collection, Bentley Historical Library, University of Michigan)

MANITOWOC, WISCONSIN, AUGUST 14, 1932

I found Captain Edward Carus at his modest home awaiting me. I had written him from Green Bay. He is about seventy-five, and good for that many more years. He's about five feet, four inches tall, stocky, bald-headed, talkative, and very much "the captain." He said he was not interested in sailor songs, stories, and the like, as sailors sang only when drunk or nearly so, and Lakes history would be better off without them. He was interested only in "historical facts" and photographs, not in any "sailor foolishness." He said he had never taken a drop of liquor nor visited a sailor waterfront hangout in his life. He was much worried about labor unions and socialism. He has what's right and what's wrong in the world pretty well determined.

In spite of my interest in worthless sailor lore, he warmed up surprisingly, invited me into his den, and nearly bewildered me with his Great Lakes scrapbooks, and more scrapbooks—a shelf of two dozen or more thick volumes. In them were photographs of hundreds of vessels, both early and modern, and records of their building, dimensions, owners, careers, and fates abstracted from government and other reports. The books also contained licenses and newspaper and magazine clippings, including a long list under his own name. He has sailed for over sixty years, forty of them as master, and has collected information about most of these years. He began as a boy in sailing vessels and early transferred to steam.

He evidently valued his scrapbooks very highly, as they were about all he had left from a lifetime of sailing. Yet, an hour or two later as I was about to leave, he suggested that I take four or five of them along with me to examine during the evening. I returned these the following morning and he at once handed me four others. This process continued until I had examined them all.

In the evening of my first day in Manitowoc, while I was at the Eighth Street bridge watching a big car ferry come in from Lake Michigan, someone called my name from behind, and to my surprise it was the captain. He was wearing a ship officer's cap with the word "master" embroidered in gold thread above the visor. We were soon joined by others and each addressed him as "Captain." One of the arrivals was Mr. Edwin Shuelte, owner of half the city and a big yacht. He stopped to consult the captain about a Lakes trip he was planning. I carelessly lighted a cigarette and offered one to each man in the group. From the captain came the prompt response, "No, thank you, I haven't sunk that low yet!"

Mr. Shuelte told me later that Captain Carus "brought out" practically all the vessels produced by the Manitowoc Shipbuilding Co. during the war and tested each on the Lakes before it was delivered to the owner. He added that the captain rules his crews with an iron hand. And then, smilingly, he said that Captain Carus was in charge of the company's employment office. "It is said that the only question he asked a prospective employee was, 'Are you a sailor?' If the answer was yes, the man had a job, but if it was no, the quick response was a disgusted, 'Well, what the hell do you know about shipbuilding? Get out of here!'"

MANITOWOC, WISCONSIN, AUGUST 16, 1932

Called at the home of Captain Timothy Kelley, eighty-four. He came to Manitowoc as a boy in 1856 and has lived here since. He was a captain at the age of twenty-two. He sailed schooners until 1882 and then took up steam. His last schooner was the *Wells Burt*. He has a painting of her in Buffalo with a tug coming alongside. She was a very pretty boat. He recalls hearing sailors chantey in Buffalo harbor as they weighed anchor. People would line the docks to hear them. Ocean sailors in considerable numbers came up to Buffalo from New York and from New Orleans to Chicago in the spring and would return in fall. He recalls hearing "Shenandoah," "Roll and Go," "Sacramento," "Broad Missouri," and "Rio Grande." They also chanteyed when making sail, especially if there were many ocean men in the crew. Sailors then were largely Irish, English, and American. Scandinavians came later.

Sailors had some songs they'd sing when not working, but they were usually kept busy because it was easier to keep them under control. He does not recall any of those songs.

Sheboygan, Wisconsin, August 17, 1932

I called on Mr. William Houghton, who was quite pleased at my visit. He had sailed more than twenty years and retired about thirty years ago. His shop is decorated with marine photos and a couple of pretty bad paintings. One photo is of a tug, "the smartest one on the Lakes," on the Chicago River. He said she used to come up past Two Rivers, Wisconsin, to find tows. The photo shows a broom hoisted over the cabin indicating a "clean sweep" or challenge to any tug who wanted to race her.

He often heard chanteys on the Chicago River as schooners were towing out and making sail. At times, a whole fleet would be at it. He could not recall words, but said he liked to hear them and always joined in. They also had songs that they sang in the fo'c'sle: popular songs of the time, some ocean songs, and some the sailors made up about trips and Lakes disasters and other events. He said he hadn't thought about them for thirty years and couldn't recall any. He told of a fleet of schooners going through the Straits of Mackinac and all trying to pass the others. He was at the wheel of the *Mechanic,* a very good sailor, and stayed through two watches, "giving her all she'd take." The *Mechanic* steadily passed all of them, except one big one, and they raced for some time before he succeeded in getting to windward and ahead. "Those were the days! We had to work like hell—and all hours—but we always went back the next season."

Sheboygan and Port Washington, Wisconsin, August 18, 1932

Another glorious night. Have just returned from a couple hours' walk about the town and up over a hill to the westward. Still a white moon, clouds floating beneath, and a silvered lake below. A little tired.

Captain Manning Kilton was at his home when I called this morning. He is a stocky man of about seventy-five. He has been on the Lakes since he was a boy. He spent twenty-five years up to a few years ago as captain of a tug that towed big rafts to Ashland, Wisconsin, from various points on the Lake. Towing rafts is pretty slow, about a mile per hour, "an' you're tied to 'em no matter what happens, and Superior gets pretty rough in the late fall. If you let go, your raft is apt to go to pieces and get in the lanes of the steamboats." He once found a big freighter—or rather the after half of it—on the rocks on one of the southwest Superior islands. The freighter had attempted to make the lee of the island to avoid a bad storm and struck on a shoal. The storm cut off the forward crew and all were lost. The after crew got away in boats. He said he knows no songs and is no singer. "You don't hear many songs on a tug."

Milwaukee, Wisconsin, August 20, 1932

Weekends are bad days for this business. One spends hours and miles to find them and they're not in.

Began the day at the post office. Three letters, all good ones. One from home and from the university containing a check. Took the check to the first bank I found, the Wisconsin First National, and they wouldn't cash it. Then went to the Marine National and got the money only after showing a pocket full of identifying material, the letter accompanying the check, and explaining what I'm doing. Either the university or I don't look so good.

Finally found the building of the Milwaukee Tug Boat line. Found three big tugs laying at dock and only a watchman on duty, Mr. James M. Leaman who, he told me, came to the Lakes in 1872 after a few years on the ocean. He was mate on the *Wells Burt* and *Moonlight* mentioned in the song. He left the Lakes in 1885 and was on the police force for thirty-five years. He knew parts of "The *Bigler*'s Crew," the "*E. C. Roberts*," "The *Persian*'s Crew," and "The *Fayette Brown*." He used to hear them often when he was on sailboats.

Made the rounds of the big boat company docks, but nobody home. Found Captain (now mate) Owen Gallagher of the Grand Trunk ferry *City of Grand Rapids*. Said he'd been on car ferries for twenty-five years. "Steamboat men don't sing, and I've forgotten all I ever knew." He is from Beaver Island and recognized all the titles I could recall from there. The second mate is also from Beaver Island and recognized them, but could suggest no others.

In the evening, I called at the Grand Trunk car-ferry slip when the *Milwaukee* came in. I found Captain Cavanaugh and Mate C. H. McCauley, both of whom I'd seen earlier in summer at Grand Haven. A car was waiting for Mr. McCauley. He said he'd be on the boat Sunday afternoon and to call about 3 p.m. if I could. Captain Cavanaugh was quite talkative. His home is here in Milwaukee. He gave me some more names and checked over those I have to indicate the best ones. He is quite interested in Beaver Island. He told of peculiar boat wrecks on shore and natives stripping the cargoes, numerous stills and beating the fishing regulations. He was much interested in the songs I've assembled. He said this work should have been twenty-five years ago. "You could easily get a book full then. . . . The old sailboat men, the windjammers, are pretty well gone now and none of the later generation know any songs. Singing was a part of the day's work for those old fellows." He could remember the chorus of "The *Bigler*'s Crew" and bits of the stanzas, part of "The Red Iron Ore" and a few others. He gave me a stanza of a canal song, but I have mislaid it and can't locate it now. He mentioned the song about the schooner *Moonlight*.

I had two flat tires today, the first since winter. The first went on returning from the Grand Trunk docks. The spare went flat as I was coming out to the street on the dark, winding cinder road that leads to the slip. It was not a very good place to lay over and wait for the tire man at 10:30 p.m. with a couple of suspicious characters in the offing.

MILWAUKEE, WISCONSIN, AUGUST 23, 1932

Some better today. Ready to pack for home last night.

Found Peter J. Marder, chief engineer for the Milwaukee Tug Boat line, at his home. Mrs. Marder is the sister of Mrs. Captain Manus J. Bonner of Charlevoix. That opened the door. He has been on tugs most of his life. He recalls hearing early sailor chanteying and songs about the schooners *Ironsides, Likely Belle,* and *Amazon,* but he knows no words. His daughter and wife reminded him of an old song about a young captain and wife who each evening both looked at the moon at the same time. The captain was lost in a wreck and the wife continued the practice alone.

At Joys Brothers office, ship chandlers from the early days and the sons of a schooner captain, I found John Joys, who could recall hearing sailors sing, but not what. His brother Carl used to know some. I tried to find him, but he was out.

[Although Walton's journal does not mention a subsequent meeting, the song notes he took in addition to his journals credit this extensive version of the widely known "The Timber Drogher *Bigler*" to Carl Joys.]

> Come all you jolly sailors and listen to my song,
> It's but a few short verses and will not detain you long.
> In Milwaukee in October I chanced to get a site
> In the timber-drogher *Bigler* a'hailing from Detroit.
>
> Watch her! Catch her! Jump up on her juberju,
> Give 'er the sheet and let 'er howl, we're the boys to put 'er through,
> You should've seen 'er howling, the wind a'blowin' free,
> On our passage down to Buffalo from Mil—wau—kee.
>
> It was on a Sunday morning, about the hour of ten,
> The *Robert Emmet* towed us out into Lake Michigan.
> We set sail where she left us, in the middle of the fleet,
> The wind was from the south'rd, an' we had to give 'er sheet.
>
> The wind chopped 'round to sou'-sou'-west, an' blew both fresh and strong,
> And plowing through Lake Michigan the *Bigler* she rolled on.
> And far before her foaming bow the silver spray did fling,
> With every inch of canvas set, her course was "wing and wing."
>
> The wind it hauled ahead, my boys, as we reached the Manitous;
> Two dollars and a half a day just suited the *Bigler*'s crew.
> From here unto the Beavers, we steered her full 'n' by;
> An' we laid 'er to the wind as close as she would lie.
>
> We made Skillagalee and Wobble Shanks, the entrance to the Straits,
> And might have passed the fleet, had they hove to and wait,

But we drove 'em all before us the prettiest you ever saw
Clear out into Lake Huron through the Straits of Mackinac.

We made the light at False Presque Isle, and then we boomed away;
Courses and tops'ls straining for the isle of Thunder Bay.
The wind it hauled 'round, we laid on 'er starb'rd tack,
With a good lookout ahead, m' boys, for the light of Point Aback.

We made the light and kept in sight of Michigan's east shore,
A'booming for the river as we'd often done before.
But where's the schooner fleet we raced all through the night?
Can that be sails ahead, just glimmering in sight?

We plowed on down Lake Huron, the wind was steady and fast,
Port Sanilac's off to starb'rd, the river's ahead at last.
And when off Gratiot Light our anchor we let go,
Till the *Sweepstakes* hove in sight, and took the *Bigler* in tow.

The *Sweepstakes* towed eight schooners, an' all of us fore 'n' aft,
She towed us down the St. Clair and stuck us on the Flats.
She parted the *Hunter*'s tow-line in trying to give relief,
An' the *Bigler* smashed head on into the yawl of the *Maple Leaf.*

She towed us down and left us outside the river light,
Lake Erie for to wander and the blusterin' winds to fight.
The wind being fresh and fair, we paddled our own canoe,
Her nose points o'er the dummy, we're hell-bent for Buffalo.

We made the "Eau," flew by Long Point, the wind was a'blowin' free;
We howled along the Canada shore, Port Colborne on our lee.
What light is that ahead that grows as we draw near?
It's like a blazing star, it's the light on Buffalo pier.

An' now, my bully lads, we're in Buffalo port at last,
Under Rood and Smith's Elevator, the *Bigler* she's made fast.
An' in Tommy Doyle's saloon we'll let the bottle pass,
For we are jolly shipmates, and we'll drink a social glass.

An' now my song is ended, I hope it pleases you:
Let's drink a health to the *Bigler,* her officers and crew.
I hope she sails for many a fall in command of Cal McKee,
Between the ports of Buffalo and Mil—wau—kee.

Found Captain W. A. Ashley, about seventy-eight, at his home. He is
secretary of the Milwaukee local of the Shipmasters' Association. He was on

schooners in the 1870s and twelve years after and then on steamboats. He said there was lots of singing and chanteying on the early sailboats and on some of the steamboats as well, and ashore. He believes that ninety percent of the early boats, especially the schooners, had songs about them. Sailors were always making up songs about the boat and her crew and trip. He said a man named Cunningham of Port Colborne, Ontario, composed "The *Bigler*'s Crew." Also known as "The Timber Drogher *Bigler*."

Ashley said songs were sung often in the shore "variety shows," old-time shore vaudeville shows that catered to the sailors. He said he retired from the Lakes a couple of years ago when business began to drop off and had never been over to the lakeshore to look at the water since. Took a business trip on the lake once, but has no desire to go on the water or to see it.

Aboard the SS *Missouri*, August 24, 1932

Am now about halfway across Lake Michigan, going east. Decided to use one of the complimentary trips from the Wisconsin-Michigan Transit Company.

The engines are just starting, the boat vibrates, and she begins to move. We're now back across to Milwaukee. We will arrive about 6 a.m. I came over most of the way up in the pilothouse, on the first officer's watch. We put in to Muskegon to unload and load some freight and passengers and then came on down here. We left Muskegon as darkness came on, again in the pilothouse. There were no lights there except that shining down from the stern mast light. The *Alabama* followed us down. Captain Richardson is a tough old sailor—about the oldest now on the Lakes—and the first mate says he is the best. He had considerable company whenever he was in the pilothouse so far. I expect he'll turn in as soon as the boat gets out past the breakwater light. Am going back up in the pilothouse. I like it. Sleep some other day.

Milwaukee, Wisconsin, August 25, 1932

Expected to be in Racine, Wisconsin, tonight but here I am.

I had a fine trip last night coming back across the Lake. I was on deck and then in the pilothouse until about 3 a.m., and then I turned in for a few minutes as the boat arrived on this side and whistled for the bridge to open. I've decided that in my next life I'll spend most of it on water.

I called again at the Federal Building and found Captain Henry Ericksen in his office this time. He is inspector of hulls, is about sixty and very friendly and interested. He had a number of years on salt water in both sail and steam. He liked the old chanteys and wrote out one for me that he'd heard on ocean schooners and on the Lakes. He used to like to hear black West Indies men chantey. "They just couldn't work at all without a song—and they were damn good at it. You couldn't tell what they sang, but they put lots of life into it." He was alongside a "tall Frenchman" at Antwerp, Belgium, one time when both vessels were making sail and the two crews had a sort of a chantey contest "and was there chanteying!" I won't forget a second chantey he gave me. The chorus of the first was: "Hurrah,

Racine.

Entrance to the harbor at Racine. (From *Picturesque America*)

boys, heave her down." The second song was "Leave Her, Johnny, Leave Her":

I thought I heard the Old Man say,
Leave her, Johnny, leave her!
"Just pump her out, then draw your pay."
It's time for us to leave her!

There was a ship that went to sea,
She was not the ship that she might be,
The times are hard, the ship is old,
And there's six feet of water in her hold.

Our hands are sore, our backs are humped,
And half the Lakes went through her pumps.
We pumped all night, we pumped all day,
We pumped and pumped the whole damn way.

We pumped all day, we pumped all night,
And her pump rods shine just like a light.
The ship is old and would not stay
She shipped it green both night and day.

The Old Man's cross-eyed and cannot see,
The mate was drunk and on a spree.
The cook's best meat was old and tough,
And of his stew, none was enough.

The ship's a sieve, both fore and aft,
Leave her, Johnny, leave her,
And now, by God, we've pumped our last!
Leave her, damn her, leave her!

     I called at the Marine Union twice. There were about thirty men hanging around, old and young, some playing cards, some laying on the floor, others shaving, haircutting and washing clothes and several walking the floor. The hall was dingy and dirty and dark and the men mostly "down-and-outers." Some told of a "Big Tim" who used to be there often, but who's now at the company hospital. They said he had been on the Lakes all his life and would know a lot of songs. I drove out to the "County Institutions Buildings" on the west side of the city, but no one in the office knew anything of any "Big Tim" sailor there. I talked with a half dozen old sailors and finally one of them told me that "Big Tim's" real name was Mike Sullivan. None of them ever knew any songs. I located Mike in a ward of the hospital with a bad heart. He wasn't feeling very well and seemed quite worried. He said he knew a number of songs about Lakes boats, and I decided it would be worthwhile to go back tomorrow after he's had a night's rest.

One of the attendants in the general office told me of a man named Horace House who was a great fiddler, had played in theaters a season or two, and who has made a collection of Lakes songs and tunes. This sounded pretty good to me. He said I'd find him at the "Milwaukee Rescue Mission."

Back downtown, I learned at the mission that Mr. House had been at the company "alms house" for a year. There were about a hundred men—certainly a forlorn looking group—awaiting a handout. A tragedy here in big numbers.

Had a small lunch. Gave my eats money and some more to an old fellow who appears about at the bottom.

Kenosha, Wisconsin, August 27, 1932

Found Alec Crangle at his post tending the Main Street bridge. He sailed the Lakes as a boy and is now about seventy. He said he used to hear and know a number of Lakes songs. He had some written down, but hasn't known where they are for years and hasn't sung any of them for thirty. Could recall only the following, which one of my canal songs recalled to him:

> "All haste, all speed," our captain cried,
> "For we are sorely pressed,"
> The engineer sang out from the bank
> And the mule, she did her best.

> Chorus:
> > And her bones today lie in Whitefish Bay
> > Five hundred miles away.

I found "The Equinox," Harris Christanson, a jolly Norwegian, working in his backyard. "Goddamn it all to hell, this is the only place I can find any work to do now." He is about sixty-five and sailed as mate with Captain Evan Johnson for twenty years. Before that, he was on the oceans for a dozen years. "Got married and had to stay nearer home." He said he used to sing "The *Flying Cloud*" while on ocean and Lakes boats. He said he used to know many ocean chanteys, "but them damn songs are never twice alike. You just join in the chorus after the chanteyman sings the verses." He also knew a part of "The *Bigler*." He tried to give it but got stuck, so I helped him. He said there was a stanza talking about head winds blowing the boat back to the Straits after it had gone out in northern Lake Huron:

> We squared away for Cheboygan,
> Cheboygan in the Straits.

He told of sailors singing in saloons in Buffalo—"Canal Street in Buffalo, that was a hot old street"—and in Cleveland and Chicago. "I mind one time taking old Mike McKann uptown in Cleveland to get his wrist fixed up when he'd cut it. We stopped into a saloon to get a little drink and we got in a fistfight all about his wrist and then the damn fool got some salve from the bartender and when I seed him next he was rubbing it on his coat sleeve. The next morning when he see'd what a mess he'd made of his coat he just said, 'Well, bejesus, my arm's better,

Kenosha Harbor.

A tug tows a two-masted schooner past a light marking the entrance to Kenosha Harbor. (From *Picturesque America*)

anyway.'"

     I went to the Coast Guard station. Captain Christopherson, now about fifty, had spent much of his career at Whitefish Point Station on Lake Superior and for a few years at Chicago. He was there at the time of the *Eastland* disaster and helped remove about fifty bodies from the hull of the boat. He also took passengers and crew off the *Milwaukee* when she sank in Lake Michigan in 1929. He sailed a few years in the late 1890s, but heard little singing or other lore and knows none.

     After lunch, I called on Captain William Barnett, and spent most of the evening with him. He was on sailboats as a boy and then took up steam. He was a captain of Pere Marquette car ferries out of Ludington, Michigan, for many years and then bought out a fish business about twenty-five years ago and has lived here since. When on the car boats he said he practically always had a number of Beaver Islanders in his crew and told of incidents that he'd heard about the islands. "They're a great lot. No others like them in the world." He told of John McCann getting in a jam with conservation officers for fishing in restricted waters and out of season. McCann was lifting nets with a big haul when he saw officers coming and dropped the end of his net where he knew he could find it and pulled around the island through a narrow, shallow channel with the state boat coming fast on his tail. "Poor man, m' heart breaks with compassion, for he'll never make it. It's wrecked on the cruel rocks he'll be." And sure enough, he was, and John went back and picked up the rest of his nets and went home. A couple days later he went back and helped them.

     At another time, he went over in Lake Huron and strung his nets in Canadian waters. [Canada banned U.S. commercial fishers from Canadian waters. Those who broke the law were called fish pirates and could have their equipment or boats seized.] He got away with it for a while, but one day he heard that a Canadian cutter was on his tail. They left their nets there until the next foggy day, and then he and his crew went back after them. They were lifting a great catch when they heard something ahead and it turned out to be the government cutter. The officers put them under arrest, took their fish and nets and took them under tow. However, in the fog the cutter ran aground on a bar and couldn't get off. The officers ordered the fish tug to come alongside and in an attempt to lighter the cutter loaded the nets, boxes of fish and other material onto the tug. They then had the tug pull, but it couldn't move the larger boat. John then suggested they transfer some of the cutter's coal, so they did and the tug squared away to pull again. It went out to the end of the line and pulled until the engines were about full power. Then, the tug cut the line and disappeared into the fog and came home: fish, nets, and extra coal.

     Captain Barnett said he once had a Beaver Islander aboard who wasn't much good, "superstitious as the devil," and lazy. Once, when the man was wheeling and Barnett was on watch, "Old Mike" asked to be relieved, saying he hadn't had anything to eat that evening. Barnett said he knew Mike just wanted to go down to the galley to sit down and smoke, so he told him all right, to go along.

He then called a watchman, a young, nimble chap, to take his place at the wheel and as soon as Old Mike left the lee'rd pilothouse door, Barnett told the watchman to climb down one of the windward stanchions and be in the galley when Mike arrived. So, he was sitting there looking unconcerned as Mike came in. Old Mike looked at him and backed out, looking quite perplexed, and started to the companionway to go above again. As he did, the watchman climbed back up to the pilothouse again as Mike got back. Barnett said Mike stood in the door and stared at the watchman at the wheel, whistling as though nothing had happened. Mike stood a while, said nothing and then turned and went below to his quarters. When they got into port, he quit.

WAUKEGAN, ILLINOIS, AUGUST 28, 1932

Found Harry Parmalee and his brother George at their bachelor shanty. They are about sixty-five. Their father was a salt-water sailor who came to the Lakes when the boys were in their early teens, then sailed the Lakes and fished. Harry said his father was quite a singer and all of them used to sing—even on their fish boats— mostly ocean songs. He remembered particularly "High Barbaree," "The *Cumberland*'s Crew," "Black-Eyed Susan," "A Wet Sheet and a Flowing Sea," "A Canadian Boat Song." He said that often while rowing in when they had no wind they'd sing some of the chanteys: "Homeward Bound," "Haul on the Bowline," "Sally Brown," "Blow, My Bully Boys, Blow," "Rio Grande," "Shenandoah," "The Black Ball Line," "Santa Anna," and others.

Harry said the sailors that he'd heard sing would usually put Lakes names in their songs and they'd make up new ones to fit their times. [The brothers' version of "Sally Brown" went like this.]

> Oh, Sally Brown is very pretty,
> Way, hey, roll and go!
> Prettiest gal in all the city,
> Spend my money on Sally Brown!
>
> Sally Brown, she's a bright mulatto,
> She drinks rum and chews tobacco.
> Seven long years I courted Sally,
> But she was always a dilly dally.
>
> Oh, Sally Brown, I long to see you,
> Oh, Sally Brown, I'll n'er deceive you.

CHICAGO, ILLINOIS, AUGUST 29, 1932

I drove to the home of Mrs. F. L. Thorpe, whose son, Harvey, said she rented rooms. On her suggestion that it would not be wise to leave anything in a car parked out overnight, I toted the ton of stuff I've been hauling around and never using into her basement. Then, after lunch, I spent half the night with a city directory and phone book trying to locate some of the addresses of men whose names I've collected all along the way. Found most of them, except Ole Olson—or Olsen—who lives with his son Olaf. The Chicago city directory lists thirty-eight "Ole Olsons" and thirty-one "Ole Olsens" and thirty-five "Olaf Olsons" and twenty-eight "Olaf Olsens" and no Ole and son Olaf at the same address. If the Democrats insist on killing the 18th Amendment [prohibiting the "manufacture, sale, or transportation of intoxicating liquors" and their importation and exportation] and the Baptists on keeping it, they both might be satisfied by having it changed to apply to Ole and Olaf Olson or Olsen instead of as is.

Chicago, Illinois, August 30, 1932

No more days like this one, please, sir—whoever has charge of such things. Ninety-four in the shade and Chicago's shade comes mostly from the smoke and dust in the air. I would hate to be sentenced to many days of this. Rattle, bang, rush, and roar and the odor and fumes of auto exhaust everywhere and crowds of people hurrying in all directions, and men begging on all the streets. What luxury a cold bath and a measure of quiet here on Wilson Avenue!

Spent part of this morning looking up some names I didn't get to last night and trying to arrange a few calls. Took a bus to the U.S. Marine Hospital first, as it was on the way downtown. [The Chicago Marine Hospital was one of many set up to serve sailors through the United States Public Health Service, created under the Treasury Department in 1798 to treat merchant seamen for cholera, yellow fever, and other ailments caused by unsanitary conditions. This loose network of locally controlled hospitals was reorganized in 1870 into the Marine Hospital Service, with headquarters in Washington, D.C. This was changed in 1902 to the Public Health and Marine Hospital Service and truncated in 1912 to the Public Health Service. Today it is part of the Department of Health and Human Services.]

Man at Information Desk said I must see Miss Dunn, the head nurse, before I could see any of the men there, so I waited about an hour for the return of Miss Dunn who, when she came, said that Mrs. Gage, the social services secretary, would have to be seen, so another wait while Mrs. Gage had her noon lunch and then she informed me that the permission of Dr. Trask would have to be obtained as "the government is very strict on allowing anyone to see the patients." Dr. Trask would not be in until after 2:30 p.m. and from noon until then no one was allowed to interrupt the sleeping hours, etc., so I decided to go on downtown rather than to sit two hours waiting for the doctor to return. I went to the Sailors' Union of the Great Lakes on Clark Street.

Chicago, Illinois, August 31, 1932

I called at the Sailors' Union Hall and found Robert "Brokenback" Collen, of uncertain advanced age, with bleached sandy hair around a considerable bald place. Big, reddish freckles on his face, neck, and forearms, faded eyes, and an under jaw that was slightly off-center. His oversized coat and trousers had evidently been worn for some time. He had a pronounced starboard list when he walked and a

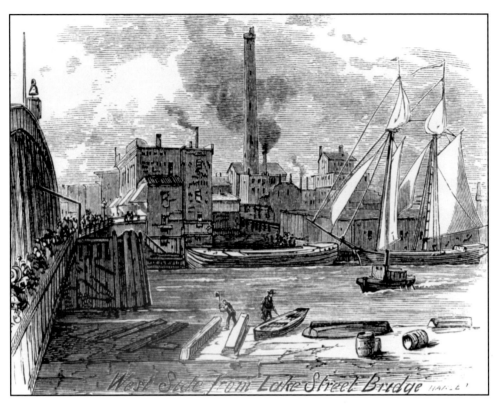

People cross over the Chicago River on the Lake Street Bridge, at left. (From *Picturesque America*)

pleasant Irish flavor when he talked. He said that his father was Irish, his mother Scottish, and that he was born in Belgium. According to his account, he ran away from home and went to sea as a cabin boy when he was ten, and sailed the oceans for years, mostly in English square-riggers in the India, Australia, and China trades. He and a half-dozen shipmates in 1880 came to the Lakes by way of New York and Buffalo. They then sailed in grain and ore schooners as long as sailing vessels lasted. His salt-water friends drifted away, and he hasn't heard from any of them or from his family in over thirty years. And now he's old, out of a job, somewhat crippled, and floating about Chicago.

While working temporarily in a Cleveland area shipyard once, scaffolding gave way under a vessel, and he was seriously injured so that he had to stay in the Cleveland Marine Hospital for over twenty-one months. After that, his friends called him "Brokenback Bob." He was quite vague about his present livelihood, but the union hall business agent said Collen came there frequently, ostensibly looking for a job onboard ship, but that he hadn't worked for years. He stays at various free missions and cheap lodging houses, and is in and out of the Chicago Marine Hospital, "where he'll probably end his days."

Weeks before Walton ever reached Chicago, sailors directed him to the songs he would find in the memories at the U.S. Marine Hospital at Buena Park. (From postcard)

Collen knew fragments of many sailor chanteys, but had no idea where he had learned them. He said crews always worked to chanteys on ocean ships and on the biggest Lakes vessels when they had a dozen or more men forward. He added that he "used to be a perty damn good chanteyman" himself, but "can't much mind 'em anymore. Dem chantey songs, yuh can't learn 'em, yuh just sing 'em—whatever yuh think of or remember at the time." He said he had an old shipmate, Jim Yonkers, who "knowed all 'em old songs," and he'd bring him along tomorrow, so we made an appointment for nine o'clock.

When asked about amusement songs, he replied, "Sure we had 'em, lots of 'em." Most of them, he said, came from shore free-and-easy vaudeville shows, "but some we made up ourselves. Any real sailor can make up a song about a ship." He could recall only a few stray lines and stanzas.

He stated that some Lakes sailors went down to salt water for the winter months when Lakes navigation closed, but some others, who had no other place to go, stayed in waterfront boardinghouses. They paid the proprietor for their board, lodging, and "anything else the boss could think of," out of their wages the first month of the new season. Many men lived this way year after year. He had spent winters and between-trip intervals in all the larger Lake ports, "but Buffalo was the place!" Then followed accounts of entertainments, saloon brawls, harbor ladies, fights with Erie Canal men, and of sailors being drugged, robbed, and dropped through saloon backroom trapdoors into the old canal.

He said he had been shanghaied "more 'n once'd" on ocean ships and "twic'd on the Lakes." Once he woke up on a Lake Superior ore schooner out of Ashland, Wisconsin, and "another time when I got sober I was a coal-passer on a damn steamboat out of Toledo, Ohio."

During my afternoon visit to the U.S. Marine Hospital, I was told several times that I should see a big Irishman who had been there for some time, and went by the name of "Mountain Dew," or simply, "The Dew." So, I called in the evening and inquired for him. Finally, an attendant asked if he owed me any money, and when I assured him that there was no money involved, he said, "You wait here and I'll get him." In a few minutes, he returned with "The Dew" in tow—a real Irish stage prizefighter. He was probably in his late sixties, tight-cut hair all over his head, about two hundred pounds and an Irish brogue a yard thick. I explained that I was looking for old songs that the Lakes schoonermen used to sing, and asked if he'd sailed much on them.

"Zhurr lad, an' I've sailed on dem Lakes damn near since dey was foist made." For an hour or more he told me of the vessels he'd been in—ocean and Lakes—the far ports he knew: London, Capetown, Sydney, Hong Kong, San Francisco; the saloons where he'd "clean de house," and on and on. Then he told me of the accident that put him in the hospital when he and two friends fell into a twelve-foot basement "an' cracked me head an' half me bones. An' what makes me so goddamn mad is dat I was stone sober. Me an' me partners was jus' takin' a shortcut to have a bit of a drink an' b' Jesus Christ, if we didn't all walk right into dat damn hole."

After he got out of the basement hole, I asked him how he got the name of "Mountain Dew."

"Dat iss me name—well, I think I was christened wid somet'ing else onced, but dat was so long ago I 'bout forgot what it was."

"Who first called you by that name?"

"One of me friends call me dat fifty years ago in a saloon, I t'ink it was in Sydney, Australia. De damn fool said I was all de toim a-drinkin' sailor whiskey—what dey call Mountain Dew—an' b' Jesus Christ, dat's de only name I ever gits since."

Finally, we got back to the Lakes.

"An' do I ever know dem ole songs! Zhurr, an' I knows 'em all. Many's a noight me an' me partner would be singin' 'em till daylight fur dem ole sailor bums in de saloons. Ever' toim we sing 'em a bit of a song, dey gets us a drink till we damn near drink de place dry.

"Zhurr, an' I knows de *Annie Peterson,* an' she was one hell of a good ship, an' dat iss a good song dey made 'bout her. Many's a drink I've had from a-singin' of it, an' if only I had my teef, I'd sing yuh a bit of it right now. A man jus' can't sing widout his teef. De ole doc here, he says dey was ulcers, py-ree-ah an' udder troubles in me teef, an' I figures dey was real bad, an' I says to de doc, 'all right, Doc, rig up yer heaving gear an' haul 'em out, an' . . .'"

"How does that song about the *Peterson* start?"

"Well, now, me lad, an' if I had toim to be thinkin' it out, an' had me teef, zhurr an' I'd be a-singin' of it to yuh."

"Could you just give me the words without singing them?"

"Jesus Christ, lad, now you wouldn't want a man to spile a good song by jus' a-sayin' it!"

Considerable pumping failed to get even a line. Each of a number of other song titles and fragments I had been trying to complete got about the same response, so, to check on his wide knowledge of Lakes songs, I invented a couple of titles and tried them. "That is a pretty good song about the schooner *Lizzy Riley.*"

"Ah, zhurr, an' it is that, an' many's a toim I've had a bit of a drink from a-singing of it. One toim . . ."

"And that song about the *Mary Downs,* do you know it?"

"Zhurr, lad, an' I do, an' it is a foin song, an' if only I had me teef."

Hospital visiting hours came to a close, and as I was leaving, "The Dew" got between me and the door and with much solicitude suggested that I return the next day—"An' maybe yuh'll have a bit of tobacee wid yuh, an' I'll have me friend Foghorn—an' b' Jesus Christ, he knows every goddamn song." And so the day ended.

CHICAGO, ILLINOIS, SEPTEMBER 1, 1932

Began the day at the Sailors' Union again, and there was "Brokenback" Robert Collen playing a game of solitaire and at another table was his friend Jim Yonkers. Bob explained that his friend wasn't feeling very well again. "I didn't find him until near mornin', and now look at the damn fool." Jim was weaving in his chair, red-faced, hair in his eyes, ragged, and pretty far gone since last night. "He's too damned ignorant to know any of dem songs anyway. If he knows any when he's feeling better, I'll send 'em to yah." Collen then pulled some old yellow paper out of his pocket on which he'd written out some lines and notes, and from it gave me two songs, one a Lakes version of the old chantey "Homeward Bound," and the other he called "The Canaller's Lament." He explained that "Homeward Bound," which they used sometimes in weighing anchor, might not be "quite right because sailors always put the names of any places and ships in that they wanted to and often they didn't make any sense, but we all joined in on the chorus, anyhow."

Oh, fare you well, we're homeward bound,
Good-bye, fare you well; good-bye, fare you well!
Oh, fare you well, 'tis a joyful sound,
Hurrah, my boys, we're homeward bound!

We're homeward bound, the Old Man did say,
We're homeward bound this very day.
Come man the good caps'n, heave hearty and strong,
Come sing a good chorus, for 'tis a good song.

This anchor we'll weigh, and the sails we will set,
And the friends we are leaving we leave with regret.
Though we leave with regret, it's happy I be,
For a lass in Buffalo is a-waiting for me.

Oh, fare you well, we're outward bound,
We're outward bound for Buffalo town.
We're outward bound with wheat in her hold,
'N' we'll crack on the canvas and then let 'er roll.

The wind is nor'west, an' it's steady and strong,
We'll reach to the Straits as we send 'er along.
Oh, down the long Lakes with a bone in 'er teeth,
With her lee rail under, we'll lead the whole fleet.

Oh, Buffalo town is the right town for me,
In Buffalo town we'll go on a spree.
Oh, I think that I heard the Old Man say,
I think that I heard the command to "belay."

Collen was unable to recall anymore. I gave him some money, which brightened him up considerably. He said he'd write up anymore he could think of or get from any old sailors, and would send them to me. I told him I'd make it quite well worth his time. Think I'd better see him again while in Chicago.

I went to the Newberry Library and found Washington Park out in front filled with an assortment of crowds. They were listening to patent medicine hawkers, prizefighters, entertainers, fakirs, and speechmakers including representatives of the Ex-Servicemen's League—a man who was recently chased out of Washington, D.C.—socialists and one red-hot who is going down to Washington and overthrow those who work there and set up a people's government and then go to Wall Street, and "get their dirty millions, clean it and give it to the people who ought to have it."

I got off the bus a few blocks from the rooming place and walked slowly along the remaining distance. Was stopped by three men and two women—very hungry and the women "lonesome."

Chicago, Illinois, September 2, 1932

I went to the steamboat inspection office and found Inspector William Nicholas. He said that, when he was sailing, he'd heard many songs about the old schooners and some of the things they did. He still knows part of "The Red Iron Ore" and "The *Bigler*" and others. He used to sing one about the *Lizzie A. Law*, but cannot recall it now. He also said he'd often heard a song about the schooner *Nellie Reddington*. When he first began sailing on the Lakes, the sailboats would often be so thick in the Chicago River that it was very difficult to get through. The southbound boats would all come out when a north wind came along, no matter how hard it blew and they'd race all the way down and the first to arrive got tugs at once and were taken direct to the docks and got the best places. He recalls several blows when the schooners came in so fast the tugs couldn't get them all in before they'd drag their anchors and pile up on the beach. "A good breeze would blow them all down in great numbers and the tugs would drag them in from one to six at a time if they could get lines on that many. It was a pretty sight and lively times."

He is glad somebody's trying to get the songs together. "They'll make a great book, if you can get them, but it's pretty late now. Had you come around about ten years ago when —— were alive, you could have got plenty."

Stopped at the Marine Hospital again. "Brokenback" didn't show up, nor did Jim. The business agent asked if I had given him some money, and to my reply that I had, he said, "Well, you gave him too much. He'll not be around now for several days." [That autumn, Collen answered several letters addressed to him at the sailors union hall, and in each one, he enclosed some song fragments. In mid-winter, his letters stopped.]

I got a group of ex-schoonermen together and found they knew about my earlier visit and had been talking about old songs. One asked if I had a song about "The *Handy No. 2*." One went through "The *Bigler*," much as I have it. I read through many of the fragments I but got only vague responses. One known as "Sheets" ever since he took bed sheets aboard a vessel, knew parts of a song about "The Crack Schooner *Moonlight*" and others filled in. "Tug Boat George" said he had sailed in her. One called Gus began a chantey and "Foghorn" joined in as did others, and I got parts of a number. I inquired about "The Dew," but no one knew where he was.

CHICAGO, ILLINOIS, SEPTEMBER 3, 1932

Saturday isn't a very favorable day for finding people. Several people I attempted to locate were away for the weekend and Labor Day.

Inquired for Mr. Carl Sandburg and learned that he is at Harbert, Michigan, engaged upon a book about Mary Todd Lincoln and will be there until fall. [Carl Sandburg, writer, poet, and folklore collector, had left the *Chicago Daily News* in May. His book, *Mary Lincoln: Wife and Widow*, was published later in the year. *Abraham Lincoln: The War Years*, the second part in Sandburg's six-volume biography of the former president, won the Pulitzer Prize.]

No luck at the Chicago Historical Society building. They've had a grand opening, but the new building is still closed and the old one and the material will not be available for public use for a month.

After this came some shopping and then about three hours in the Chicago Art Museum. I nearly had to spend the night in the building as I got locked in one of the rooms. An irate janitor said he told me it was closing time, but I didn't hear him. The museum has a pretty fine collection.

In the evening, I came up to the Marine Hospital again and found "The

Dew" this time, but he couldn't give me anything. "I know all of 'em, sure an' I do, but I can't think of a damned one now, an' it's the truth, I'm tellin' yah."

An old, lanky washed-out appearing man came up and The Dew introduced me to "Gasoline George," another tugman who apparently got his name for once mixing up his liquids. The gasoline is running pretty low now.

Waukegan, Illinois, September 5, 1932

Labor Day, and still nobody home. Decided to drive up to Waukegan to call on lightkeeper S. C. Jacobson. Found him talkative and friendly. He began sailing on schooners in the 1890s, then hiring out to steamboats and later transferred to the Light Service. He has been trying to recall some of the schooner songs he once knew. Sang and talked "The *Julie Plante*," "The Red Iron Ore," "The *Bigler*'s Crew," and "*Sand Patch*" [also called "*Sam Patch*" or "Yim Yonson"]:

> Yim Yonson ship from lumberyard upon de scow Sam Patch;
> He didn't know his starboard bow from oft de forward hatch.
> He make big bluff before he sail that he ben sailor man,
> But when de trouble struck de scow, Yim had to show his han'.
>
> De scow ben in de cordwood trade. She sail from Sister Bay,
> An' Yim he would be handyman 'till off Twin Points one day
> When yust like finger snap a squall on de wood scow flew
> An' made her stan' on her beam's end an' call up all de crew.
>
> De captain swore like crazy man, an' at Yim Yonson yell:
> "Yump up an' rif dat tops'l queek, or it ben gone to hell!"
> But Yim, he say, "I will not stir from dis cahutan stanchion;
> Der ben ten tousand tops'ls, yes, but only one Yim Yonson!"
>
> An' dat's how Yim, he lose his yob, an' no more go to sea—
> At sailin' he ben greenhorn, sure, an' always want to be.
> Ven he was kicked from off de ship, he heard de captain swore;
> But said, "I'd rather lan' dis vay dan float along de shore."

Mr. Jacobson tried a song about a Lake Ontario vessel, but could only recall:

> And when upon our starboard tack
> Port Dalhousie did loom
> We all stood by upon the deck
> To tip the long jibboom.

He said the song told of a timber drogher that carried a team of mules aboard for loading and making a trip to the Upper Lakes [Huron, Michigan, and Superior]. He said that a vessel going through the old Welland Canal had to unship its jibboom and tip it up against the foremast in order to navigate the locks. He could not recall where he had learned it. He also recalled the following from an Erie Canal song:

So haul on your towline, boys,
Stand by your sorrel mule.
Low bridge, everybody down,
Don't stand there like a fool.

When asked about signs and superstitions, he said that most sailors were worried about mirages that sometimes appeared in the late season on the Lakes. He recalled seeing one on Lake Superior once when on an ore schooner. They were not far out of Marquette when the wheelsman called their attention to some schooners that appeared in plain sight and that disappeared over the horizon and later appeared again. Some of the men said they were ghost ships and a sign of disaster. Some of the crew wanted to get off when they got to the Soo, but the Old Man wouldn't let them. Jacobson said that one time he saw the Outer Island Light on Lake Superior when on the way to Ashland, Wisconsin, and about 70 miles from the light. They then lost it and later picked it up again. Some of the crew— including himself—were quite worried. He added that most sailors didn't want cats aboard, nor women. Both bad luck. Starting a trip on Friday was bad. He never heard of any vessel getting close to a ghost ship.

St. Joseph and Ann Arbor, September 8, 1932

Arrived in Ann Arbor at 2:30 a.m. Changed plans and omitted Grand Rapids for the present and came on to the end of the trail.

I began this day by calling on Mr. O. C. McCauley, lightkeeper at St. Joe. He's about sixty-five, a former Beaver Islander, and has spent most of his life on and about the Lakes. He referred me to several men on Beaver Island.

Called on former sailors Charles and Vasco Roberts, brothers about sixty-five to seventy and seventy-five to eighty. Charles seemed to be quite unfamiliar with any of the early Lakes lore and Vasco, who has been tending the State Street bridge for the past fifteen years, was on the verge of a nervous breakdown as the result of an accident a week before. It seems he opened the bridge about 4 a.m. Sunday after the insistent blowing of a coal freighter to get through. The gates at either end of the bridge wouldn't close, and for the first time in his fifteen years, he opened the bridge without them. Just as the boat had cleared, a closed sedan with six people in it came roaring down the street and plunged fifty to sixty feet out into the river. Four of them got out and two drowned. He couldn't talk about anything else.

Captain Charles Morrison, now eighty-two, began sailing the Lakes with his father at age fourteen in 1864. He said he never could sing himself but would join in with the others. He said the early sailors, which were about half salt-water men, made up songs about the boats, crews, and trips and sang them as well as many others while working about the deck and while relaxing in the fo'c'sle. They also chanteyed while making sail or weighing anchor. One could hear them any time the boats were being towed out of the Chicago River. One day in the 1880s, he counted more than five hundred schooners in the Chicago River and on the trip to Muskegon for a load of lumber. Most of his sailing was on Lake Michigan in the lumber trade. He changed to steamboats as they took trade from the slower sailboats. He spent two years on the Pacific. "They don't know what real weather is there. They tried to laugh at me because I'd sailed on frog ponds but, by Jesus Christ, I never saw anything in two years sailing on the Pacific to be at all as bad as some of the November and December gales which we have out here every fall, and them lumber hookers would go out into them and think nothing of it. I tell yuh, they was sailors in them days!"

He was wrecked about two-thirds of the way over to Milwaukee once and was in the water hanging to some wreckage for eight hours before being picked up.

In evening drove on to Paw Paw Lake to the home of Van B. "Soub" Ludwig, where I'd called once at the beginning of the summer, thereby completing the circle. He is now about seventy-five and living alone with Mrs. Ludwig and has been hit pretty hard by the times. He told of the Ludwig band. His oldest brother was captain of the *Mary Ludwig,* the next brother was mate, Soub was the cook, and three other brothers were in the crew. Each one could play several instruments. They could often play when passing other stops or in port. Supplemented by a number of other players, the band took second in a state competition at Saginaw one time. As the brothers got ships of their own and left, the band broke up. He said they didn't sing much, but played a lot.

And now, back in Ann Arbor for a campaign of letters to bring in promised material and to assemble the material I've collected.

Finis.

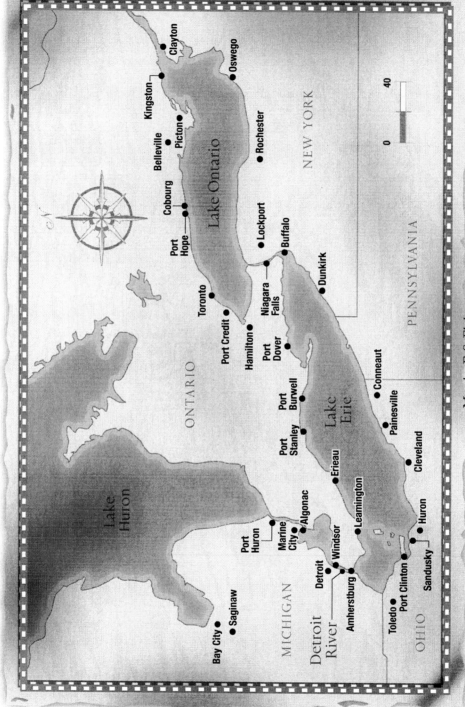

Lake Huron

Bay City
Saginaw

MICHIGAN

Detroit River

Port Huron
Marine City
Algonac
Windsor
Detroit
Amherstburg
Toledo
Port Clinton
Sandusky

OHIO

Learnington
Huron
Cleveland
Painesville
Conneaut

Lake Erie

Erieau
Port Stanley
Port Burwell
Port Dover
Hamilton
Port Credit
Toronto

ONTARIO

Niagara Falls
Buffalo
Dunkirk
Lockport
Port Hope
Cobourg
Rochester

Lake Ontario

Picton
Belleville
Kingston
Oswego
Clayton

NEW YORK

PENNSYLVANIA

N

0   40

Map by F. S. Fluker.

CHAPTER 2

1933: Southern Lake Huron, Lake Erie, Lake Ontario

When the dark waves are wildly rolling,
On old Ontario's rocky shore,
When the seabirds are idly soaring,
Remember those the waves roll o'er.
    "THE SCHOONER JENKINS"

Walton's 1932 circle tour of Lake Michigan encouraged him to visit more places. Accounting on October 31 for his expenditure of faculty research money, Walton wrote, "I spent the summer traveling on and around Lake Michigan talking with all the older Lakes sailors that I could find. I didn't locate as many songs as I had hoped, but did get some and titles, subjects, and stray lines and stanzas of a considerable number of others." By November, he was already charting a course for the southern end of Lake Huron and around the Lower Lakes of Erie and Ontario.

Over the winter, Walton continued to draw out his contacts from the summer of 1932. Mail carriers brought scraps of song from Robert "Brokenback" Collen to Walton and carried thank-you notes and spending money back the other way. One of Collen's letters brought the song "Up Anchor":

We've got the rusty mud-hook up,
    She's green with Chicago slime;
We're sailing with a gale of wind,
    No more of city's grime!
We'll head for the old blue waterways,
    And mates, we'll drink our fill
Of winds that hail across the bow
    And through the hatches spill.

As Walton's collection grew, his circle of informants shrank. Captain Edward Carus, whom Walton met in 1932, wrote on June 27, 1933, "I must ask a favor of you, that is not to send any articles for suggestions or corrections and do not give my address to anyone. I have been sick this last winter and am feeling miserable now and can not put my mind on

Ivan and Lynn Walton with Springer Spaniel and birddog Duke at their Ann Arbor home in 1935. (Courtesy Lynn and Sue Walton)

anything, and I thank you very much for your flattering letter, but I feel like letting go my anchor."

With his sources dwindling, Walton lengthened his interviews, letting his informants wax on about the facets of sailoring that they knew best. Some knew no songs at all but were deep with weather signs, greenhorn tales, or stories of boardinghouses or the transition from sail to steam.

And Walton learned that different territory meant different tales. While in canal country in 1933, he heard about canallers, lock tenders, and tugmen. Few men who had worked on tugs had any song in them, but they were loaded with insight on the fading days of the windjammer. They recalled how they had used their wits and their fists and sometimes traveled the length of a great lake to pick up one of the ever-scarcer schooners just for the price of a tow through the river.

The homesickness and the "Night, Pete" signoffs that characterized his first summer disappear in the 1933 journal. He had learned that he needed some visitors or company during the long summers. So, in 1933 he celebrates a reunion at Buffalo, where Mildred and Lynn came to visit him. Though happy to have them nearby, he didn't stop his work for them. They waited in the car while he interviewed one informant and, for amusement, Ivan, Mildred, and Lynn took in a comedy film, *Tugboat Annie*, in which a waterfront captain and his wife try to raise their son to be a sea captain.

The summer of 1933 had a couple of subplots. One was the *Lyman Davis*, one of the last working lumber schooners on the Great Lakes. Walton had heard of the speedy vessel in 1932 and had been given a photo of it at Muskegon. The boat was named for owners Lyman M. Mason and Charles Davis. As the *Davis* sailed through the piers at Muskegon for the last time on May 7, 1913, William Brinen Sr., one of its later owners, died at his home up the hill from the docks. The doctor called it a stroke.

On July 25, 1933, Walton interviewed Captain E. J. Buzzard, about eighty, who had served on the *Davis*. A week later, at Toronto, Walton learned that the vessel was to be burned as a public amusement, much like executions had once been carried out in town squares. It incensed Walton and he ran into other sailors who were outraged by the proposed spectacle.

One of the more tantalizing but fruitless leads of the summer were the storied song sheets of Dave and Mose, clothing merchants in Buffalo. Several men told Walton they had seen or even handed out the merchants' popular fliers. The clothiers catered to sailors and tried to attract them by marrying advertising with sailor songs of the day. Walton inquired about the song sheets at several places but came up empty-handed.

Nationally, the country was taking an upturn, though it would come too late for some of Walton's old sailors. They would not all live to see the new president, Franklin Delano Roosevelt, lead the nation out of the Depression. In June, the Twenty-first Amendment to the Constitution repealed the Eighteenth Amendment, ending national Prohibition. Michigan had been the first state to approve the amendment and dry days would be over by year's end.

In an event that would have great significance for Walton and his work, the widow of inventor Thomas A. Edison gave an old-fashioned cylinder-style recording machine to John Avery Lomax. He and his son Alan used the machine to capture ballads of the American "folk." Like Walton, they were gathering what they could while they could. Their work would be the basis for the Archive of American Folksong in the Library of Congress. Alan later recalled, "For us, this instrument was a way of taking down tunes quickly and accurately; but to the singers themselves, the squeaky, scratchy voice that emerged from the speaking tube meant that they had made communicative contact with a bigger world than their own." Walton would later agree.

Port Huron, Michigan, June 21, 1933

The first day out, the summer of 1933. Somewhat of a slow start. Just had car overhauled, which made a cruising speed of twenty-five to thirty-five miles per hour all the way from Ann Arbor. Arrived about 1:30 p.m. after many honks and "what-to-hell" looks by passing motorists.

Port Huron, Michigan, June 22, 1933

I found ex–schooner captain A. M. Conkey sitting on the side porch of his home, and he seemed quite pleased to have someone stop in to talk. He is eighty-two, about six feet, three inches tall, erect and well built, and forceful in his speech. He said he began sailing in 1862 when he was twelve and continued over half a century until the steamboats drove the old schooners off the Lakes.

"Yes, sir, I've been on every goddamn lake, and many's a time, and in all kinds of weather. I began as a boy when I ran away from school because of some trouble. That was a long time ago, but I'm a'tellin' you right now, lad, in them days there was real sailin' and real sailors. There wasn't no lights or ranges or dredges an' every other goddamn help that keeps them steamboats off the shore. In thick weather, we made our way the best we could without any foghorns to steer by an', by God, we got there! An' I'm a'tellin' you something else, and I've always said it, by Jesus Christ, that if there had been some of the old schooners out on the Lakes a few years back when all them freighters went down, they'd a rode 'er out and come into port. [Conkey may have been referring to the Great Storm of 1913. It killed almost 250 men and sank 19 vessels.] By Jesus Christ, I'll be goddamned, but they'd just spread their wings an' ride right over them big seas. But them goddamn steel freighters just blow right down into 'em an' what t' hell can they do?

"Yes, I knowed the schooner *Shupe*—knowed 'er well, every spar in 'er. The day she was lost a few miles up the beach here, I came along astern of 'er in the *Magruder* an' saw she was makin' heavy work of it, an' I offers old Captain Miller a line, but he says, 'No, I'll make the river all right,' but by God, he never did. When I got in an' made fast, they was a-hurryin' around gettin' help to go out and get 'er off the beach where she was a-poundin' to pieces. I hurried up, and there he was hard aground an' the seas a-rollin' over him. They wanted me to go out in a surfboat to help get the crew off, an' I says, 'hell yes, sure I'll go out.' I wasn't afraid of nothin' in them days. But as I was a-getting in the boat, I says, 'Who's a-goin' to run this damn thing?' A young feller says, 'I am,' an' I says, 'No, you're not, if I'm a-goin' in 'er.' He was the Old Man's nephew an' wanted t' rescue 'im. I says, 'there ain't no damn tugman a-livin' that knows how to handle a boat in seas like this.'

"Well. They went out without me, an' every damn one of 'em was drowned except Dan Lynn. My oldest boy went out in the surf 'bout a mile or so down the beach with a line around him an' pulled Dan in. The crew of the *Shupe* was lost, too. There was a song wrote about 'er called, I think it was, 'The Cruel Waves of Lake Huron.'

"Yes, there was singin' in them days an', by Jesus Christ, some of the prettiest damn singin' I ever heard. Get a bunch of sailors in a saloon and how they'd sing! Sure, I knowed the '*Bigler*'s Crew,' an'—an'—ain't that hell, now? I knowed a hundred of 'em, but now I can't mind a one! I had a bad sickness last year and damn near died, an' since then I can't mind a damn thing."

I recited a few lines of it.

"Yes, that's it, and there was one about the *E. C. Roberts* that tells of bringin' ore down from Escanabie, an' there was others, a lot of 'em, but I just can't mind 'em.

"Oh, yes, I knows a song about the schooner *Fayette Brown*. She was out of Cleveland. Old Captain Bradley owned her and he had 'em put a crew of niggers on her, an' the white sailors didn't like it, an' they made up a song that tells about it. An' there was a song about the *Annie M. Peterson*. She was a small vessel and carried only grain, an' she could show her stern to all of 'em. The *Lizzie Law* was another fast one. I mind one time when the *Law* and the *John L. Danforth* came down the Lakes racin' for Buffalo, an' a tug went out to tow 'em through the rivers [St. Clair and Detroit] an' just astern of 'em was a little two-masted schooner, the *Golden Fleece*. The tug took 'em alongside of 'er, but the *Danforth*, which was astern of the *Law* in the tow, refused to take 'er line, so he took 'em around again, and still the *Danforth* wouldn't take it. Well, the tug captain was pretty hot by this time, an' took 'em around the third time, but before they come up to the *Golden Fleece*, he hauled 'em up close an' he told 'em to take that line or, by God, he'd show 'em a few things. They said they was in a hurry, but he told 'em he didn't give a goddamn if they was, but to take that line, an' they did. When they dropped the tug below Bar Point [the mouth of the Detroit River], the *Golden Fleece* outsailed 'em both and was in Buffalo fifty-five minutes before either of 'em came in.

"The *Law* was built here in Port Huron. I saw 'er launched down near the mouth of the Black River. She was as pretty a goddamn ship as you'd ever see. There was a song about 'er, too, an' one about the big five-masted *David Dows.* A sailor I had with me once from Milwaukee knowed it and promised me a copy, but I never got it. She was made into a tow-barge and later lost off Chicago. I mind one time we was to windward of 'er as she let go 'er tug off Bar Point, an' when she came around to the wind, by Jesus Christ, we had to square away before it to keep from gettin' hit. She carried a lot of canvas, but she was too damned awkward for the Lakes.

"Some of 'em schooners was pretty a sight as—well, there ain't a goddamn thing on this earth as pretty as a ship carryin' all 'er canvas before a good breeze! There was the *Moonlight* an' the *Atmosphere,* an' the *Likely Belle,* an' I mind one called the *Sunbeam.* I knowed 'em all, but I can't mind 'em now. Crowds of people used to gather along the river right here in Port Huron to watch a tow of schooners comin' up an' all a-makin' sail an' crews a-singin', an' as soon as they'd let go they'd square away for a race up the Lake. They'd never stop for any kind of weather.

"It took from eight to ten or twelve hours to tow up the [Detroit and St. Clair] rivers, an' less goin' down. Most captains would spread some canvas when the wind was fair and help the tug. The crew always had to scrape the sticks down and do any repair work necessary when under tow, an' at times keep a good lookout for sparks from the tug, especially when they was a-burnin' wood an' workin' hard.

"Sailors always would chantey when they had a good audience. I mind one they'd use when workin' the caps'n up for'ard—'Oh, Shenandore, I love your daughter, I . . .'—ain't that hell now, I can't fetch it. Chanteys made the work light, an' a good chanteyman was always a good man in a crew. Some captains would pay 'em extra wages. At Buffalo, sometimes there'd be thousands of people about the harbor a-listenin' to the sailors an' a-watchin' 'em work, an' some tryin' to sell 'em every goddamn thing. An' they was always a lot of whores a-hangin' around and every other buildin' was a saloon.

"Oh, we had many ways of foretellin' weather, lots of 'em. And we didn't have no goddamn gov'ment bureau that's always wrong. A real sailor could tell at least a day ahead what weather to expect and never miss. There was sun dogs and rings around the sun an' moon, an' the way the sun rose and set, an' the clouds, an' wind, an' also them goddamn gulls—they'd tell yuh what weather was a'comin'. An' I could feel weather in me bones. I don't know how, but I could. I can't explain all them signs to you, but we always knew what weather to expect and was ready for it.

"Ghost ships? Yes, I've heard about 'em, but I never ran afoul of one. An' there was unlucky ships. By God, you couldn't get a crew aboard some of 'em.

There was the *Colonel Cook* that sunk the *Lady Elgin* with about three hundred lives. By God, they changed her name damn near every season, but the sailors knew 'er. She was always a-losin' 'er sticks or sails or some of 'er crew. An' there was unlucky men, too. There was old Captain Miller, who put a vessel on the rocks in Georgian Bay an' another on the Flats [in Lake St. Clair] an' lost the *Shupe* out here off Port Huron, an' he also lost a lot of men. By Jesus Christ, it got so bad he couldn't get no crew.

"No, sailors don't like no cats aboard. No sailor does, an' ships don't like 'em either, nor women. Some sailors wouldn't ship on a vessel with a woman cook. An' St. Elmo's fire? You mean corposants? I never see'd it but once. There was a bright glow up about the mainm'st head, and it damn near scared some of the crew to death. They was sure some of 'em was a'goin' to lose their lives right away, but they didn't.

"Yes sir, lakesmen was a hell-'f-a-lot better sailors than ocean men at everything but mendin' lines, an' sails, an' riggin'. Them shellbacks would be scared damn near to death in a blow if there was a lee shore in sight. They wanted lots of sea room. We got along all right together, but we'd both knock hell out of a landsman who wanted a fight.

"It was them damn sailor unions that killed sailin' on the Lakes. They got the wages up so high that sailors flocked in from all over, an' there wasn't enough jobs for 'em. Owners also began to bring in Swedes an' Norwegians—goddamn roundheads we called 'em. After workin' like slaves on the oceans, they thought wages and livin' on the Lakes was pretty goddamn good.

"I mind one time I was sailin' the *Magruder*—she was flat-bottomed, what you'd call a scow-schooner—an' could go anywhere there was a heavy dew. Well, I was sent with 'er over to South Fox Island in Lake Michigan to get the engine an' riggin' out of a goddamn steamer that was on the beach there. When we arrived, we found that them damn Irishmen that haunt them islands had about stripped 'er. We did get most of 'er engine and bottom plates, but we had to dynamite 'em loose. When we got all that was worth carryin' away, we had several boxes of dynamite left an' I had it brought aboard. And do you know, them damn roundheads was afraid of it and wouldn't sail with it aboard. I had it all taken up on a sand hill and buried and, by God, it's still there yet if them damned Irishmen haven't blown themselves to hell with it.

"Another time, I was in Manistee harbor for some lumber, an' old Louis Sands, who owned a number of vessels, wanted to carry all the lumber from there in his own boats, so he padlocked a bridge we had to go through. We waited there until dark, but he wouldn't let us through, and he put a watchman on the bridge to see that we didn't. Well, I got an idea, and I sent up town an' got a couple quarts of whiskey, got the watchman drunk, took his keys, opened the bridge and went in, got a load of lumber and got out before old Sands heard about it. But when he did, as I heard later, Jesus Christ, was he mad!

"I was mate on a vessel once that went into Cheboygan, Michigan, an' loaded up with lumber. The captain was a bull-headed fellow, an' loaded 'er full without watching 'er. An' she sat as solid in the mud as though she'd growed there, an' we couldn't get 'er free. Hell, but he wouldn't lighter none. Well, I says to him, 'Capt'n, would you like to go out of here in a hell of a hurry?' An' he says, "Yes, but I ain't a-goin' to lighter none.' I says, 'lighter, hell! Get 'er ready an' have all hands up, an' I'll have you off damn quick.' So, he did that, an' while he was a-gettin' some sail on 'er, I went a block or so up where the dam was across the river. There was nobody around, so I went out on it, opened the sluice gates as wide as they'd go an', Jesus Christ, how the water poured through—enough to float a battleship! I managed to get the top gate shut, but the bottom one I couldn't move. I happened to look up just in time to see the whole goddamn Cheboygan police force a-comin', an' did I get out of there in a hurry! I ran like hell down past where the vessel was just beginnin' to move, swam out, and got aboard, an' by God, we didn't dare to go back there all season.

"My oldest boy, Charlie, is now sailin' one of them big Steel Trust boats. He passed down a couple of days ago an' will be a-comin' up about tomorrow or the next day. He's the best goddamn skipper on the Lakes—yes sir, the best. He always blows me a salute when he passes through. He sailed one of old Captain McDougall's pigs for awhile, but now he's got one of the biggest freighters there is. Them pigs was the goddamnedest lookin' things that ever hit water. [Alexander McDougall designed a line of low-riding steamers characterized by rounded sides and blunt bows that allowed the waves to roll right over them. This appearance earned them the names whalebacks, cigar boats, pigboats, or simply pigs.] There oughta been a law ag'in 'em. They'd just root their damn snouts down into the seas an' how t' hell they ever come up, I dunno. My boy Arthur is a good sailor, too. But I'm a-tellin' you, lad, sailin' ain't like it used to be, no sir, not by a hell 'f a lot."

Port Huron, Michigan, June 23, 1933

Spent the afternoon with Captain T. J. Crockett, former grand secretary of the shipmasters association. He is now sixty-four and had thirty-seven years on the Lakes. He began as a "boy" on the schooner *E. C. Roberts*. He spent a number of years on her and then changed to steam. He was a master at twenty-seven, but lost his leg in an accident in 1929 and retired. He's now in the coal business. He implies he was a pretty hard man aboard ship. He said there was little or no singing on steamboats and he couldn't remember much of it from early schooner days.

Bay City, Michigan, June 27, 1933

Called at several places in the late afternoon and evening. Found only Samuel Cranage, sixty-eight. His family owned Lakes boats, mostly grain and coal, and then they came to him. He never sailed except as a passenger. Captain McNeil, who worked with them for many years, was much of a storyteller and singer. They acquired a boat in Chicago one spring and got her ready to sail first that season, as it happened, on Friday. Captain McNeil fussed around doing all sorts of minor jobs until after midnight Friday before starting out for the season. He stoutly denied being superstitious, however, and of having any objection to starting out on Friday. Another boat which lay alongside did start out that Friday and during the day Sunday they overtook her. She had her pennant at half-mast and they learned that the skipper had fallen, injured himself, and died. Their sailors were all convinced that this accident was due to beginning the season on Friday.

On one occasion, they were locking through the Soo with another vessel and Captain McNeil asked the other captain if he knew what boat that was and he replied yes, and that all the men had their bags packed for emergencies. It was a "hoodoo" ship and all sailors were afraid of her.

Mr. McGinns, a bridge engineer over sixty-five, had two years on schooners and then took up steamboats. He also was on river tugs and said there had been sawmills on both sides of the river, nearly to Saginaw. "Barn door" schooners came up from Montreal after square oak timbers for transport to ocean boats for Europe. Timbers were loaded in the stern through the doors with horses on the windlass.

Men who worked the canals were a tough lot, he said. There was much fighting between them and Lakes sailors and lumbermen. The first deprecation— an insult or song—and a big fight was on. There were "variety shows" all along the riverfront with "ladies" by the hundreds. He recalls "Gentle Annie," who was the big, husky "boss whore" of the river.

I found L. S. Foot at his home on my third trip there. He is about seventy-four and intelligent, a peculiar old bird. He is thin, somewhat stooped, with a high collar, a dirty shirt, and the seat of his trousers hanging about to his knees. He has an immense library, he says about ten thousand volumes, and old pioneer curios of various kinds which are stored all over his house from his attic to the dank, musty basement. He is a book collector—not a book reader—and assembles them from rare-book dealers all over the world.

"What are you going to do with all these books when you're through with them?"

"Oh, probably give them to somebody or some college."

I think I better talk with the university librarian about getting some ideas in his head. He has hundreds of his books piled up like cordwood—pretty rough on rare old books.

Captain Porter Stewart, eighty-nine, was on schooners during the Civil War. He carried supplies and prisoners from Sandusky, Ohio, to Johnson Island in the bay there on Lake Erie. [The Union Army imprisoned Confederates on Johnson Island during the Civil War.] He towed up and down the St. Clair and Detroit Rivers "hundreds of times." "The most beautiful sight a man can ever see is a tow of schooners on a bright day with canvas up."

He is very deaf and difficult to talk with. His daughter, Mrs. Joe Hirschmann, helped. She said he sang very little, but enjoyed hearing others. He said sailors were a tough but happy lot. Boats were always racing and would pull up to windward of each other and steal wind and in going by would tauntingly drop a towline over the stern as if the other boat needed an assist. That was also a challenge for a race. Told of one skipper-owner who was such a "big hog" that the men said seagulls stopped following his boat because he was too cheap to even throw the scraps overboard. He has seen hundreds of schooners at a time trying to beat up or down the St. Clair River get stranded and have to wait for a tug. "A schooner under all her canvas is a beautiful sight."

PORT HURON, MICHIGAN, JULY 5, 1933

Police Court Judge Eugene Coté says the proprietor of the Atlantic Hotel has a heart that's all right. She's kept a home for down-and-out men for years and never turns any away. If they can't pay, they stay just the same. She tends them when they're sick, feeds them, looks after them, plays pool with them, sleeps with them, etc.

I called at the Atlantic Hotel on Quay Street, a former sailor hangout and "tough joint." It was pretty well down and out. The proprietor, Pidgie Conway, with her youthful glory of former years pretty badly wrecked, was there. Also, about a dozen nondescript men of various stages of non-prosperity, two of whom were pretty much intoxicated. Pidgie said her memory was pretty bad. She had heard men sing a great many times, but never learned any of their songs. She asked if I had heard the song of the schooner *Shupe*, which sank just north of Port Huron. She gave me names of some men who she thought would know some of the material. I then called at several of the addresses. Two were bootleggers—one drunk and the other out—and the third place was a whorehouse and pretty well out. Clairmont doesn't seem to be Port Huron's society street anymore.

I found Captain William J. Small, over seventy, at his home-office on Quay Street, where he operates a dredge and dock company. He is a big Irishman. As a boy, he sailed on schooners and tugs and then had fifteen years in the Coast Guard Service, mostly at Port Sanilac, Michigan, north of here. At the time the schooner *Shupe* was lost, his crew came down and he lost five men and experienced all the sensations of drowning. He seems to be much interested in Lakes lore and says he is glad somebody is trying to preserve some of it. He wants any of it that may be published. He said a number of former sailors hang around his office and he'll get from them anything he can and send it to me.

Told me of Captain Alexander "Pat" Gallarneau who lives in a little shanty at the foot of Quay Street, just south of the Sarnia, Ontario, fishing docks. I found him as he drove up in his old Ford truck. He is pretty well down. He said he'd see me at Small's at 4 p.m. He was there ready to "word me a song" about an old tow schooner, the *Oliver Cromwell*.

> On November first in eighty-nine from Port Huron we set sail;
> The wind blew from the north'ard a sweet and pleasant gale.
> The *Lowell* was our puller, a staunch and noble craft,
> She was followed by the *Cromwell* with three before the mast.
>
> Oh, the *Cromwell*, she's a goer, you can bet your gold on that.

She leads them all before the wind 'n' she's hell upon the tack.
With Stone at the wheel, his eyes fixed on Dunn,
Keep clear of her snoot, my boys, How the old tub can run!

Our captain's name was Gallarneau, our mate was Mister Dunn;
We took the lead of all the fleet, you bet that she can run.
When we arrived at Bay City, no load there could we get,
So we made fast to a boom, my boys, to keep out of the wet.

They kept us all a-working from morning until night
For fear we'd go ashore, my boys, and get a little tight.
With washing and a-scrubbing 'n' a-working down the spars,
But we stood it all quite pleasantly like jolly old tars.

I took the song down, and started on the tune, when I discovered it was the same as the ocean song "The *Flying Cloud.*" The crew made it up, he said. It's about him and his mate and the boat, which kept the men busy at the pump most of the time. He said sailors were "all the time a-making up songs, but nobody tried to remember them, or ever wrote them down." He said Buffalo saloons were great places for singing. His father would not allow his men to chantey when making sail or hoisting the anchor. It made them work too slowly, "but I never bothered my brain about it." He could not remember any of them. "They were just anything—nothing to remember." He said he might be able to word some other songs for me as they came to him. Captain Gallarneau said he began helping his father [Peter Gallarneau] on schooners in 1879 and was on the Lakes until about twenty years ago. He was in sailboats, barges, tugs, and steamboats. [Records show that Gallarneau had actually begun as second porter on the *Susan Ward* in 1863, just after he had turned fifteen.]

Captain Gallarneau told me about a woman named Peggy who—in hushed tones—"was a damn whore" and now lives with "Squint" Carpenter on Clairmont. He said he and some others had "learned her" more than twenty-five songs and she used to sing them when about half drunk. At the address he gave me I was told she had moved. At the second address, she was "out." Will try again tomorrow.

PORT HURON, MICHIGAN, JULY 6, 1933

I called at Fred Bennett's store on Clairmont. He is over fifty and comes from a family of Lakes sailors: father, brothers, and several uncles. All are big, rough, brutal, old-time sailors, according to Bennett. He sailed himself as a boy and has been collecting old marine curios all his life. The second floor of his little store is all but filled with parts of old ships, logs, instruments, books, pioneer articles, coins, and whatnot. He knows all the old marine characters in the river section of the city. He gave me names of a number including "Danny" McDonald, fifty to sixty, a waterfront ne'er-do-well, Jacob Leighton, late seventies; Sylvester "Ves"

Ray, an old schooner captain and roustabout, and others who "probably wouldn't know a hell of a lot." I spent several hours on their trail without success.

I went aboard the passenger steamer *Tashmoo*, which was tied up at the dock.

I found Captain Bud C. Willis, fifty-eight, on his houseboat at the foot of Broad Street. He says he has spent about forty years on the Lakes but "a real sailor can't get a job no more. Yes, there was always some fellow in a crew that'd make up songs, and we'd all sing 'em when we got about half drunk in some shore saloon. They were all around. I never tried to remember any of 'em."

"Write 'em down?"

"No sailor ever thought about that. They were songs everybody knew, and if they didn't, they'd make some up." He recalled hearing a song in a Toledo saloon about three years ago concerning the "pig" *Alexander McDougall.* "There's almost no singing no more. Sailors don't gather like they used to when all sailors were sort of brothers, even though they were fighting each other most of the time. They'd drink and sing and fight all or part of an evening."

He's seen many Jacob's lanterns—St. Elmo's fire—on the masthead while on Lake Huron on foggy nights just before or after a storm, a dull glow about the top of the masts. They meant bad luck, and some thought they meant death to the one who first saw it.

He told of a crew that began a season on a Friday and then blew a main gasket, which delayed them about a half day. They ran into some "damn heavy weather" that washed away part of her deckload and one man had an arm broken—all on that very first trip. "Now, tell me, why did that bad luck happen?" Only one answer to that.

A woman aboard also brought bad luck. She couldn't pull or pump in an emergency, and the "Old Man was probably with her nights, and a vessel doesn't like that."

"A sailor can't make nothing, no more. Those big fellows have it all. The government spends millions of dollars dredging out deep channels for 'em so they can make all the money. Well, if I was one of 'em? I s'pose I'd like it."

Captain A. P. Chamber, about sixty-five, had a grouch on and wasn't very talkative. No, he "never heard no songs." "No sir, I'd never take a boat out to begin a season on a Friday. One time there was some owners who set out to prove that there was nothing in this Friday business, so they met and decided to build a boat on Friday, signed the contract on Friday, began work and finally finished her on Friday. Well, sir, she began her maiden trip on Friday and was never seen or heard of again." That settled that. Not much poetry in his soul.

Found Captain Andrew "Andy" Bonnah at his home on Ontario Street and was greeted with, "What do you want?" He's about sixty-five and five feet, five inches—and the same in circumference amidships. He doesn't object to talking. He admits that he is about as good as ship captains get, but has been out of a job the last several years. The times are getting very bad and he worries about what we're coming to. He said he sailed the best-constructed and equipped wrecking tug on the Great Lakes for years, and when others put into port on account of bad weather, he put out, and stopped for nothing. He was laying in at Cleveland awaiting orders when the big blow of 1913 struck and piled up a lot of steel freighters all around the Lakes, especially on Lake Huron. He received a telegram from the owners to come up to Lake Huron as soon as possible and he started "in the teeth of the storm." During the next few days he pulled a dozen or more vessels off rocks, shoals, and beaches and towed them and others to safety.

He once heard a sailor song in a Buffalo theater about two vessels that collided and sank in Lake Erie, but "I never paid no attention to any damn songs nor other sailor nonsense."

SARNIA, ONTARIO, JULY 8, 1933

Captain Edwin A. McGregor is over eighty, dignified, friendly, and clear-minded. He said he made his first schooner trips on the Lakes as a boy with his father during vacations. In 1868, he began a full-time sailing career, largely in the grain, ore, and coal trades. That lasted for fifty-four consecutive seasons. He was a mate in the 1870s, and a master in the 1880s. His vessels carried large numbers of immigrants, including crowded deckloads of Mennonites from Buffalo, New York, to Duluth, Minnesota, on their way to the Canadian Red River district, and other immigrants to Minnesota and Wisconsin. He stated that two hundred to four hundred of them would live mostly on the schooner's deck in all kinds of weather. Only a few could be quartered below. They carried some freight in the hold, but most of the space was occupied with the immigrants' belongings, including household things and much farming equipment. To conserve space, they would lash wagon wheels and similar equipment to the shrouds [ropes or cables stretched from the masthead to the vessel's sides] and other convenient places.

They had very limited medical facilities and very seldom any professional care, and deaths aboard were not unusual. They put the bodies ashore at the nearest ports for burial. They tried to avoid bad weather out on the water, but were not always successful. When caught in heavy blows, many of the passengers would become seasick, and living conditions became pretty bad. Births also took place on the trips, generally in some makeshift quarters and, at times, marriages. When no clergyman was aboard McGregor, as shipmaster, performed the ceremony. About the only means of entertainment the passengers had was singing. He couldn't understand their language, but he thought most of their songs were religious hymns.

He said he had seen the Lakes "covered with sail" during the 1880s and 1890s, "and some of the vessels were as beautiful as ever sailed. But they're all gone now. The big wooden steamships and the still bigger steel freighters took the trade from the slower sailing craft. The size and tonnage of the vessels increased as the channels, locks and harbors were deepened, and today one of the big freighters can move enough cargo in one trip to keep a fleet of the old schooners busy all season." He added that sailors on the Lakes today are very different from the crews of the old schooners. "You can't tell a sailor now from a landsman." The schoonermen,

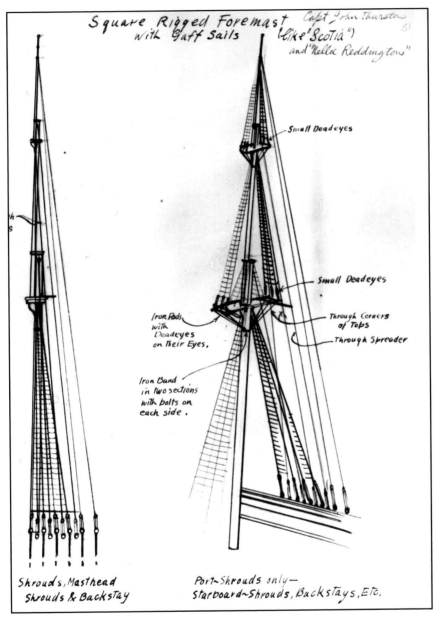

Shrouds and other features of a square-rigged foremast drawn by Loudon Wilson.
(Courtesy Historical Collections of the Great Lakes)

however, were largely drifters. They kept largely to themselves when ashore in the numerous waterfront boarding and entertainment houses where they squandered their wages but enjoyed themselves in the process. They were scorned and victimized ashore, but they were very jealous of their skill aboard ship, and many of their songs expressed their own scorn of landlubbers.

"Most of them were great singers. They worked to chanteys aboard ship when permitted, and entertained themselves in shore saloons with their songs. Most saloonkeepers encouraged singing by providing free drinks to any sailor or group that could sing a good song, especially if the others present applauded. The songs brought in trade. And I wish you could have heard some of the singing I've heard in schooner fo'c'sles. Most of the old sailors could sing many songs—it was a part of their trade—and as they went from vessel to vessel, they always had an audience. I enjoyed listening to them, but never thought a time would come when I'd wish I'd written some of them down. Sometimes, a few lines come back to me when I think about some of the crews I've had, but they're pretty well gone now. About the only song I can go through now is the "*Bigler*'s Crew," and all lakesmen knew that one. The old schoonermen were also practiced liars. They liked to tell of the great things they'd done and seen aboard ship and ashore, and the great storms they'd weathered."

St. Clair, Michigan, July 10, 1933

Called at the St. Clair-Courtright ferry office and talked with John A. Miller, whose father had a long sailing career, mostly in Detroit and St. Clair River tugs. Miller remarked that competition to tow schooners through the rivers became very keen as the sailing vessels began to be replaced in the 1890s. He said the skippers resorted to all sorts of ruses to get ahead of each other and at times would go the full length of Lake Huron or Lake Erie looking for a tow.

He said his father sailed the famous tug *Champion* in her last ten years, and was in command when the popular lithograph *The Champion's Tow* was made. It shows the tug taking a long line of sail vessels by the Detroit waterfront on their way from Lake Huron to Lake Erie. It now adorns the walls of many marine offices about the Lakes. I haven't kept a record of the number of tugmen who are reported to have sailed in this most famous of river tugs, but the number would compare favorably with the number of American ancestors who came across the Atlantic on the *Mayflower*.

Captain Frank Meno, sixty, who lives just north of the city limits on Riverside Drive, has assembled a real fund of information, clippings, and photographs. He is interested largely in the engineering end of it. He was going to some school meeting shortly after I arrived in the evening, so I looked through one of his scrapbooks. In it I found a version of "The *Bigler*" with a last stanza slightly different from those I have:

> And now my song is ended and I hope it pleases you
> Here's a health unto the *Bigler*, her officers and crew

Seth Arca Whipple's painting *The Champion's Tow* was a fixture in sailor homes and hangouts. Painted in 1878, it was mass produced as a chromolithograph and widely copied. (Courtesy Henry Ford Museum and Greenfield Village)

I hope she'll sail the rest of the fall in command of Captain McKee
Between the ports of Buffalo and Milwaukee.

This is a beautiful night. I can see out across the river from my room—a near-full moon hanging low over it and making a wide path across the water. Two big boats are just passing. The river buoy blinks in mid channel and across, the shore lights of the Canadian side.

St. Clair, Michigan, July 11, 1933

Found Henry Anderson in his vegetable garden picking bugs off his potatoes. He is about eighty, blond, big, and slightly stooped, and talks with a pronounced Swedish accent. He said he was born in Sweden and, when about seventeen, went to Kiel, Germany, where he learned to be a ship's carpenter. After sailing the oceans for several years as "Chips" [a nickname for carpenters], he came to the Lakes and made his home at St. Clair and his livelihood working as a ship's carpenter, as a rope and steel cable splicer, and as a sailor.

He stated that he sailed for a number of seasons in the schooner *E. C. Roberts,* and recited "The Red Iron Ore" which tells of its trip to Escanaba for iron ore. He said he had learned it aboard the vessel. He added that a copy was tacked up on the schooner's cabin door, and that all sailors on that vessel soon learned it. He also stated that the old schooner spent her last three years tied up around a bend in the Pine River and that her bones are still there, just back of the city golf course.

I drove up to Marysville, Michigan, to see Captain Harvey Kendall. I found him at home with his son Earl, who is about forty, and quite pleased to see me. Harvey said that about forty years ago he was mate of a Ward Line propeller, which carried copper from Houghton and Hancock, Michigan, to Cleveland and Buffalo. They used Negro deckhands most of the time. They would recruit a crew of fifteen to twenty in Detroit and carried from six hundred to one thousand tons and it was all loaded and unloaded by hand trucks. The deckhands were powerful men and not any trouble. They would work them all day and all night with only short stops for eating and then they'd sleep most of the trip back and shoot craps the rest of it.

He said they were great fellows to sing and did most of the time when working. One would start a song and others would join in on the chorus and when he ran out of ideas or lines, another would take it up and then another.

He recalls one Sunday when loading at Hancock, Michigan, that the men sang so loudly that a delegation came down from a Houghton church to ask him to quiet them so they could go on with their services. "Not to be outdone, they sang a church hymn that you could hear to the sky all the while those men were going back and, by God, they could sing."

He said it was quite impossible to remember any of their songs as they were never twice alike. One trip back from Superior in the fall they got frozen in Mud Lake and he put the deckhands out cutting ice to free the vessel. They didn't like it at all and they made up lines about it. Some were:

> I'm a-going back down south, where de sugar cane grow.
> I'se a'going far, far away from dis frost and snow.

He could also recall the chorus:

> De captain's in de pilothouse, ringing de bell;
> De mate's down between decks, giving the niggers hell.
> Who's on de way, boys, who's on de way?

They'd sing this while trucking the copper on or off the boat. There was no beginning or end to it. They just couldn't work without noise—something to keep them going. Striking a bell or the mate's "bawling and cussing" at them would do it. They'd also yell at each other to get to work and seemed to like it.

Earl Kendall mentioned a couple of Irishmen, Tom and Bill Manion, who live on a small farm a few miles west of St. Clair.

Tom, about sixty-five, was working in his garden when I called, and he seemed to be quite pleased that an excuse had come along for him to sit down. Both his health and his finances seem to be in a bad way. He wiped the perspiration off his face with his cap. His graying hair and beard had had no attention in some time and his well-worn shirt and trousers hung loosely on his gaunt frame. He said he had sailed a few seasons, but had worked in the lumber woods near Alpena, Michigan, about twenty winters. He has been a fiddler all his life, likes to play and takes his fiddle with him wherever he goes. He entertained the lumbermen "hundreds of times" and has supplied the music for country dances around St. Clair for about forty years.

He recited several well-known lumber camp songs including, "The Foreman John Monroe," "Morrissey and the Black" [a version of "Morrissey and the Russian Sailor," about a bare-fisted ring fight], and others, which he said he had learned "in the woods."

In response to a request to hear some of his fiddle tunes, he willingly invited me into his kitchen, which was in about its last stages of holding together. He got his fiddle, tuned it, and then, incredible as it may seem, held a traditionally strung violin by his right hand and shoulder, and the bow in his left hand and "fiddled" one tune after another until I had to leave for another appointment.

I arrived at Captain Small's office in Port Huron about 7 p.m. and found Sylvester "Ves" Ray waiting for me. Small had the job of raising the gasoline launch that blew up at the Seventh Street bridge last week, and expected to work all night on it. Captain "Bob" Thompson didn't show up, either, and Ray didn't seem to be very desirous of going after him, so we spent the evening together.

He's pretty old and somewhat enfeebled, but his mind and memory are clear and he likes to talk. He ran away from home at age thirteen when his brother-in-law gave him a beating, and he's sailed all over the Lakes from Duluth to Chicago to Quebec until a few years ago. He is full of incidents. He gave me a version of "The Red Iron Ore" and a fragment of a song about the schooner *Africa*.

He mentioned the chanteys "Away, Rio," "Heave Her Up and Bust Her," "Broad Missouri," "Rolling Home," and "The *Dreadnaught*." [Ray also recalled "A Trip on the *Lavindy*." Part of the song came back to Ray that evening and he dictated the rest of it to Small for a letter to Walton the following summer. Ray seems to have written the song himself, borrowing from "The Timber Drogher *Bigler*."]

> Come all you young sailors and landlubbers too,
> An' listen to a song that I'll sing to you;
> It's about the *Lavindy*, the schooner of fame,
> Likewise her bold captain, Billy Parker by name.
>
> We set sail on a Saturday from Port Huron dock,
> All hands to the halyards they quickly did flock;
> "Yo-hee!" and "Hi-ho!" the mate he did bawl,
> An' we soon spread our wings, gaff tops'ls an' all.
>
> The tug dropped our line, an' we heaved it onboard,
> With the wind on our quarter, up Lake Huron we roared;
> The wind it was fair till off Thunder Bay
> When we hauled 'er up close and for Mackinac lay.
>
> We tacked through the Straits in the dead of the night,
> The sky it was cloudy but the beacons showed bright;
> Tall schooners and steamboats we left on our lee,
> As we rounded the Shanks and Skillagalee.
>
> . . . .
>
> Now we're again on the big lake in a record time,
> So I will conclude and finish my rhyme.
> This song it was made while we was under way
> By a curly headed sailor by the name of "Ves" Ray.

I asked him about sailor beliefs and he said they had no end of weather signs "and you could depend on 'em, too":

Rainbow in morning, sailors take warning.

Sundogs in the morning, back at night means a fair evening.

An opening in a ring around the moon indicated the direction of wind the following day.

You could depend on having a breeze with both the rising and the setting of the moon.

If the moon "stands up"—the long axis up and down—that means good weather
If the moon "lays down"—long axis across—it will rain like hell.

Wind from the eastward and the sundown clear,
For that night there will be no fear.

The bright end of the Milky Way indicates the direction of the wind the next day.
Shooting stars also show the direction of the wind.

Gulls coming into port in the morning mean bad weather.
Gulls on the inside [between the boat and shore], bad weather on the
    outside.

It's now past midnight and a waning moon makes a good path across the
river out in front of my window. Several freighters have gone up and down as I've
been writing, the deep-toned whistles the only sound in the night.

Marine City and St. Clair, Michigan, July 12, 1933

Captain Walter Stover, in his seventies, said he wheeled in the tug *Champion* and
in others when the old schooners were getting scarce. He said they'd go as far as
Buffalo and the Straits of Mackinac or the Soo Locks for a tow and get paid for
only the river. He said that on one trip down Lake Huron from the Straits they
had six schooners and the *Annie M. Peterson* was in the tow. A breeze came up and
her captain put up all her canvas and towed the three schooners that were behind
her out to one side as fast as the tug *Champion* was going until her raffee sail gave
way and then she fell back in the towline. "She was about the smartest schooner on
the Lakes in her day."

St. Clair, Michigan, July 14, 1933

Captain William Kenyon, ex-master in the Detroit and Cleveland line of luxury
passenger boats between Detroit, Cleveland, and Buffalo, suggested that I visit
Charles "Major" Leach, an old-time schoonerman: "He'll tell you plenty!" I found
him at home with his two ex-sailor brothers, William and George, all in their late
seventies or early eighties, and also a sailor grandson. All were quite willing to talk.
During a considerable conversation, mostly with William, the major, a wiry, super-
active individual, dashed in and out of the room several times with only brief
landings. As he was about to cast off once, I remarked to him, "I understand there
were some pretty good vessels and sailors on the Lakes along in the 1880s." That
set him off:
    "Jesus Christ, yes! I've see'd more 'n a hundred, yes, more 'n a hundred and
fifty of 'em in Buffalo harbor one time, and b'God, there was real sailors, too!
There ain't no real sailors no more. Hell, anybody who can drive a horse can drive
one of them steamboats up and down here. B'God, they've got every little bend
and bump in the bottom of the whole damn string of lakes and rivers marked for

'em and they carry electric range finders and radios an' every damn thing they can think of to help 'em, an' still they run aground, have collisions and founder in storms. B'God, when I started there wasn't a range or buoy, or a damn thing the length of the rivers and damn few along the lakeshores, and we went out in all kinds of weather and in late and early season. I've been out on Lake Huron day and night when it was snowing and freezing and the wind blowing a gale, and we'd fetch up where we wanted to go.

"Them fellows on the freighters ain't sailors. Hell, they'll take any damn farmer or coal heaver that comes along and call him a sailor when he doesn't know his ass from a hatch, and couldn't splice a line to save his own damn neck. In my day, you had to know every damn thing about a boat, an' it took you years to learn it.

"Sailors was proud of bein' sailors, an' they had only contempt for fellows like they take now, and also, b'God, we had to know—an' I mean KNOW—the Lakes, an' how to lay a course in any weather to any port on any of 'em. It wasn't all marked out for us on government charts. An', b'God, we wasn't slaves to no big steel corporation that might order us around. The captain in them days was captain, and once he cast off, he took orders from nobody.

"Them fellows on them freighters are just damn slaves to the machinery and big corporations. Some man who never sailed a day in his life sits in a soft chair in Cleveland and orders 'em around all the way to Duluth. . . . We worked like hell day and night sometimes, and in all kinds of weather, but we stayed at it. Sailors was always finding fault with everything, and the mate would cuss 'em around, but, b'God, in them days the men was proud of bein' sailors and they was real men!"

Finally, we got to songs again and Charles told of Captain Frank Meno asking him one day for a copy of "The *E. C. Roberts*." He said he copied off most of it, all he could recall, and sent it to him, and had not heard from him since. On learning that I had it, he asked if I'd send him a copy and I promised to do so. George said, "Yes, we sang all the time, and especially when ashore in some of the hangouts. Did you ever hear of the Golden Dollar Bar in Detroit? It was run by Jim Bielman, but you'd never see him—only the girls. It was located down on Monroe between Library and Randolph. He had another one called the Silver Dollar Bar nearby. There was lots of drinking and singing and fighting there. Atwater and Franklin Streets were all sailor boardinghouses and sporting houses then. We had a song we used to sing about:

> Come all ye girls of Detroit town (or any other place)
>   And take advice of me.
> And never let a sailor lad
>   An inch above your knee.

. . . .

He'll double reef your mains'l, girls.
    And down your tops'l, too
No storm can throw him off his mark
    And him you'll sorely rue!

Martine Beebe, seventy-two, a red-haired Scotch-Irishman, said he had heard of this sort of material and had often heard sailors singing, but he was primarily a shipbuilder, like his grandfather, father, and son. He was foreman in a plant building ships for the U.S. Shipping Board during the war. He said the old windjammer sailors were a queer lot. They never did any work they didn't have to, and then not quite all of that. They'd never tell the captain or mate about anything they'd see that went wrong with a boat. It could fill up with water and sink and they'd never say a word, although their lives depended on it. Also, they'd never tell a new man anything right, but would fill him up with all the wrong information they could.

ALGONAC AND ST. CLAIR, MICHIGAN, JULY 18, 1933

In the early evening, I drove back up to St. Clair to see the Leaches again. Found William and Charles at the latter's home. The night after my previous visit, some of the songs they sang in old schooners and gathering places started running through William's head and he couldn't sleep all night. About midnight he got up, awakened his nephew, who copied off several and they had mailed them to me at Ann Arbor. "And those ain't all. I seem to have a hundred of 'em that flit across my mind and get away, but I'll write out some more and send 'em to you." He was greatly pleased that I'd driven that far to see him. He wanted to hear some of those that I have, so I read a number to him. Charles said he'd received "The *E. C. Roberts*" I sent him, but it wasn't just like the song as he knew it. He will send his version as soon as he can copy it down. Those old fellows seem to be the real thing, real old-time windjammer sailors.

AMHERSTBURG AND LEAMINGTON, ONTARIO, JULY 24, 1933

Found Mr. David Hackett, seventy, at a club playing cards. He was very friendly and interested. His grandfather and father were river pilots and tugmen and his family kept the light on the south end of Bob-Lo Island for about a hundred years, he said. He is much crippled by rheumatism. He said he was mate on a steamer in Lake Superior in late November one season when he was young and they battled a bad storm for seven hours. He was out, soaked and cold in all of it, and rheumatism developed soon afterward. He is much interested in this and wants to help. He said he has heard sailors chanteying "hundreds of times" as a tow of schooners would be making sail while going past the light preparatory to letting go of the tug at Bar Point Light. He had known parts of "The *Bigler*," "The *Roberts*," and had heard "The *Fayette Brown*" many times. An old sailor who died in the village a few months ago used to sing it often, he said. He had a copy of it once and loaned it to a young lady reporter on the local paper.

Loudon Wilson's sketch of the steam tug *Bessie*, built at Fair Haven, Michigan, in 1880. The *Bessie*, built to carrie bulk cargo in shallow waters and small ports, sank in 1899 with 1,000 barrels of salt after colliding with the steamer *W. S. Ireland* near the head of the Detroit River's Belle Isle, not far from Algonac. (Courtesy the Historical Collections of the Great Lakes)

LEAMINGTON AND ERIEAU, ONTARIO, JULY 25, 1933

The morning cometh and I beginneth on an unsuspecting shoemaker who once did sail de windjammers. Mr. Charles Irwin, seventy, began sailing as a boy in schooners and continued thirty some years until he lost his voice. He was quite pleased to talk about "them old days when we worked like beggars, but we liked it." He knows "The *Bigler*'s Crew" and a few lines of "Buffalo Girls." He says that often while he's working alone some of the old vessel songs get running in his mind and he can recall most of them. He promised to send me any more that he can recall.

On my third trip to his home across from the post office, I found Captain Edward Winters, about seventy, who was supposed to be an old vessel man, but who turned out to have spent all his sailing days on steamboats. He told of one occasion when he was at the wheel out of Buffalo when they ran into a bad storm and a light appeared on the end of the steering pole. He told the captain, who immediately ordered "hard to port." They wallowed in the trough for a while and then aimed for the pier at Erie, Pennsylvania, and finally made it. They had to lay in for three days doing repairs and restoring the package freight, which was mostly

The lumber schooner *Lyman Davis* under way from the docks at Muskegon, Michigan, in the 1880s. The design on the vessel's transom is the log mark of Muskegon County's Mason Lumber Company. Logging companies used marking hammers to brand the ends of their logs to help identify their timber at the sawmills. (Courtesy Ivan H. Walton Collection, Bentley Historical Library, University of Michigan)

fine liquor. The captain was an old windjammer captain and said that about twenty years earlier he had seen a light like that and shortly after lost his boat in Lake Huron.

I came on to Erieau, and located one old vessel man there, Captain E. J. Buzzard, about eighty, in the Lake View Hotel. He said he was born near Pontiac, Michigan, and raised in Port Huron and began sailing in windjammers at the age of fifteen. He remained on the Lakes for twenty seasons and then married a Canadian lady and left the Lakes to go into the hotel business. He said he made much more money there, but lost it in oil. He is a great old fellow to talk and is much interested in Lakes sailing. His memory is pretty good on early matters. He said there were many places in my version of "The *Bigler*" that were wrong, so he gave me the "right" way. He also gave me all he could recall of a song about a "Dredge at Gravelly Bay":

I was a handsome nice young man, I hailed from Cleveland town;
And for daily occupation I teamed for Johnnie Brown.
And all day long I'd sport and play, my joy I ne'er begrudged,
'Til I was sent to Gravelly Bay to work upon a drudge.

I had not been in Gravelly Bay scarce one day, two, or three
Before a very fair young girl fell into love with me
Saying, "Mike, my man, give me your hand, from you I'll never budge;
With you I'll stay on Gravelly Bay and work upon the drudge."

Her mother standing at her door says, "Please, don't make such noise,
And another thing, you're far too young to trust among those boys.
And that young man that holds your hand, if I can rightly judge,
Has just the eye that'll make you sigh before you leave the drudge."

"Now, mother dear, don't be severe," my darling then did say,
"Never eyes so fair, or such black hair, was e'er on Gravelly Bay!"
I took her to my bosom then; the world did me begrudge;
And for many a day she got my pay, while working on the drudge.

He said he sailed in the *Lyman Davis* when she first came out in
Muskegon in the early 1870s and said she could outsail anything she ever met on
the Lakes in her day. Buzzard said the *Davis* had a sixty-two-foot boom and he
recognized a picture I have, except he said she carried no raffee sail when he was
on her. He also sailed on the *Golden Fleece* and mentioned the *Annie M. Peterson*
and said it had the highest mainmast on the Lakes and was "a smart sailor." He
had heard a song about her. He said the *Davis* is still owned at Kingston, Ontario.
He told about sailing, buying and selling schooners, episodes, and histories of some
old ones.

Amos 'n' Andy came on the radio and spoiled all chance of getting any
legends, etc., and, as he was going away for the evening, I departed and drove to
Port Stanley for the night.

Port Stanley, Port Burwell, and Port Rowan, Ontario, July 26, 1933

Captain Mark Berry, a rather heavy, deep-voiced, clear-eyed, and friendly man of
about eighty-two years, said he began sailing on the Lakes in the middle 1860s at
the age of fifteen. With the exception of two years in the American Navy and two
more on salt water, he continued until he retired a few years ago. He was in sailing
vessels as long as they were around and reluctantly changed to steam. He said that
most of his sailing on the Lakes was in the grain trade, Chicago to Buffalo, and
they usually had about ten men aboard. A trip required from one to three weeks
each way, depending on the weather, and about the only way the men had of
entertaining themselves, particularly in the dogwatches 4–6 p.m. and 6–8 p.m., was
by singing, "and some of them damn sailors was pretty good."

Riding out a sou'wester under the lee of Long Point on Lake Erie's northern shore. (From *Picturesque Canada*)

He recalled two men who were with him a number of seasons and who were "great musicians." One played a violin and the other a banjo, and both were good singers. Whenever the vessel tied up in port, these two would play and sing and a crowd of people would gather to listen. When they went ashore, they got all the free drinks they wanted in shore saloons, and often were called on to take part in the "variety shows" the big saloons provided to entertain sailors.

He remembered one up-trip [from Buffalo to Chicago] when they ran into a bad blow in the Straits of Mackinac. It became worse when they got into Lake Michigan, so they pulled in under the lee of some islands there and dropped anchor in company with twenty-five or thirty other vessels to wait it out, and they didn't get away until the next morning. In the early evening, some men on another vessel began singing and the nearby crews called for more, and then another group took over, and finally "my men" joined in. Then, the crews around in every direction really shouted for more and "made a hell of a racket." The singing continued until after midnight. "It sounded pretty damn good there in the night when about all you could see was other ships' lights weavin' about."

When they arrived at Chicago and tied up, some sailors were awaiting them and "they about kidnapped" these two men, and took them to a big saloon that provided a variety show. They played and sang and had all the drinks they wanted on the house until they got too drunk to continue.

Captain William Dale, about sixty, spent all of his sailing days on steamboats. He now has a grocery store. He said the old windjammer sailors were a lot of liars. There never was much glamour to the sailboats, it took them weeks to get anywhere, and they could not carry a cargo when they did go, he said. There was but little singing on the Lakes at any time. He can recall that, as a boy when just south of Sarnia, Ontario, on the St. Clair River, he used to hear the sailors chantey as they towed by, putting up their canvas to make ready to let go out on Lake Huron. He never paid much attention to them.

At Port Burwell, I called at the home of the lightkeeper. As he was telling me of the different kinds of material, a group of young ladies in bathing suits came along and wanted to see the light, so he took them up, saying he'd be right back. I waited about three-quarters of an hour and finally he did come back. His supply of Lakes information came from an 1863 keeper's record book, in which he noted down boats, etc.

Bronté, Oakville, and Port Credit, Ontario, July 29, 1933

This day has been hot! Sweltering, and the inside of my car much like an oven!

Went through Bronté this morning on my way to Oakville, and there learned that there are some old lakesmen still in the village. I went back. Found Walter "Doc" Thomas, about seventy, at his little house. He was lying down, and seems not at all afraid of work as piles of it are lying all about: dirty dishes, clothes, paper, etc.

Thomas is a bachelor and keeps the government light at the end of the pier. He has rheumatism in one knee and seems to enjoy lying down better than stirring around. He seems to belong to a group who sailed together on old schooners, went to the Buffalo and Cleveland variety shows together, and, until recently, would gather at times during winter evenings and sing. "B'God, sometimes damn near all night. We'd have a little to drink and then each one would sing and we'd all help out on the chorus."

In the group were "Doc," Billy Churchill, Billie Gillman, Maxie Belyea, and some other irregulars. As far as I could learn, they sang anything they could think of after each one sang his pet song. Belyea sang "The Curtains of Night," or "I'll Remember Your Love in My Prayers"; Gillman, "The Snake in the Grass"; and Doc, "The Old Armchair."

Doc couldn't recall much. They hadn't gotten together for several years now, but he did know part of a Lakes song about the schooner *Jennie P. King*. Doc decided to get Churchill to help him out, but he was in his sailboat all by himself about a half mile at on Lake Ontario.

I then called at the home of Mr. Belyea and found him ill in bed—about finished—so I didn't talk with him.

I found Mr. Gillman at his little refreshment store selling ice cream cones and soda water. He is in his early seventies and hasn't been on Lakes boats for thirty-five years. He said they used to sing a lot in schooner fo'c'sles and usually had several musical instruments. He knows "The *Bigler*," "The *Flying Cloud*," several Irish songs and some American songs popular at that time. Mr. Gillman's father sailed Lakes schooners for many years and he said he and his brother used to sing much about boats and storms, but he couldn't recall what. Mr. Churchill came in while I was there, so I met him as he tied up and went over to Doc

Thomas's with me. Together they gave me most of "The Curtains of Night," which has a very attractive air, part of the song about the *Jennie P. King*, a stanza of "The *Maggie Hunter*," "The Ship That Never Returned," and "The *Lady Elgin*." I pumped much, but there were no more songs.

In Port Credit, Ontario, lives Al Hare, seventy-two, sailor-singer, friend of everybody, musician, and great-granddad of a number of boys. He drives an old Model T Ford and now has a canoe and boat livery. I found him at his boathouse—or rather, shack—sitting on an old ragged couch, telling stories, and whittling out something for a ten-year-old boy. He came up to the subject of songs like a hungry boy to eat. He knows and sailed with Thomas, Churchill, and others of Bronté. He recited "The *Bigler*" and added some to "The *Maggie Hunter*" and a chorus to "The *Jennie P. King*." He mentioned a song about the *Belle Sheridan*, which went ashore near Willards Bay, seven miles from Brighton, Ontario. The crew members were all from the McSherry family and all were lost except one son. He said he hadn't sung the songs for twenty years.

When I asked him about "The Curtains of Night," he said he'd sung it "hundreds of times" aboard sailboats. He tipped back his big, fat head and in a cracked voice cut loose on it and I wrote out the parts I didn't have. Then he thought of a printed copy that he had obtained a few years ago from a radio station. We boarded his old Model T and pushed off for his home. I assume he was a better sailor than he is a driver.

His wife fished out the book and he insisted that I take it, adding that one song was all he wanted in it and that he knew it. He had several crayon drawings of some "fore 'n' afters" [two-masted vessels, one forward and the mainmast aft] that he sailed. He had drawn them himself and then with much pride pointed to some that his son, who is an architect, had drawn. While talking, he explained that there wasn't so much fun in living as there was years ago. "Then, nobody had to worry about a job or enough to eat and people were friendly and ready to help each other, but now every man is for himself, each is trying to get what the other has, only a few have jobs and none are happy."

In the evening, I drove on into Toronto and hunted up a room just across Saint George Street from the Toronto University campus. Downtown, I got off on a side street some way and it was pretty narrow and shopkeepers had their stuff pulled out past the curb and all the cars I met were dodging those piles and driving all over the street. I almost had several head-ons. Some of the drivers honked their horns, and others shouted. I didn't know at what or why. An old lady beside a projecting fruit stand says, "Where're you goin' young man?" I plowed on through the yokels, running one fellow's Ford up on the curb, but he was driving on my side of the street. And then, at the end of the block, a car came dashing in on my side again. We both stopped dead a couple of feet apart and a cop came over. I settled back to hear him talk big talk to the driver of the small truck, but he walked right past him and says he to me MANY things and among them that that was a one-way street.

Toronto, Ontario, July 30, 1933

Sunday in Toronto seems to be Sunday. Everything seems to be closed except the sky and streets. Haven't been down to find out if the Lake was taken in for the day. Went for a walk after breakfast this forenoon and after circulating around and through the university campus, I came out in front of Knox Presbyterian Church just as the faithful were entering. The organ music sounded pretty good and I have a constitutional weakness for it, anyway, so I went in, planning to leave when the music was over. However, an usher steered me away from a back seat I was aiming at and took me down about one third of the way and I had to stay through a sermon on the glories of the Christian life, past, present, and future. They're going to have a great time when they all get to Heaven.

Toronto, Ontario, July 31, 1933

I spent practically all day in the editorial offices of the Toronto *Evening Telegram* reading the marine clippings of Mr. C. H. J. Snyder. Wanted to have a talk with him, but he will not be back from Europe until the end of this week or first of next. He has written a couple of books on Lakes matter—all with a pronounced Canadian bias—and has for many years been very much interested in Lakes happenings, particularly during the war and schooner periods. Since early in 1931, he has been running a series of copyrighted articles called "Schooner Days," which are mostly narratives of unusual schooner experiences told in first person. There ought to be much material of this kind for a very interesting book.

Toronto, Ontario, August 2, 1933

I visited Sunnyside beach this morning, where I learned the old "fore 'n' after" *Lyman Davis* is tied up. Mrs. Thomas [Margaret] Hume of Muskegon, Michigan, gave me a post-card-size picture of her while I was in Muskegon last summer, and I've heard of her racing qualities from time to time while she was in the lumber trade on Lake Michigan. She's now at the breakwater near the beach and is being fitted out for visitors at ten cents per during the exposition. The report is that she's to be burned as an advertising stunt, as was the *Julia B. Merrill* last year. I wonder if the momentary pleasure of the morons who would gather to see a fire would be worth more to Toronto than the educational value of such a boat as a permanent exhibit of one of the best of the old Great Lakes lumber hookers? I went aboard her, but none of the men working there knew anything about her history—or much else, for that matter.

Captain Alfred Thomas, who is in his seventies, was at his home on College Street when I called about 5:30 p.m. "When the sailboats were all gone off the Lakes, I tried a steamboat and stayed on her about a month and quit. None of that for me." He began on schooners as a boy in the 1870s, and stayed on them as long as they lasted. He told of being on Lake Ontario one day when he was about fifteen. The owner was the captain; his oldest son was the mate. A younger son and Thomas were the crew. The captain was changing something on the main

Three men and a woman on the deck of the *Lyman Davis*. The open-sided box attached to the mast in the foreground is the masthead light holder. When a vessel was at anchor, a white lantern or light was placed in the box and run up by cables to the top of the mast. (Courtesy Ivan H. Walton Collection, Bentley Historical Library, University of Michigan)

boom while the mate was forward and the younger son and Thomas were aloft, when a puff of wind hit the boom and knocked the captain into the water. He had sailed all his life but could not swim a stroke. The mate jumped in after him and his father grabbed him and both went down. The two boys climbed down as fast as possible, lowering the yawl boat and pulled for them, but just got a glimpse of the two as they disappeared. They rowed around and could find no trace of either. The boys got back aboard and brought the boat back to Port Hope.

Port Hope, Ontario, August 4, 1933

Richard J. Edmonds of Port Hope, Ontario, began sailing on the Lakes in 1866 when twelve years old and became a master when twenty-one. He sailed schooners until 1896, when he transferred to steamboats. He said that steamboating was not real sailing, and he quit after two seasons of it. He added that he "grew up on the old windjammers," and "would like to do it all over again." Life aboard the old sailing vessels was always intriguing, at times demanding and dangerous, and frequently exciting. In the 1870s and 1880s, the larger schooners generally carried eight men forward and four aft, and half of them forward were "salties." The crews practically always sang chanteys when both watches were on deck "walking the capstan" or "on the halyards." Singing put life into the work and seemed to lighten it.

He recalled hearing work songs about "the Rio Grande," "Shenandore," "Santa Anna," and many more which told about "any damn thing the leader happened to think of," but he never tried to remember the lines. He added that he never paid attention to any of the sailors' stories or customs, as long as they did their work.

In the heyday of the old schooners in the 1880s, they could always get cargoes, and they carried large enough crews so that the work aboard was not particularly strenuous. In the 1890s, however, when steamboats began to take the trade away from the slower sailing vessels, the owners cut the size of crews, and hurry and drive became the order of the time. Many vessel officers, trying to maintain earnings and please owners, would no longer permit the reduced crews to work to chanteys as it made the work go too slowly to suit them. The vessels were not "kept up," nor given new canvas when they needed it, and the old days were over.

Edmonds stated that the old schooners were well adapted to the traffic of their day. Being fore 'n' aft rigged, they were easier to handle and could sail closer to the wind than could the square-rigged vessels characteristic of the oceans. They were also much less expensive to build and equip, and could navigate shallower harbors and channels than could steamboats of equal capacity. Because of these advantages, shipyards sprang up all about the shores; and two- and three-masted schooners of from three to six hundred tons capacity "covered the Lakes" from Chicago and Duluth to the head of the St. Lawrence River.

Most of the old sailing vessels obtained their cargoes through ships' brokers located in practically all of the ports, and delivered these cargoes to any

Making Lake Ontario's Port Hope in a storm. (From *Picturesque Canada*)

assigned port. The first vessels into a port got the choice unloading docks and also any waiting cargoes, so vessels were always racing each other and carrying all the sail they could stand and frequently more. He often carried lumber from the Saginaw River to the St. Lawrence; iron ore from Escanaba and Marquette, Michigan, to Lake Erie ports; grain from Chicago and Milwaukee to Buffalo and at times Oswego; coal and general cargoes anywhere.

They seldom stayed in port on account of bad weather. In late November and early December, when rates and wages and risks were high, they kept going as long as they could get a cargo and vessel insurance, and some skippers would take chances without it and continue until near Christmastime. During darkness or in fog, which is frequent in late season, or in snowstorms, they had to sail by dead reckoning. They had no government navigation aids, and not enough sea room to heave-to and wait out a storm, as lee shores were never far away. They had to keep going whether they could see anything or not, "an' by God, we got wherever we wanted to be!" Whenever a vessel got caught in a hard blow from the north in late season, it would ice up and sink lower and lower in the water under tons of added weight. Some vessels disappeared with all hands.

COBOURG, ONTARIO, AUGUST 5, 1933

About a hundred yachts of various descriptions were anchored in the harbor until between 5 and 6 p.m., when they got away, the band playing, cannons, crackers, and a harbor full of emptied bottles—southeast for Fair Haven, New York, on the first leg of the annual race. They made a very pretty sight as they stood off across the lake, row after row as the different classes got away.

Edward "Ned" Navin of Cobourg, Ontario, a slender, active, medium-sized man in his late seventies, said he began sailing in schooners in 1878, when eighteen years old, and continued for twenty seasons. Most of his trips were on the Lower Lakes, and he'd been through the old Welland Canal "hundreds of times." When he began, only one medium-sized vessel could go through any of the canal's locks at a time. On the levels between the locks, each vessel was towed by one or two teams of horses or mules, depending on the size and the draft of the vessel. A few carried their own teams on the forward decks for towing, but not many.

"It was not difficult to get up a scrap there. Some of those canal hands were as tough as they come, and they'd drop their work and fight anybody, especially any sailor who criticized them, or anybody, for anything." In wet weather, the mud on the towpath would at times get knee deep, but the vessels had to be kept moving. At midnight Saturday, the canalmen all stopped working, and all vessels the length of the canal had to stay wherever they happened to be until Sunday night, when work resumed. By Sunday noon, the harbors at each end of the canal would be filled with vessels waiting to go through. Many others would be waiting on the various levels.

Occasionally, some vessel would jam a lock gate and hold up traffic, and it might take several days to make repairs and get the vessels moving again. "Then, there'd be high times aboard some of the vessels. Men would gather on any boat where they'd see anything going on or hear some music—someone playing a fiddle, a banjo or mouth organ, or anything else—and some sailors were pretty good at it. There'd be singing and at times step-dancing, and tales of what different men had done—mostly damn lies—and this would go on most of the day or night." The men liked songs about sailors, but they would listen to any popular songs of the day. Sometimes someone would "get up a dirty take-off" on some popular song and sing it, but these were few in number.

Mr. Navin half sang and half talked part of the song about the loss of the schooner *Antelope*, "The *Persian*'s Crew," "The Red Iron Ore," "The E-ri-o Canal," and all of "The Sailor's Alphabet." [This is what he recalled of "The *Antelope*," also known as "The Shores of Michigan."]

> On the sixteenth of November, from Chicago we set sail;
> Kind Providence did favor us with a sweet and pleasant gale.
> With our canvas spread all to the wind and our hearts as light as air,
> We left Chicago far behind, our colors flying fair.
>
> On the seventeenth in the morning, an angry storm did rise;
> And fearful billows loud did roar, and dismal grew the skies.
> We reefed her down, made all things snug, and then contrived a plan
> To save the life of the *Antelope* off the shores of Michigan.
>
> On the eighteenth in the morning—and what I say is true—
> The ice upon our riggin' froze, and the cold winds fiercely blew!
> And no one thought in a few short hours that very afternoon,
> Some would be froze and some be drowned—the *Antelope* was doomed!
>
> The cold increased, the tempest raged, the huge seas loud did roar—

With our canvas gone, both anchors out, we were drifting toward the shore!

Our deck was coated with tons of ice, but not a sailor knew,
Some would be froze and some be drowned of our big freighter's crew.
The huge seas raked her fore and aft, the cold wind loud did roar,
We struck stern on and swung broadside to our doom on Superior.

Cobourg and Picton, Ontario, August 6, 1933

No movie shows today, no baseball games, nobody home, no nothing. It is Sunday in Ontario. Called at the bachelor shack of "Ned" Navin this morning to learn if he had thought of anything else. He said he thought he had omitted part of a stanza for "The Schooner *Antelope*," so he went through it again and added four lines to the second stanza. Could recall no others. Said he sailed only about eight years as a young man and hadn't tried to repeat those old windjammer songs since. He said he had heard hundreds of them.

By accident, I found Captain Patrick McManus, about seventy-five, sitting in front of his house. I found him to be quite talkative after he finally warmed up. He knew nothing at first, but gave me part of "The *Maggie Hunter*" and part of "The Rock Island Line," which tells of a sailor leaving a boat to work on the railroad.

On one trip he made in a barge, two women passengers were aboard and the mate was sore about it and said something bad would happen before they arrived at Marquette, Michigan, where they were bound. Sure enough, as they were being towed through the rapids at Port Huron, the line parted and they drifted back, scattered traffic and finally came to against spiles on the Canadian side. The mate said: "Didn't I tell you?" Women always bring bad luck to a boat. The steamboat *Jack* of Kingston was a hoodoo boat, always in trouble, hard to steer, and sailors wouldn't go on her if they could get any other. A bird perching in the rigging in port was a good sign, but out on the Lakes, bad.

Picton, Ontario, August 7, 1933

Went to Wellington about ten miles away on the lakeshore, where there was said to be a super gala affair. It consisted of a few thousand people walking about looking for something to happen, which didn't. I almost won an automobile for twenty-five cents. Had No. 4411 and the winning number was 26–something. Couldn't tow it around, anyway.

In the forenoon before going, I visited Captain Marcellus "Sully" Palmetier, who retired a couple of years ago after a half century on the Lakes. He is a very friendly man and is very much interested in this subject. He thinks the proposed burning of the *Lyman Davis* at Toronto is a crime. He knows parts of "The *Bigler*" and "The *Persian*'s Crew." Has heard "The *Fayette Brown*," "*Maggie Hunter*," "*Jennie P. King*," and a number of others. He gave me the lines of a song about "Moses Dulmage," who drifted around Lake Ontario from here in December and was lost.

In response to my question about Lake sailors' beliefs or superstitions, he said there were quite a number that were believed by some men, but of course these men were a small minority. However, many who professed not to be superstitious had various ways of getting around them. For example, many, perhaps a large majority, would not begin a season on Friday. They'd have something else to do that day. Women aboard were thought by many to bring foul weather or other bad luck. Cats, especially black ones, brought vessels bad luck. A half-grown kitten came aboard once when Captain Palmetier's boat was trading out of Cleveland and he carried it several blocks uptown when going there. When he returned, the kitten was back. They left it aboard and, shortly after leaving, ran afoul of a gale and bad weather all the way to the Detroit River. As soon as possible along the river, some of the men put it ashore. He has seen sailors getting off a vessel many times when rats were seen leaving. Changing a boat's name was bad:

> Change the name and not the letter,
> You change for worse and not for better.

A vessel bearing the name of a dead man will not prosper. He sailed on Sundays, but doubted he gained anything by it.

Weather, especially the wind, was quite important to the old schooners. The skippers watched the wind very closely and always sailed to take advantage of it. They would always figure to get a "slant" if possible to the port they were bound to. Many of them, especially in the early days, would not carry barometers and depended entirely on various signs.

In lowering, heavy weather, a patch of clear sky in the west "the size of a Scotchman's bonnet" indicated clearing off and fine weather.

Sun setting behind clouds meant dirty weather before morning.

A wind will come out of an open place under clouds on the horizon.

Wind usually came from the general direction of the heavy, or big, end of the Milky Way—a sure sign.

A circle around the moon meant an approaching storm. It was as many days away as there were stars within it.

Northern lights usually indicated northerly and colder weather.

Gulls flying low over the water and following the boat far out meant good weather; gulls flying high and hugging the shore meant bad weather.

Some boats were considered unlucky, or hoodoo'ed, and were always in trouble of various kinds—going ashore, losing parts of their rigging, collisions, losing or injuring men, losing cargoes, etc. The schooner *Undine* of Hamilton, Ontario, was one, also the *Delaware*. Men would not ship in them, if they could get another.

Some sailors were quite given to observing hunches and would get off a boat or miss a trip if they had a hunch that something was going to happen. Captain Palmetier told of two experiences of boarding a vessel for a trip and then changing his mind. In one case, the vessel was lost, and in the other, she had a very bad trip. He has heard of many others.

Frequently, before sailors would sign up for a trip they'd look at the pumps. If they "had cobwebs on them" and were not much worn, it meant the boat didn't leak and they wouldn't have to do much pumping. But, if the pumps were shiny from use, nothing doing. "Some mates would throw dust over the pumps to fool them, but they couldn't make cobwebs."

There were many lucky and unlucky signs. A slight list to port as a vessel was towing out indicated a lucky trip. To starboard, unlucky. The new moon first appearing over the port quarter meant good luck for that "moon." To kill a seagull either intentionally or otherwise would cause the boat to go down.

A pretty hard lot of men hung around and worked on the Welland Canal. The canal hands and sailors were continuously fighting. The crews of rival boats also were fighting much of the time when together. If one boat would interfere with the other either intentionally or not—"I'll be back in a few minutes." At this, the whole crew would come, except the boy left aboard to watch, and there'd be a grand rough-and-tumble out on the bank or towpath. There was also much singing and having a good time. Palmetier said some crews would have one or two who could play some instruments and sing and others so inclined would collect around. When the boats were tied up together, they'd often play and sing most of the night. The sailors liked sailor songs most, but sang others, as well. There were many salt-water men among Lakes crews and they'd sing ocean songs and many of the lakesmen learned them and sang them. He mentioned "The *Flying Cloud*," "The *Cumberland*'s Crew," and "The Ship That Never Returned."

Picton, Ontario, August 8, 1933

In the evening, I drove out four miles along the bay to the farm of Captain William Bangard, seventy-six, who began at fourteen years of age and retired two years ago. He was just finishing his chores. We sat out on the front porch and talked a couple of hours and during that time, stray stanzas of songs came to him. He gave me a few of the "E-ri-o Canal" and two of the "*Jennie P. King*." He thought he might recall some others, so I gave him my address.

He said there was a good song about the schooner *Sweetheart*. The crew got it up one trip. She was a big, awkward, three-masted schooner, very hard to steer and always in trouble. She carried timber. He said there were hundreds of songs drifting about, though sailors were always making them up. Usually, they didn't last very long, but sometimes one would "take" and be sung all around the Lakes. I asked about their general nature, and he said they were frequently built along the pattern of some other songs and told about anything that was outstanding about the vessel or her trip. When I asked about parodies, he said that they were quite common—mostly indecent—but didn't last long. Then I asked about obscene sailor songs and said he had often heard people refer to such songs, but never heard many himself when he was "before the mast or afterwards." He said most of the sailors were not much different from other people, but they liked to play up to their reputation and gave the impression they were "pretty tough." Not many of the songs he had ever heard them sing were what might be called indecent. They always talked pretty rough and were experts at profanity, but that was traditional.

I asked Captain Bangard if he'd ever heard of the "Black Dog of Lake Erie," and he said he had. About the time he began sailing, a story went around the Lower Lakes of a captain who killed one of his men in a dispute. Shortly after that a big, black dog appeared before the cabin seemingly from nowhere and would snarl and bite at him. The next time out, the boat went down. The boat was supposed to be cursed. "Of course, there was nothing in it, but that was the story."

When returning to the home where I'm sleeping, I stopped at the gasoline station of Captain Nelson Hudgins. We got talking about "The *Maggie Hunter*" and, with what I have, he recalled what I think is the remainder of the tune.

At this point, a car drove up and reported another car a couple miles away out of gas and asked him to send some out. Hudgins had no car, so I offered to take it out. His helper went with me and we found an old Model T on the sidelines and poured into it some gas and still it wouldn't go, so we towed it back, the motor dragging all the way. When we examined it under the gas-pump lights, we discovered that the throttle wire had become disconnected. We fixed it and the driver then thanked me profusely and then went merrily on his way, Model T, wife, and four offspring. Then a group of young people came along for ice cream cones and other forms of depravity and so ended the day.

Picton, Ontario, August 9, 1933

Found Tom "Topper" Sinder, a solidly built man of about fifty-five years, working in a local harness shop. He said he began sailing in schooners in the middle 1890s and stayed at it for about twenty seasons. He implied that he knew all the old sailor songs going, but when questioned about titles and specific lines, he could give none. I've noticed that practically all former schoonermen with whom I have talked seem to feel that they should know many such songs and imply that they do. Such knowledge seems to have been taken for granted among schoonermen, the same as knowledge of how to do any necessary manual work aboard ship.

He was quite fluent about some sailor hangouts in the larger ports, especially Clark Street in Chicago. There, "Hinky Dick" was a well-known gathering place for sailors, with a bar over one hundred feet long where one could get a beer and a sandwich for five cents and board and lodging during the closed season of navigation for forty dollars. According to him, Canal Street in Buffalo "was the toughest damn street in the whole country." In Montreal, "French Mary," a big, husky female who was her own bouncer, kept a well-known place down along the harbor where rivermen and sailors stayed while in the city.

William Head, a slender, active man of seventy-eight, spent all his adult life until a few years ago on the Great Lakes. He sailed in "the old windjammers" for twenty-five seasons, beginning in 1875, and then fished for thirty more years, mostly in eastern Lake Ontario. Most of the schooners at the time carried coal or any other available cargo to the Upper Lakes ports, and timber, ore, or grain back down. They had no difficulty getting cargoes, and times were good. When the steamboats finally took the trade away from the sailing vessels, he took up fishing.

As a young man, he sailed several seasons in the old schooner *John Bigler* about which the song "The Timber Drogher *Bigler*" was written. He said the schooner was built primarily for carrying squared timbers from the lumber ports on the Upper Lakes down to the eastern end of Lake Erie or Ontario for transshipment down the Erie Canal or the St. Lawrence River. The vessel was built bluff stem and stern and had the maximum dimensions permitted by the locks in the Welland Canal. "She wasn't much on speed and made a great commotion in the water when carrying all her canvas before a fresh breeze." She had ports built in her bow and stern that could be opened for loading and, of course, closed and caulked when out on the Lakes. The timbers were dragged aboard by means of a line to the vessel's capstan. When the hold was full, they loaded more on the deck.

He recalled loading "some pine sticks" off Marquette and Grand Marais, Michigan, on Lake Superior, that were four by five by twenty feet "and more" and "not a knot in them." They were too big to come in the loading ports and had to be hoisted by strong tackle onto the deck. He also recalled once lying to at anchor for nine days out in deep water off Grand Marais loading timbers. The weather was cold and changeable, and several times they had to "slip anchor," and move further out into Lake Superior for safety.

Rafts of timbers were towed out to the waiting vessels by tugs and loading them was always a cold, wet, disagreeable job and the full crew was kept busy at it from daylight until dark. At night, they always had a hot meal and all the hot coffee they wanted and then the crew usually sat around a stove in the fo'c'sle and sang songs for a while. Only one man stood deck watch during the night.

The second mate had a good voice and the song about the *Bigler* was one of his favorites. Most of the crew learned it from him. He would sing the stanzas alone and all would join in on the chorus. They sang many songs this way and Mr. Head was still able to recall parts of several.

When asked if he knew the song about "The Schooner *Fayette Brown*," he at once recited several stanzas. He said that during a sailor strike in Cleveland that song was printed on big cards and distributed all about the harbor, and he thought he still had one of them somewhere.

Mr. Head said that a sailor named Clark from Buffalo wrote songs about most of his trips on the Lakes. He spent his money freely and after it was gone, he would make the rounds of the saloons in whatever port he happened to be in and sing these songs for free drinks. "I once heard that he finally drank himself to death." He added that before he himself sailed the *Bigler*, Clark made a late-season trip in her. Grain rates at this time were always high. [Rates rose as winter crept toward the Lakes and grain farmers still needed to get the year's harvest to market before navigation closed.] The Old Man decided to bring down a load of wheat instead of lumber from Milwaukee, and the song tells about the trip, "and it's a good one!" He said he always understood that Clark wrote "The Red Iron Ore" song that tells about a trip of the schooner *E. C. Roberts* from Escanaba, Michigan, to Cleveland with iron ore.

"Another song that I know Clark wrote—an' it's also a good one—is about a canal schooner that loaded timbers at the Straits for D. D. Calvin's rafting yards at the head of the St. Lawrence River. She carried a pair of mules on her fore deck for towing through the Welland Canal and for working the capstan while loading. The song tells about it." He recalled the opening stanza and several others.

He thinks the proposed burning of the *Lyman Davis* at Toronto is an outrage.

BELLEVILLE, ONTARIO, AUGUST 10, 1933

I left Picton about 8 a.m. for Belleville and began the day's occupation there, but with small results. I inquired about for some time, but got traces of only about a half dozen sea houses that sounded at all promising.

Mike Meehan, a barber in his late seventies, an ex–windjammer sailor and Irishman, was the first visit. Found him living in a one-room habitation behind another house. He began sailing as a boy on the whole chain of Lakes and later had his own vessel and sailed mostly in the coal trade on Lake Ontario. He sold her to New Orleans during the war period for $4,000. "That was the biggest mistake of my life." He thinks he would be rich now had he kept her. He has an enlarged close-up photo of her framed on his walls. It was taken as she was coming up with all her canvas on and billowed out with the near bank as a foreground.

He says he heard many songs years ago on the Upper Lakes. He remembers hearing a good one about the loss of the schooner *Asia* on Georgian Bay. He said many schooner officers would not permit whistling aboard their vessels. Some thought it would bring a gale of wind. He has heard mates go aloft and whistle for wind when becalmed. He has also seen and heard the captain stand on the after deck and "curse God almighty for not sending wind. The captain of the *Maggie Hunter* did that one trip I made with him. I was pretty scared and expected we'd all be lost. I wouldn't sail with a man who did that. It's a wonder we wasn't all lost. I've heard of vessels having their sails torn to ribbons and damn near wrecked after someone in the crew did that."

He told of a rich Brighton, Ontario, vessel owner named Proctor who was owed some money by a man who died. He seized the body to get his money from the man's relatives. The people around said that a big ball of fire appeared over his house night after night to plague him. "I was in one of his boats that season and, as we were laying to at anchor off the harbor there, a light bigger than a streetlight came upon our main truck. We were scared as hell, but nothing happened."

I then drove on to Kingston. Got the first mail since Toronto. I had a bacon and eggs birthday dinner all by myself, then got a room, and took a long walk about the Queen's University campus and downtown and the waterfront and now here and the end of this day.

KINGSTON AND GARDEN ISLAND, ONTARIO, AUGUST 11, 1933

A day of promises and some meat. Almost everyone I inquire of thinks that only captains know anything about the subject, when some Irish before-the-mast, happy-go-lucky rowdy would know more than a shipload of captains. All the old schoonermen are "captains" anyhow. They got that way like Southern "colonels," so I take 'em all and have found frequently that those praised highest as knowing most of the lore usually know little or nothing of it and, on several occasions, some "aw-he-doesn't-know-a-damn-thing-about-sailing" will have something. So, I can't pass any of them up.

I inquired at "The Sailors' Institute," a marine rescue mission and home, and got the name of Captain Israel LaRoche on Wolf Island. Then I asked at the offices of a couple of coal companies who have been connected with sailing for a half century or more, and skippers of a couple of ferry boats who have been around here a lifetime. They all begin with, "Well, there used to be hundreds of them around here, but them old captains are all dead, now. If you'd come a few years ago . . ." Then comes an account of what some of then would have given me "if." I settle back and wait for an opportunity to get back to today and usually learn of a few possibilities. I've learned that I can't depend very much upon what one sailor says of another who is still living, especially if living nearby. They all depreciate each other.

At Garden Island at the head of the St. Lawrence River, I found John Ferguson, still very active in his late seventies. He said he sailed before the mast and as a mate for over thirty years in timber droghers carrying squared timbers from Saginaw River, Georgian Bay, and Lake Superior ports down to Calvin's "rafting grounds" off this island. He was also captain of a barge in the same trade for a number of seasons. He has lived on the island in the same house for forty-three years.

Garden Island was the headquarters of the D. D. Calvin Co. operations that William Head had mentioned. It rafted timbers down the St. Lawrence to Montreal and Quebec. The Calvin family still owns the whole island. In the boom days of the timber trade, the island had a shipbuilding yard here that employed from fifty to one hundred fifty men year after year. The rafting grounds, where the timbers were first pulled from the vessels by horses and later by steam power, was on the down-river side of the island. The timbers were formed into large rafts and sent down the river with fifty to seventy-five men on them and all in tow of one of Calvin's steamboats. The men had to guide the rafts all the way, and take them through the rapids in "drams," or smaller rafts.

These raftsmen were mostly Indians, Frenchmen, or "half breeds," and they were all daredevils. Three hundred to five hundred of them came up the river to the island every spring as soon as the timber droghers began to come in, and they worked until navigation closed. The work hours were from daylight until dark, with time out only to eat. Old D. D. Calvin controlled all of it. He wouldn't allow any drinking or rowdyism. He fought the sailors' union and imported men from Scotland to sail his vessels, and finally took the masts out of his timber barges and towed them behind his steamboats.

There was much singing among the raftsmen, particularly in the bunkhouses and on the rafts going down the river. Their songs were all in French. The raftsmen especially liked to sing at their work. They were not much as sailors, but they were very skilled rivermen. Most wore bright red sashes all the time. The sailors on the vessels that brought the timber down from the Upper Lakes had songs about their trips, also.

I met James Captain, a robust, active, and friendly man who looks much younger than his eighty-four years, at Kingston. He made his first trips on the Great Lakes sailing vessels when he was fourteen, and at twenty-four became master of one of D. D. Calvin's timber-carrying schooners. He remarked that there were practically no government aids to navigation at that time, "and we had to know the Lakes pretty well—every bump and bend in 'em." Altogether, he sailed the Lakes for over half a century, mostly in the timber trade between the Upper Lakes and the "rafting grounds" at the head of the St. Lawrence River.

On one wall of his home's living room hangs a large picture of a two-masted timber drogher with all her canvas up. On one side of it is an enlarged photograph of the harbor at the Port Colborne end of the Welland Canal with about thirty vessels of various kinds at anchor awaiting transit down to Lake Ontario. On the other side is another photograph of the Port Dalhousie harbor with fifty or more vessels at anchor waiting to go through to Lake Erie.

Captain James Dix stated that the timber vessels he sailed in usually carried a team of light horses, or at times mules, on the foredeck for towing each way through the Welland Canal, for working the capstan and occasionally when raising heavy canvas. He said the horses would sleep standing up, and became pretty good sailors. They would always stand with their "after end" to the wind, and shift position after the ship came about while tacking. It was the "boy's" job to feed and handle them and to clean the deck.

When they used local horses to help in the loading, they had the problem of getting them off the vessel and ashore. They tried various methods, but the most workable one was to attach a long line to a horse's halter, lead him up on top of the deckload of timber even with the top of the rail, and then three or four men would give him a quick push overboard. "He'd make a big splash, but always came up all right and would head for the shore. They were pretty good swimmers. We'd help them along by the line to their halters. They always made it, and it didn't seem to hurt them any."

He sailed a few seasons for Corruthers and Gumm of Kingston. They had five timber-carrying vessels:

> The "*Hydrobad*" and "*Bangalore*"
> The "*Elm,*" "*Ox,*" and "*Singapore.*"

Kingston, Ontario, August 12, 1933

Saturday night of another week, ten minutes to Sunday. This has been a long day. Much hunting but with small results.

Shortly after noon, I visited the parks where the old heads gather for their daily reunion. Found Captain Dix and another old lad quarreling like a couple of two-year-olds over whether the *Blue Nose* now at Chicago for the World's Fair can

In this photo, taken inside the breakwater at Toronto, a man affixes an advertising banner to the mainmast of the *Lyman Davis*. It teases: "Come bid me farewell." (Courtesy Ivan H. Walton Collection, Bentley Historical Library, University of Michigan)

carry passengers. Later, a couple of others expounded in detail on the superiority of Canadian-built boats and sailors to all others, especially American. Gar Wood of Detroit won the speedboat races from "that Englishman" because he bribed the crew—"it's an absolute fact. How else could he have won?" [The 1931 Harmsworth Regatta at Detroit was one of history's most controversial races. In it, Wood's Miss America team was declared the winner over English challenger Kaye Don's Miss England II team. Wood had crossed the starting line too soon, disqualifying himself, and Don followed close behind, also becoming disqualified. The race was won by the Wood team's second boat. Wood was accused of being unsportsmanlike and pulling a "Yankee trick."]

Then came a long explanation of the superiority of the old schooner sailors to the present steamboat men. "And they call themselves sailors! Christ, almighty! Get one of them a mile off his course and he'd never get anywhere!"

I brought up the *Lyman Davis,* which was owned here before she was taken to Toronto to be burned to entertain some morons. I thought the *Lyman Davis* would be a good way to get back to common ground and some Lakes songs, but immediately in some unaccountable way there broke out a hot argument on whether she carried a raffee sail. The old lad who stoutly maintained that she "never carried no damn raffee" got so ruffled that he trudged away home. [Photos showed that the *Lyman Davis* had, at times, carried the triangular foresail.] I then tried them individually, but got nothing.

[Thousands gathered on June 29, 1934, to see the *Lyman Davis* burned off Toronto. Toronto's *Evening Telegram* wrote the next day, "Burned to the water's edge and wracked by the explosions of powerful fireworks, the stout little schooner, which was born in a Muskegon shipyard 61 years ago, was towed to deep water shortly before 2 a.m. and sunk by a dynamite charge in her bottom. . . . Even the most thoughtless of the watchers saw in the sinking vessel something more than the destruction of an inanimate thing. They had a feeling that out in the centre of the oil-fed flames, the bursting bombs and roaring rockets, a personality and what, until then, had been a living memory of inland sailing fleets, was quickly dying. . . . The vessel's destruction had the character of an execution. She was made to take that last short voyage, even as a condemned person is made to walk to the gallows, and she did so in the ignominious tow of a sooty tug."]

HENDERSON'S HARBOR AND OSWEGO, NEW YORK, AUGUST 14, 1933

Explored Oswego for the lay of it and then called at the business place of John S. Parsons, in his late sixties, a ship's chandler. His father was a sailor and chandler before him. He says he's been connected with Lakes sailors for about sixty years.

Two old sailors were present and I heard of more songs in the hour or so with them than in any one place I've been yet. Every few minutes some one of the three would mention one and Mr. Parsons would give part of it.

Mr. Parsons mentioned and recited parts of songs about the *Gilbert Mollison*, the steamer *Bay State*, the schooner *M. J. Cummings*, the schooners *Hastings*, *Moonlight*, *George C. Finney* and a French patois song about the scow *Look and See*.

"Bound Away on the *Twilight*" and "A Trip on the *George C. Finney*" are passage songs modeled on the widely known "The Red Iron Ore." ["The *Twilight*" starts this way:]

> She's an iron ore vessel, a vessel of fame,
> She sails from Oswego and the *Twilight*'s her name.
> She trades to Superior where the stormy winds blow,
> Bound away on the *Twilight* for ore we go.
>
> Now the *Twilight* has left the old Cleveland pier
> And the boys and the girls, they give us a cheer.
> Saying "There's the bark *Twilight*, her canvas all set,
> May she have pleasant weather from here to Marquette."

Will get what I can of these from him tomorrow. They said a blacksmith's helper and former sailor named Peckham composed a number of them. I spent part of the evening in the city library.

Night.

OSWEGO, NEW YORK, AUGUST 15, 1933

A flat tire for a morning greeting and the tire man's "I'll send a man right up" took an hour and nearly another one to repair it. Then breakfast and an empty call to post office and back to the office of Mr. Parsons.

A gruff old fellow was in, and both were reading newspapers. It was evident Mr. Parsons wasn't inclined to talk much in front of "Mr. Gruff," but he turned to his desk and wrote out for me all he could recall of a song, "The Schooner *George C. Finney*":

> Come all you bold sailors who follow the Lakes,

And in a canaller your living do make.
I'll sing you a song of the winds and the seas,
Of a trip up the Lakes, and I hope it will please.

Oh, the *Finney* is lying now at the salt dock,
And the boys and the girls on their deck they do flock;
They give us a cheer when away we must go—
Bound away to Chicago the *Finney* must go.

We arrive at Dalhousie, and our work is begun,
We heave up our jibboom and our anchors take in;
We unship our catheads, our bowsprit also,
We've boarded our boat, through the ditch we must tow.

We towed all that night, and all the next day,
Until we reached Allenburg where a tug there did lay.
The tug *Minnie Battle,* she took us in tow,
And out in Lake Erie she then let us go.

Now the *Finney* is booming up the Lake Huron shore,
We shaped her a course as we'd oft done before;
Through Saginaw Bay with a fair wind we sailed,
Past Thunder Bay Island and the False Presque Isle.

Now the *Finney*'s in Chicago, made fast stem and stern,
We'll go to Pete Kemmer's and spin a long yarn.
Here's a health to Jack Preston, who gave us a treat
For arriving in Chicago ahead of the fleet.

He also wrote out what he could of "The Schooner *Moonlight,*" and also
scattering stanzas of songs about "The *Bay State,*" "The Schooner *Oriole,*" "The
Good Scow *Alice Strong,*" "The *Fayette Brown,*" and one stanza about "The
Schooner *M. J. Cummings.*" He may be able to recall more tomorrow. "Mr. Gruff"
left and "Wild Jack" came in and held the stage until Mr. Parsons left for noon
lunch.

His place of business seems to be an old sailor's last stand. From time to
time, individuals come in, usually without any greeting either way, and sit down on
a coil of rope, a box, or one of the few old chairs available. Then, they read
newspapers, argue politics, and in response to a question about the old-time
sailing, they argue the relative merits of sail and steam, cargoes carried, disasters,
sailing records made, and the men who made them.

Mr. Parsons's "office," a room about fifteen feet square and a ceiling at least
twelve feet high, contained so many ship models and other mementos of sailing
vessels that there was scarcely enough space left for his roll-top desk and chair. The
four walls, except for the door and window spaces, were completely covered with

paintings, drawings, and old photographs of earlier Lakes vessels, about four-fifths of them under various sailing rigs. He was seemingly able to give the name, home port, fate, and any other information about any of them. He stated that he had purchased a few of the pieces, some were loaned to him "years ago by individuals who forgot to come back for them," and others were "gifts by former vessel owners and their families who didn't know what else to do with them."

Mr. Parsons said that a Tom Peckham, who died in the 1880s, wrote quite a number of songs, including the ones about the *Antelope,* the *Oriole,* the *M. J. Cummings,* and the *Mollison.* Peckham was "quite a singer," who composed many songs about schooners on which he sailed, and sang them in port saloons all about the Lakes for free drinks. He added that someone a few years back contributed several to the local newspaper.

Mr. Parsons said that Tom's son Ben is a former sailor, singer, fiddler, fisherman, and handyman who lives on the lakeshore on the west side of the city.

There was another man living here about that time named Patrick Fennel who wrote under the name of Shandy Maguire some stories and songs. Mr. Parsons said Fennel wrote "The *Persian*'s Crew" and "The *Isaac G. Jenkins*" and some others. Captain William Bangard of Picton, Ontario, had told me that a man named Clark wrote those two, "The *Bigler,*" and some others. Someone else, I don't recall who, said they were written by a man named Kelly. Well, they were written and by the different ways they're sung, I suspect some additions and modifications by succeeding singers.

Mr. Parsons also mentioned "The Stately *Southerner,*" "The *Dreadnaught,*" "Away, Rio," "How We Paid Paddy Doyle for His Boots," "Shenandoah," "Rio," "The *Cumberland*'s Crew," "The Schooner *Hesperus,*" "Whiskey Johnny," "Boney Was a Warrior," "*Julie LaPlante,*" "*Flying Cloud,*" "Harry Bail," "Gerry's Rock," "Little Brown Bulls," and some lumber camp songs. He said that a French patois song that he'd heard many times called "The Launch of the *Angelique*" was in the *Marine Record* a few years ago.

When I asked him what proportion of the sailor songs were what might be called indecent, he said "very few." Often someone would get up a smutty parody to some new song, but these never lasted long.

On the matter of beliefs or superstitions, one wouldn't notice them except at some times. The feeling that beginning a season on Friday was unlucky was quite general. Blaspheming would bring bad luck or even destruction to a boat and crew. Rats leaving a boat generally made sailors worried, if not convinced that something was about to happen. Some boats, as well as men, were "Jonahs." Whistling aboard ship was unlucky and might bring a gale. When becalmed, he had seen sailors deliberately whistle toward the sky for a wind, also scratch the mast, throw small coins overboard and often change wheelsmen. Someone else added that it was a common belief that weather would be "scoffed off" by the moon when it came up. Different ones in the group mentioned the usual weather rhymes.

Met Thomas "Race" Callahan, eighty-two, on a street near Mr. Parsons's chandlery. He told of one captain who he had sailed with as a boy who usually carried a small pig aboard that he believed could "smell" weather and indicate approaching storms by the direction it would sniff the air. "Race" seems to be quite a character. Parsons had said that Morgan Robertson, a writer of sea stories from here, got much of his information and ideas from "Race." He's a small man weighing about one hundred twenty and can still dance. Is good for a hundred years, at least. Parsons said he'd been dismasted and wrecked a number of times, but "nothing could kill him."

I found Ben Peckham a few miles west of downtown in the shade of a tree at his rundown lakeshore home, working on a model of a schooner. He was a tall, lanky, stooped man of about seventy-five, suffering from arthritis and a bad heart and was very talkative. He apparently had no teeth, and when he extended his chin in a gesture of satisfaction, it and his nose seemed to meet, and out of the background protruded his heavy gray moustache. His clothing was long past its prime and he gave evidence of much time having elapsed since his last bath. He stuffed great quantities of scrap tobacco into his port cheek and, after he got it satisfactorily packed away, he more or less regularly made shots at the none-too-near bucket. At about six feet his score was pretty good, but at a longer range his hits and misses were about equal.

He was pleased that I had come to see him, and he talked continuously, one subject suggesting another. He said that his father and three brothers were all sailors. He himself began sailing when a boy in the 1870s, and sailed all the Lakes and in every kind of vessel and weather until about twenty-five years ago, when he took up fishing "an' other work." He added that he hadn't been able to get any work for some time and was about to lose his home for back taxes.

He stated that his father, Tom, ran away from home when fourteen years old while his father, in turn, was "a-learnin' him blacksmithin'." His family didn't know where he was for months until a schooner was wrecked a few miles up the Lake Ontario shore in a late November blizzard and Tom was listed in the Oswego newspaper as a member of the crew who reached shore safely. Tom Peckham sailed for many years, and all the time made up songs and he and other sailors sang them. When he got too old to sail, he again took up blacksmithing. Ben said his father "made up dozens and dozens of songs about every damn thing." Ben was in the crew of the *M. J. Cummings* when she was dismasted in a storm on Lake Ontario and reported lost and his father "made up a song about it from what I told him." Tom made up songs about most of the vessels he sailed in, and he got free drinks in any port he happened to be in for singing them. Ben recalled his father jotting down new songs at home and then going downtown to a saloon to sing them.

Peckham recalled "The Dredge from Presque Isle" and attributed it to his father. It tells of a tug's trip across Lake Ontario to pick up a harbor dredge and tow it back to Oswego. It begins:

> The night was fair, the sky was clear, no ripple on the sea,
> When King he came into the shop and thus he says to me:
> "We're going on a pleasure trip." How good that made me feel.

And then he said, "If the weather's fine, we're going to Presque Isle."

It was quite late in the month of August, and, if I remember right,
We went onboard the *Sumner* tug at nine o'clock at night.
Bill Bishop cast off the mooring lines, Captain Dobie took the wheel,
And the stern being nigh, he let 'er fly to the place they call Presque Isle.

About the hour of five next morning, the light was right ahead;
Says King to Captain Dobie, "Sir, the *Sumner* is not dead."
"Oh no," says Captain Dobie, proud, as he held the *Sumner*'s wheel,
"There's no tug afloat can beat this boat from Oswego to Presque Isle."

Oh, now that we are landed safe, and made fast to the dock,
Machinists and dredgemen and others, too, around us then did flock.
Then down to breakfast we all did go for mutton chops and veal;
About then, says I, "The boys live high on dredges at Presque Isle."

My blessing on that good old cook, I think her name was Ann,
She gave us each a pile of grub to fill a twelve-quart pan.
There was pickled feet and pork and beans, and also Irish veal—
You'd laugh and cry to see the pickles fly when we were in Presque Isle.

Onboard ship he was considered a "lucky wheelsman" and was often sent aft to wheel when the wind would go down "and, b' God, she'd damn near always come back." He also mentioned throwing small coins and other things overboard for a wind. At times, the sailors would get out the towline and make it fast to the forward timberhead [as a sign they were looking for a tow] and "that would bring a wind."

When asked if he had any manuscripts of his father's songs, he said that shortly before his father died, his friend and "pardner," a man named Charles Tebo, came to visit and borrowed the notebook "in which me father wrote all the songs he liked, and them he made up himself. An' then not long afterward, Tebo himself died in Syracuse, an' we never seen that book again." He let on that he didn't know anything about Tebo, other than that he was "sort of a wanderer."

OSWEGO, NEW YORK, AUGUST 16, 1933

Three occasions of note today: This morning I got denounced by a young lady down the hall when I stopped, or should I say, slowed down, to watch the procedure as she was in the first stages of dressing inside the open door of her room; saw the Oswego fire engine truck smother and almost stall as it was going up the little hill just across the river bridge on the main street; and found some Lakes stuff, even though not so much.

Called at Mr. Parsons's office again. He could give me no more songs, but did tell me about a Mr. Steven O'Brien, son-in-law of Oswego's former poet, "Shandy Maguire," who had written some Lakes songs.

Found Mr. O'Brien, about sixty-five, at his home on Erie Street. He was just starting out to see his brother five or six blocks away, so I went along. I told him what I wanted, and he was very pleased at my interest in his wife's father and he praised him most of the way to his brother's and the return, and would not allow me to go out for lunch, so I had an Irish boiled dinner with him. He's Irish all through. His son lost his life in the World War, and his wife died last year. He's had no work for three years, and the world hasn't much summertime in it. His daughter is keeping house for him and his two grandsons—his son's sons—are also living there.

He got out two volumes by Shandy Maguire—Patrick Fennel—and I looked them through quite carefully. One was composed largely of poems addressed to railroad men, and the other was "Lyrics and Poems," published here in 1887. In the latter, I found the original song, "The Loss of the Schooner *Persian*," which evidently is the pattern for some other songs on similar occasions. I had never before seen any mention of an author. The schooner, which was from here, was lost with all hands in Lake Huron in 1869. The song is known all over the Lakes. The book also contained a poem on the "Loss of the Schooner *Isaac G. Jenkins*," also of Oswego, which was lost off Sheldon's Point, New York, a short distance from here, with all hands in a November blizzard in 1875. The poem was read at a memorial meeting held the month after.

In the afternoon, I took a walk and then went to the city library and searched newspaper files of the *Palladium-Times*. I found in the 1928 file the two poems I had just copied and one other, "The *Jenkins*," which was written on the same occasion as Maguire's poem. I had obtained parts of it from William Murray of Montague, Michigan, and more from Captain Nelson Hudgins of Picton, Ontario. Have it all, now.

OSWEGO, NEW YORK, AUGUST 17, 1933

Went out to see Ben Peckham again and found him on my second trip pretty well "plastered" and his rheumatism about forgotten. He was upstairs rummaging about when I got there after eats, and he came down with a little candy box in his hand, which he said he was going to send me, and I had considerable difficulty getting him to give it to me then. He kept telling me that he "had an idea, a hell of a big idea—and I can't tell it to you all at once, etc. Finally, it came out that he had decided to write and publish a book of songs and make lots of money. In his box I found clippings of "The Old *Bay State*," "Loss of the Schooner *Mollison*," and "The Loss of the *Lady Elgin*," a new one to me! He also had some others that I already have.

ROCHESTER AND LOCKPORT ON THE ERIE CANAL, NEW YORK, AUGUST 19, 1933

After lunch, started out for Lewiston, New York, and on to Port Dalhousie, but didn't arrive there. Called in the Erie Canal town of Lockport to see the canal and locks and to try to locate some canal stuff. A peculiar old bird tending one of the bridges over the canal gave me the following, which he said he'd heard as a boy:

> Pull in your towline, and haul in your slack,
>> Take a reef in your trousers and the kinks out of your back.
> And whatever you do you must never forget
>> To tap the mules gently when the cook's out on deck.

I did not take down his name.

"Butch" Sullivan, a square-built, heavyset Irishman of about seventy, still carries a few battle scars on his face. He began driving on the Old Erie Canal when nine years old, had his own boat when twenty, and retired only five years ago. He said he had traveled the length of the canal "hundreds of times." He always carried two teams of horses or mules, and said they and the drivers towed six-hour shifts night and day, seven days a week, unless some lock jam or other trouble interfered. Occasionally, when they towed two boats, they used two teams at a time. They usually traveled about two and a half miles an hour and made a round trip from Albany to Buffalo and the return in about 30 days. At Albany, tugs or steamboats towed them on the Hudson River to New York City and back.

He said that the men who worked on the canal boats and at the locks were "a pretty tough lot." He said that there was much fighting between crews, especially when one boat would try to take advantage of another, and between boaters and locktenders, but usually traffic moved quite smoothly. Some canal boat captains would pay a good fighter more than the customary wages, especially if they were expecting trouble. A good fighter was a good man to have along "to settle arguments."

At Buffalo, the canallers and Lakes sailors went to the same saloons and other entertainment places. "The sailors thought that they were better men than the canallers, and we had to show them that they were wrong."

There wasn't much singing on the canal boats. The men generally worked long hours and were too tired, but on occasion when a group of boats were tied up together, the men and women, too—"we usually had women cooks"—would gather on one boat and entertain themselves by singing. He added that he never could sing and, so, never learned any songs, although he often wished he had. He did, however, recall hearing a song many times that had in the chorus the lines:

> I've got a mule, her name is Sal,
> Fifteen miles on the Erie Canal.

He added that sailors in the Buffalo saloons would sometimes sing songs that made fun of the canallers, songs about the great storms, bad shoals, and even pirates they had to deal with, and "that was one sure way to start a fight."

PORT DALHOUSIE, ONTARIO, AUGUST 21, 1933

Captain Jeremiah Cavanaugh, in his late seventies, was the find of the village. He gave me a song, which he said he worked up himself about fifty years ago about the *John Bentely* on which he was sailing at the time. It has about a dozen stanzas.

An elevator towers over the Erie Canal basin. (From *Picturesque America*)

He also gave me the following two stanzas of another that went to the air of "The Ship That Never Returned":

On July Fourth in Cheboygan port,
    They went on a bum
And all that day the lumber lay
    Alongside the *Stuart H. Dunn.*

"Schoonermen did most of their singing in shore saloons. A group of acquaintances would get together and at once they'd make for a saloon and have a drink or two, and then someone would call for a song, and then each man had to sing a song, clog dance, tell a good story, or buy a round of drinks. I always had to sing 'The *Bentely.*'" Some of the old-time saloons had a sort of a stage built at one end of the bar and the men would do their stuff there. Fights also took place there. Buffalo was a great place for sailor songs.

He was in the Lake Superior grain and lumber trade for a number of years. Cavanaugh told of "hugging the weather shore" in bad weather. He was master of steamboats for many years and, when war came, went in government service as a St. Lawrence River pilot, which he had learned as a boy. He says steamboating is a job, but sailing a windjammer was much more a game and always had something new in it. Working "before the mast" on a schooner was hard work and all hours, whereas a steamboat is regular and much easier work, but he prefers the former.

He says that if present-day steamboat captains get a mile off their regular course, they're lost. None can navigate enough to lay a course according to the weather, but plow along on a course someone laid out in an office somewhere and roll and strain their boats and lose many of them and their men with them.

In the evening, I drove out to the new Welland Ship Canal to Lock No. 1, at Port Wells, New York, a new port that has only a dozen or so inhabitants now. I watched a couple of freighters and a tug go through the 46½-foot lift of the lock. That lock and its operation is a great engineering accomplishment. Turning a few switches fills or empties the big 80 by 820 by 46½-foot lock in seven to fifteen minutes, according to the speed needed. Will see those at the escarpment tomorrow.

Port Colborne, Ontario, August 23, 1933

Frank Mahaffey, about seventy, spent practically all of his many sailing years on tugs out of Port Colborne on Lake Erie. "It was a great life and we made good money until steamboats began to cut in on the old windjammers. We would pick 'em up out in the Lake off the harbor and bring 'em in, often several at a time, and get each one in its proper turn started down the canal. We also towed out of the harbor most of the sailboats that came up from Lake Ontario. If the wind was right and not too many vessels in the harbor, some of them would put up their canvas and sail out by themselves."

He added that sometimes the harbor would become so filled with windjammers that they could scarcely move. "I've counted over sixty of them tied up out there at one time waitin' to go through. Bad weather and contrary winds sometimes would hold many of 'em under the lee of the islands at the head [west end] of the lake. Then a good breeze would come out of the west and scores of 'em would come racing down the lake, most of 'em for Buffalo, but plenty for the canal. We'd be expectin' 'em an' we'd haul 'em in day and night as fast as we could. The first to arrive got first chance through the canal. Some of them old windjammer captains was pretty tough an' had reputations for speed, an' if other vessels was storming down hard on their tails, they'd carry most everything right through the harbor piers an' then, if their anchor didn't hold, there'd be hell to pay gettin' untangled. The captains and mates would accuse and cuss each other, an' if they was close enough together, they'd sometimes get into fistfights."

Bathers splash in Lake Erie as a schooner, possibly the *Oliver Mowatt,* is towed into Lake Erie at Port Dalhousie by the Canadian tugs *Alert* and *Augusta.* They are passing the light at the end of the Welland Canal. (Courtesy Dossin Great Lakes Museum)

He said that in the 1890s when the steamboats took over most of the trade, the old schooners became pretty scarce and competing tugs would sometimes go looking for tows all the way to the Detroit River and occasionally up through the rivers into Lake Huron. They would take any sailboats they could pick up all the way to the canal or Buffalo for just the price of river or harbor towing. "An' to make it worse, in the 1890s the tugboats began to cut rates." He explained that when schooners were numerous, the tugs got from one hundred to one hundred fifty dollars per schooner, depending on size, for taking them through the rivers. In the 1890s, rates got as low as forty to fifty dollars and "that wouldn't even pay for the fuel unless we was fortunate to get a half dozen or so at a time."

He continued that, in the early days before vessel owners put donkey engines aboard to do the heavy work, the canallers would carry eight or ten men and the big grain schooners to Buffalo still more, and many of the crew members would be shellbacks. The crews would always chantey when handling heavy canvas or the anchor, "an' you could hear them at either end of the canal or in Buffalo harbor when they was makin' sail to go out on the lake."

He also stated that many steamboats and tugs would take on fuel at Amherstburg, Ontario, at the mouth of the Detroit River, at first cordwood and in later years coal. It was brought aboard by dockhands, usually big, husky Negroes pushing wheelbarrows. They would shuffle along in a big circle and sing most of the time. He recalled one occasion "[w]hen we was lyin' 'longside a fuelin' dock an' a big river tug with a double high-pressure engine came along an' they started a song to the slow rhythm of the exhaust." All he could remember was an oft repeated line:

Beech an' maple, beech an' maple.

He recalled another occasion when his tug was lying alongside a big schooner off Detroit waiting to take her to Buffalo. Another schooner came along, the *Fayette Brown* of Cleveland, behind a tug, "an' the crew of our boat sang a song to the other one about: 'That nigger-lovin' Mollet that sails the *Fayette Brown.'"* He said the song grew out of a sailor strike in Cleveland a few months earlier. [The *Fayette Brown* carried an all-black crew of non-union sailors. Joseph Mollet was the captain.]

He said that he had never heard men aboard a tug sing, or even any song about a tug. "We always had a small crew and the men was always too tired and sleepy to sing, an' then, you don't feel like singin' on a tug or steamboat."

Buffalo, New York, August 25, 1933

Captain William E. "Billy" Clark, local compass adjuster and old-time schooner sailor, said he began sailing on the big grain carriers out of Buffalo in 1874 when he was fifteen. He continued on them until the end of the century when they became scarce and he then changed to steamboats. After twenty-five more years on the Lakes, he took up compass adjusting, "an' I'm still at it." He explained the intricacies of adjusting a compass to compensate for the ship's magnetism and then turned to sailboats. "That was the life!"

He said that the largest schooners on the Lakes could carry from five hundred to eight hundred tons and a few still more, and there were hundreds of them—two- and three-masters, and a few such as the *David Dows* with four masts. Three quarters of them were fore 'n' aft, or schooner rigged. Some carried a triangular or "raffee" foretopsail, which was "a very handy rig," and many spread a big square foresail for running before the wind. A square foresail would add miles to the speed, but was no good "on the wind," especially while tacking. That's why the square rig so often used on ocean vessels was rarely used on the Lakes. The few Lakes vessels that were square-rigged on the foremast "would do all right on the down trips," but were clumsy going up when they frequently had to sail "tight to the wind" and at times tack much of the way. They carried a captain, one or two mates, and a cook aft, and from six to twelve men forward, depending on the size of the vessel.

The officers, especially the captain, had to know "every foot of the Lakes," and be able to lay an advantageous course, determined by the direction of the wind

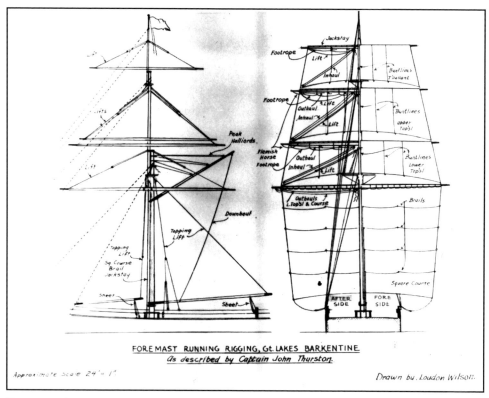

Diagram of a barkentine's rigging by Loudon Wilson. (Courtesy Historical Collections of the Great Lakes)

and expected weather. He had to be able to follow it day and night, in good weather or bad, and in late season, fog, or blinding snowstorm, which at times would last several days. He could not "heave-to" and wait out a storm as they did on the oceans—there was never sea room for that. He must keep going, and always know his exact location. Captain Clark said the men forward had to be able to take in any sail on the ship or do any other necessary work in complete darkness, the same as in daylight. The binnacle light over the compass and just forward of the wheel was the only light the length of the deck. These men were specialists and had learned their trade over several years of hard work.

He explained that when he first began sailing as the crew's "boy" he had to help the cook, run errands for everybody, and do more and more work with the regular members of the crew. The men had songs they would sing during each kind of group work— handling the capstan or windlass, hauling on halyards while setting the heavy courses nearest the deck or the lighter topsails, or hauling the sheets, or pumping. He said that he soon learned the choruses and some lines of several dozen chanteys, and got so that even when he was below and heard the men on deck sing, he could tell from their song the kind of work they were doing.

They sang chanteys at night the same as during the day, and in bad weather the same as during pleasant days.

Captain Clark added with a smile he had a fairly good voice when he was a young man and sometimes when there was no one else to lead, some member of the crew or the mate would call on him to be the chanteyman. On hard pulls, he worked with the other sailors, but when both watches were on deck working together and they were not short-handed, his job was to lead the singing. On a capstan haul he would generally sit on the capstan barrel, but when a group of men were "tailed off" on a halyard or sheet, his place was near the head of the line, and "the boy," the lowest ranking man in the crew, was at the other end.

The chanteyman would usually first sing solo lines that everybody knew, and then make up rhymes about anything that took his fancy. These work songs seldom told a story. One rhyme might be about Chicago, and the next about Liverpool and following ones about the cook, the vessel they were in, its officers, the trip, boardinghouse bosses, shore experiences—real or imaginary—or anything else the chanteyman happened to think of. Sometimes, the chanteyman's rhymes "got pretty raw," but if clever, they gave the men a good laugh. The leader had time to think up new rhymes while the crew was singing the chorus, but if he didn't, he could always fill in with an old one. The men generally would not put up with much repetition. They liked originality and humor, and would show their appreciation by the way they would bawl out the choruses.

Captain Clark said that a good chanteyman was a valuable man in the crew and some captains would pay him a little extra, even though he was "just another man forward." The chantey not only enabled the men to work in unison, but it lightened the work and kept the men good natured, especially at night or in bad weather. It also enabled them to show off before a shore audience when they were putting up canvas preparatory to leaving port. He added that the old-time sailors knew all the tunes and choruses, and liked to sing at their work. When a group began hauling on a line and no song was started, some sailor would be sure to call out, "Give 'er lip, give 'er lip!" A good chantey was much more effective than the mate's calling out, "Heave-ho," "Yo-hee," "Head up, asses down," and other such phrases.

Chanteying became less and less frequent along in the 1880s. Then, schooners began to feel competition from steamboats and their crews were reduced and the men worked harder in an attempt to continue making profits. Captain Clark concluded that "as long as the men had pride in their vessels and in their work, they showed it in their chanteys."

TONAWANDA, NEW YORK, AUGUST 27, 1933

I found Phillip Prue in the Star Hotel where he is owner and manager. He is a slender, active Frenchmen, now about seventy. As a young man in the early 1870s, he sailed a number of seasons on Lakes schooners out of Buffalo, and then about 1880 "became interested in a variety show" in Tonawanda. He catered especially to sailors and canalmen. He said that his establishment would seat about five hundred people and had a bar of "considerable size—but only for refreshments," and "some side rooms for other entertainment."

He explained that he "booked only the best stuff from New York" including singing and dancing acts, contortionists, impersonators, stuntmen, short plays, and the like. Many of the performers, when requested and given written copy, would sing sailor songs, and sometimes a sailor with a few drinks in him would get up on stage and sing. The audiences would applaud or hiss, depending on how good he was, "and some of them sailors was pretty damn good and would get a big hand."

One of the best drawing cards, he said, was a real "bare-fist fight on the stage with no holds barred" between a couple of husky sailors or canalmen, or one of each. The men would fight for free drinks and to find out which was "the best man." If these fights were advertised a little, they would fill the house. "This type of entertainment was, of course, against the law, but if a cop came along, I'd slip him a five and he wouldn't see a thing, and if a real nosey one appeared, we were only having sparring matches."

Mr. Prue added that there were a number of variety shows, or what the sailors called free-and-easy shows, along Canal Street in Buffalo, "but not as big as mine." There was no charge for admission and the patrons could stay as long as they wanted. "We made our money off the refreshments and special entertainments."

BUFFALO, NEW YORK, AUGUST 28, 1933

On returning from Tonawanda last evening, a slight knock became noticeable from one of the connecting rods in the car and this morning it was still there, so I went to a garage prepared for all day without a car and a corresponding bill. The manager of the garage said a rod "was out" and would have to be replaced at once, or, etc. He said he'd try to keep the bill under fifteen dollars. I decided to go to the post office with the car before leaving it and got a card from Mother and Lynn saying they were in Buffalo and had arrived on the morning boat from Detroit. I was expecting them tomorrow, so did not meet today's boat. After considerable chasing about I finally found them here at my room—a meeting worth a million. No more work in the morning.

In the afternoon, we went to a movie: *Tugboat Annie*. I spent the early evening in the Grosvenor Library. Mrs. Mott, who is in charge of music, had been looking through its collection of songs and found nothing of this kind. Lynn amused himself with some books and Milly and I looked through some more material, but no findings.

Later in the evening, I called at the home of Captain James Todd, who is about seventy-five. He is much interested, but could not get away until about 9 p.m. He said that most of his time in sailing vessels was as an officer and captain and that he never sang much with the men—couldn't sing, anyhow. He said he'd heard hundreds of songs, but never paid much attention to them. Singing was the most common means of entertainment. He asked if I had seen any of the

The lighthouse at Buffalo. (From *Picturesque America*)

advertising sheets put out by "Dave and Mose," two Jewish merchants who had a store at the foot of Main Street in the early 1870s and catered to the sailor trade with oilskins, boots, clothing, etc. They would circulate these sheets for advertising, each having several sailor songs printed on it and their own announcements. They circulated these among sailors for years until they were stopped by city authorities when they put out some smutty ones. He has not seen any of them for about forty years.

He told of going down Lake Superior on the schooner *Thomas Brown* and the men seeing a "ghost ship" sailing along in sections and their telling of various dire things that were about to happen. It turned out to be a mirage and later the vessel was seen to "come together" and be quite natural. He said that another time about a hundred miles from Chicago, they could see the city very clearly, floating some distance above the horizon. They could even see boats in the harbor and many buildings they recognized. I called at the home of Captain Moses Boggan, about seventy, who lives a block away. He sailed with Captain Todd before the mast for many seasons. He is not very well and could add nothing. Milly and Lynn were waiting in the car telling stories.

BUFFALO, NEW YORK, AUGUST 29, 1933

Began the day's proceedings at the Buffalo Public Library on the trail of Dave and

Mose sheets, but could get no trace of any. Then went to the Grosvenor Library with the same results. Mrs. Mott got out the folder containing some Erie Canal stanzas which were sent in, in response to some publicity given Alan Lomax's search for canal songs when he was here in the spring. I already had most of them, although some were different.

In the evening, I went to see Captain Thomas Hylant, seventy. He, too, had sailed with Captain Todd. Until retiring a year ago, he sailed the harbor fireboat. He was on her at the time of the great harbor fire when a wooden tanker caught fire and burning oil spread over the water and, in spite of their efforts, reached a big freighter loaded with naphtha and gasoline. It exploded and set fire to all surrounding boats and buildings.

He is very friendly and quite anxious to help. He knows parts of some of the songs I have. For several seasons, he was with a crew that did much singing of "all sorts of songs." He told of singing chanteys to "all work where it was 'all hands.'" He mentioned "Shenandoah," "Lowlands," "Santa Anna," "Sally Brown," and some more. He said "The *Dreadnaught*" was a good capstan chantey, and that "Marching through Georgia" was about the best one there was. Also mentioned that "Good Bye, My Lover, Good Bye," was a favorite for setting light sails. He had verses about all sorts of local things and work. When I asked about Dave and Mose pamphlets, he said that as a small boy he used to get twenty-five cents a day for taking bundles of them out to newly arrived vessels. He knows of the existence of none now. He said he never thought that anybody would ever want them.

Hylant said "tall stories" were told to him and some other boys on their first trip to Lake Superior. An old shellback told them of a great sea serpent that stayed around the Apostle Islands in western Lake Superior. It would put its head and neck up out of the water and pick men off the deck or rigging and they'd never be heard of again. Hylant said the boys were so scared they'd rarely go on deck all through there. He said there were many stories of this kind.

Dunkirk, New York, August 30, 1933

Departed the city of Buffalo this morning. I had expected to find many old sailors there and much lore, but it seems I was about twenty to thirty years too late. There seems to have been a large amount of both in the last quarter of the last century, but it's about all gone, now.

E. A. Baker, a former schooner sailor and commercial fisherman, said he began sailing on Lakes schooners out of Ashtabula, Ohio, in the 1860s, and continued for thirty years until sailing vessels became too scarce to depend on. He then worked a couple of seasons on steamboats but, not liking it, he took up commercial fishing out of Dunkirk, and he and his sons still operate the business. He added, "[F]ishing now isn't near as good as it used to be. We get much better prices for our fish, but Lake Erie is about fished out."

When asked to identify some of the song fragments I have collected, he brightened up saying, "That brings back the days," and he broke into the opening stanza and chorus about the schooner *Bigler*, and, following that, sang some couplets and choruses of several chanteys. He said he'd "been in company with" the *Bigler* many times on the Lakes. "She was a blunt-nosed old canaller that everything on the Lakes could leave astern." He added that she usually carried squared timbers from the Upper Lakes down to Kingston, but at times brought down grain from Chicago or Milwaukee. He said he had known the song about her and many others most of his life, but hadn't thought seriously about them for forty years or more. He added that a few years ago he wrote out, on request, and sent a copy of "The *Persian*'s Crew" to *Sea Stories* magazine. He also said that lines of some songs he had learned while on old schooners came back to him while he was at the wheel of their fish tug or sitting at home. He was able to recall a song called "The Michigan Girls" and a few stanzas of an ocean song about "The *Three Bells*," which tells of the heroic action of the crew as the vessel foundered in the Atlantic. He later found the entire song in a scrapbook kept by his wife. When questioned about the nature of sailor life on the early schooners, he said that "there was no harder work in the world than that on the old windjammers, and I swore off many times, but always went back. There's nothing in this world like being to leeward of a big sailboat as her canvas is filling and she's beginning to move off from her anchorage and the crew is still bellowing some old song as they set the last of the sails. And when aboard and far out from shore, there's nothing like the sound of the wind whistling through the riggin' with the masts and spars creaking and the big seas pounding the weather bow as the vessel drives along with a good breeze."

He recognized a stanza I have of an old chantey beginning, "The rats have left her . . ." and the song, "The tug towed us out and dropped us in a gale."

He told of coming down Lake Erie one night in late season when the weather had been squally and thick most of the afternoon and evening. "And that night it was so dark you couldn't tell whether your eyes were open or shut, and suddenly the whole vessel was lighted up. I glanced upward and saw the full moon shining through a hole in the clouds. It lasted only a few minutes, but during that time there was the prettiest lunar bow I've ever seen and then, as suddenly, everything became as black as before." He said that some members of the crew were much worried and said that the sudden light was a sign that they were all soon to be lost. Many sailors, he continued, are prone to consider any unusual occurrence as a sign of approaching disaster.

In response to a question about weather signs, he at once recalled a dozen or more and added that the old schoonermen had at least a hundred more, "and they were surprisingly dependable."

Ashtabula, Ohio, September 4, 1933

Decided Labor Day was a good day to begin laboring again, so I started out from Franklin, Pennsylvania. Milly and Lynn took a bus for Ann Arbor from Conneaut, Ohio. I was somewhat lonesome the remainder of the day and noticeably so tonight.

I stopped at the farm home of Captain Adams just east of Ashtabula and found him quite willing to take time off to talk sailing. He said he was born in Boston and, in his early teens and against the wishes of his family, shipped on a big square-rigger bound around Cape Horn. He "rounded the Horn" four more times and said he visited about every country in the world. He said that on one trip on the Pacific, he and a friend got fed up with the officers and ship they were on, and when the ship laid over in San Francisco to discharge some cargo, they left. His friends had earlier sailed on the Great Lakes and said that wages and living conditions were pretty good there. "So, with a couple months' pay in our pockets, we set out for Chicago by stage, railroad, and even walked part of the way, and finally made it." That was in 1880, when he was twenty-two. "We shipped on a grain carrier out of Chicago the next day, and got a dollar a day. That looked pretty good to us after getting only about fifty cents a day on ocean vessels. We also found that on the Lakes in the late season both the wages and bad weather about doubled." He said that they "took it easy" in shore boardinghouses during the closed season and then shipped out again on the first vessels in the spring. "During my third season I got a berth as mate, and five years later became a captain, and never went back to salt water."

He sailed the Lakes for eighteen seasons, mostly in the grain and ore trades. As the steamboats increased in number and size and took traffic away from the schooners, he said, it became more and more difficult to get a decent schooner. So, on one occasion when he brought a cargo of ore down from Escanaba, Michigan, to Ashtabula, Ohio, and got a chance to buy this farm cheap, he took it and has been here ever since. "That was thirty-three years ago. . . . Farm life looks real good to a sailor, particularly in cold, wet weather, but it's pretty tame."

He said that there wasn't much "real chanteying" on the Lakes, at least in the vessels he was on. "There wasn't enough men in the crews, and the officers were generally in too much of a hurry. Also, in my last years, not many of the sailors knew the old songs, and that was quite unfortunate. . . . Chanteying puts life into a crew, and a man can pull twice as much to a good song and not even know he's working." He still remembers parts of some of the chanteys he learned on salt water, "and that was a long time ago."

Captain Adams said he never lost a vessel, but came close to it on one of his last trips. He was in charge of a barge being towed by a steamboat in late November, bound for Manitowoc, Wisconsin. "We were heavily loaded with railroad iron and machinery and, when halfway across northern Lake Michigan, we ran into a northwest blizzard with snow and freezing temperatures. As the quartering seas increased, the old barge rolled more and more until I was afraid she would capsize. We had spread some canvas on the fore and mizzen masts—the mainm'st had been taken out when she was cut down into a barge—and that eased her some, but I had to signal the steamboat to head up into the wind.

"Darkness came on early and we lost sight of the steamboat, but the cable held. Spray came over the bow from the big seas and the barge became covered with a thick coat of ice and settled lower and lower until the deck amidships was almost awash and most of the scuppers plugged. We had only six men forward, including the cook. I had the wheel, and had all hands chopping ice under the direction of the mate. He came aft and reported that they couldn't keep the scuppers open and the water was washing back and forth across the deck and ice was making faster than they could chop it loose. I told him to chop the goddamn bulwarks down if necessary and get the water off the deck. When he returned to the men, half of them refused to work any longer as they were all going to be lost anyhow. All hands had been on deck since mid-afternoon and had had no food and all were soaked from head to foot and their clothing frozen stiff. I learned later that the mate grabbed a capstan bar and threatened to brain any man who stopped chopping ice, and they chopped.

"Along about midnight, the wind slackened and the seas decreased some, but we were so low in the water the steamboat could make but little headway. When daylight came and the skies cleared, we could see the dim shoreline and it was a most welcome sight. We made the harbor at Manitowoc shortly after noon, and as soon as we got tied up, every man in the crew quit, and I felt like doing the same.

"The captain of the steamboat told me that he had all the deckhands and some of the engine crew fighting ice most of the night. Some of the crew wanted to cut the cable and free the steamboat from the barge so she could make harbor and safety. He armed the second mate with a good axe and told him to guard the towpost [where the line to the barge was attached] and to allow no one near it. He also chopped ice most of the night, but always kept himself between the crew and the towpost."

Painesville, Ohio, September 5, 1933

At Fairport—the harbor for Painesville—I visited Captain Rasmussen, seventy-five, who came to the Lakes in 1878, after sailing out of Copenhagen, Denmark, in an ocean vessel for several years. In 1882, he was quartermaster on the *U.S.S. Michigan,* then back on the ocean and again back on the Lakes in the Coast Guard Service. He was pensioned off sometime back. He said that when he first came to the Lakes there was much singing by the sailors, particularly when weighing anchor and making sail. On the *Michigan,* the men always chanteyed when weighing anchor. They used six bars on the capstan with three men on a bar. [The bars radiated from the capstan like spokes from a hub.] Dick Elliott, a small man and loud, was chanteyman. He could play several instruments. All the men joined in on the chorus. Captain Rasmussen can recall only hazily the words of a few. One was: "Yo-heave-ho and a bottle of rum." Another was, "So early in the morning." He thinks there was a third: "Roll, old *Michigan,* roll." The *Michigan* carried three masts and used sails whenever there was a wind. He said sailors were kept busy and out of mischief making and taking in sails. She was a side-wheeler, the first all-steel boat ever built. She now is in Misery Bay at Erie, Pennsylvania.

Captain F. W. Elliott was sitting in the Great Lakes Towing Co. shack at the mouth of the harbor when I called in the late afternoon. His tug, the *Ohio,* was tied up nearby. He was somewhat gruff when first approached, but thawed out completely when asked about early sailing on the Lakes, and particularly about sailor songs. Mention of the song about the old schooner *Bigler* practically always brings results, and it did not fail here. He thought about it a minute or so and then leaned back, shut his eyes, and sang eight stanzas without a break. He stated that he had sailed eight or ten seasons in the old windjammers before he began tugging in 1880, "and had not missed a season since." Captain Elliott insisted that I go with him to his home and Mrs. Elliott became interested at once. Knowingly, she said, "Now, you're going to have trouble stopping him. He used to sing our babies to sleep with those songs years ago." He then asked if I knew the song about the "Loss of the *Persian*" and, without waiting for a reply, sang it complete. He also mentioned a song about the steamer *Lady Elgin,* but couldn't recall any of it. Then followed a few stanzas about the Cleveland schooner the *Fayette Brown* and lines from several he said he had learned from his father including "White Wings" and "The Maid of Mohee." He then asked if I would like to hear an original song and, again without waiting for a reply, sang several stanzas and choruses of "The Mont Line":

> Come gather 'round me lads, and I'll sing you a little song
> Of a barge trip up the Lakes, and I'll not detain you long.
> Oh, maybe you don't believe me, lads, and maybe you think I lie,
> But ship in this starvation tow and you'll see the same as I.
>
> There's one Mont, two Monts, four Monts in a row,
> And you come to the old *Republic,* the end of the rotten tow.
> We dragged up both the rivers, 'twas all the tug could take,
> And then we passed Port Huron and were out upon the lake.
>
> And when upon Lake Huron, the wind came steady and strong,
> We spread our wings into the wind, and the *Niagara* forged along.
> We crawled up the St. Mary's and finally reached the lock,
> And then upon Superior, our tubs began to rock.
>
> And when we got to Houghton, near nine o'clock one night,
> The men put up a hell of a kick and damn near had a fight.
> 'Twas all about our shoveling dirt, we wanted some extra pay,
> The Old Man said, "You can go to hell! I'll pay you off today."
>
> We spent our dough at all the bars, and then in port there came
> Another vessel from below, and we shipped right out again.

Captain Elliott explained that he once sailed before the mast in the barge *Montmorency* with four other men forward and a captain named Black, his wife as cook and the mate aft. Captain Elliott said the *Montmorency* was one of a line of old canal schooners including the *Montcalm, Montpelier,* and *Monticello* that M. F. Merrick of Detroit bought cheap down on Lake Ontario, "but whatever he paid, it was too much. He made barges out of them and towed them behind his tug, the *Niagara*, with another barge, the *Republic*, hauling coal up to the copper smelters at Houghton, Michigan, and the copper pigs from there and iron ore from Marquette, Michigan, on the down trip to Lake Erie ports." He added that "Merrick made lots of money out of them old barges, but starved his men in doing it."

Referring to the song, Captain Elliott said the barges were "old and leaky and kept the men at the pumps most of the time," and the cook was too fat and lazy to prepare decent meals. He added that slow towing behind a tug was not very exciting, at best. He said that one day "while draggin' along up Lake Huron and everybody grumbling, someone suggested that we ought to get up a song, and all agreed, but no one could think up an opening line. A little later, I happened to glance astern and saw the whole parade of the old Monts wallowing slowly along and the line, 'There's one Mont, two Monts, four Monts in a row,' just popped into my mind. The other men thought it was pretty good and one said we ought to include "the old *Republic*," which was the end of the tow, and someone then thought up a second line that rhymed with the first. I went below and found some paper and a pencil and wrote down both lines. Some time later I happened to hear one of the men singing to himself the chorus of some song beginning, "Oh, maybe you don't believe me lads, and maybe you think I lie," and two more that rhymed with them soon came to me, and I wrote them down and the men thought they made a pretty damn good chorus. Well, after that we just added lines that fit as anyone thought them up, and by the time we got out on Lake Superior, we had a song that we thought was pretty damn good. We sang it a number of times on that trip when we was sure the captain and cook could hear us, but it didn't do any good. We then sang it in a Houghton saloon and the crews of the other barges took it up. We also got free drinks for singing it in other Lakes ports. Later, I heard sailors off other vessels sing it. . . . We also made up other songs, but I guess I've forgotten them."

Captain Elliott said that men on tugs seldom sang and he never heard of any of them making up a song. The work on a tug is quite regular and much easier than on the old sailboats, "but I'd much rather be on the deck of an old windjammer any day. There's nothing on God's earth as pretty as a sailing vessel on a good breeze with everything filled."

Charles Ellsworth was in bed, not very well and very deaf, so I didn't stay long. When I asked Mrs. Ellsworth if she'd ever heard him sing these songs or say anything about them, she said that she hadn't and added that she didn't know him very well, as she was his second wife and had been married to him for only about thirty years.

Painesville and Cleveland, Ohio, September 6, 1933

I drove to the farmhouse of Captain Henry Ingraham, seventy-nine. He had gone to Painesville for some groceries and "would be right back." He arrived two hours later. He is about five foot four, thin and has heavy white hair. He began sailing at fifteen on his father's schooner and had his master's papers in his early twenties. He sailed many schooners and then went into steamboats. He lost the schooner *Zach Chandler* on the beach fourteen miles east of Cleveland in a late October gale in 1892. The crewmen took to the rigging and were taken off by the U.S. Lifesaving Service eighteen hours later.

Ingraham said there was much sailor singing at the time, especially when ashore. Asked if I'd seen any of the pamphlets circulated by Dave and Mose of Buffalo. He said there were some good songs on them.   Ingraham said his father could foretell weather very accurately. He "always knew where to go on the Lakes to get good wind and avoid bad storms." Ingraham said that one time he was heading up to Duluth, Minnesota, on one steamer while his father was on another. The captain of Ingraham's depended entirely on his barometer. After passing Whitefish Point, Michigan, in Lake Superior, his father took the longer, north-shore route, but the captain of the boat the son was on headed on its regular course through the middle of Lake Superior. When abreast of Keweenaw, Michigan, a gale had developed, which they could not make headway in, so they put in back under the point for protection. They had to lay there for three days. When going on the following day, they met his father returning from Duluth. Ingraham said his father had seen a "bad sunset" and took the northern route.

Ingraham said he always carried a barometer, but also relied on various signs that he had learned were dependable:

> If the sun rises clear and soon goes under clouds and stays there, a storm is on the way. If it comes out in a short time, expect good weather.

> If stars seem very bright and close, there'll be high winds soon.

> A bright, yellowish sunset means winds.

> Sundogs indicate the direction of an approaching storm.

> A red sunset means good weather.

Sailors were a superstitious lot. Anything that didn't go right would start some of them off prophesying "something's going to happen." Ingraham has seen many boats waiting over Friday to begin the season. He told of being up on Lake Superior once when one of his men swore that a big gull flying near him at the bow of the vessel called his name and he recognized the voice of a sailor friend who was lost on the Lakes a few years before. Ingraham explained that some thought that gulls had the souls of drowned sailors.

CLEVELAND, OHIO, SEPTEMBER 11, 1933

Captain William Summerville appears to be over eighty and said he was blind and otherwise in bad condition, but he is full of all sorts of songs and such material. He recalls hearing sailors chantey when bringing the tow rope in and doing other

Mouth of the Cuyahoga River at Cleveland. (From *Picturesque America*)

group work. The mate usually led, he said, but at times a good singer in the crew did. Songs were "about anything" and he could not recall any lines or subjects. He remembers amusement songs, as well.

He said men before the mast usually shipped for one trip and were paid off when the boat tied up—"union regulations." "They were a queer lot, and all superstitious," Captain Summerville said. He told of crews getting off if someone, while battening down, dropped into the hold a hatch cover or "strong back"—a hatch support. That would bring bad luck. It was bad to ship with a cross-eyed man, women, cats, etc.

The fo'c'sle was usually "a pretty rotten hole," often called the "dogs' hole." Men did not stay long enough aboard to want to keep it clean; they left that for the next fellow. The deck above would leak at the towing post, and the room was always damp. The straw mattresses—"donkey's breakfast"—usually were foul and lousy. Boots and socks kept the air pretty bad. Sailors usually slept with their clothes on. The room was heated by a small stove and lighted by oil lamps. Officers frequently stayed on one boat for a season, and the mate usually was "the best man" aboard and often enforced discipline with his fists. Captain Summerville had heard often of men being shanghaied, carried aboard drunk when help was scarce. They were paid from one dollar to five dollars a day, depending on the season.

Lake Erie schooners usually carried coal and package freight up and grain, meat, and ore down.

Evening, and a midnight steak roast on the beach.

Cleveland, Ohio, September 13, 1933

It's after midnight again. These are long days. I planned to work in the library and then come back here, but I wandered and went to the auditorium to a performance of the opera *Cavalleria Rusticana* followed by *Pagliacci,* and a grand affair it was. It somewhat balanced the empty day. This hunting people who aren't where the book says they are is wearing me down.

Captain Dan Henderson, who is over seventy-five, began as a boy on his father's boats and recalls tarring his hands so he'd "look like a sailor." He says that working on the old schooners was a dog's life, but he always liked it. He liked to hear the men sing as they made sail. Chanteying was very common, especially on the larger boats. A good chanteyman was often paid more than other men in the crew. He mentioned a song, "The Barque *Mary Jane,*" but does not recall the words. He says the boat was Canadian. He recalls hearing men sing in the saloon, but never joined those crowds, as he couldn't sing, and buying treats took too much money. He said his father had a high-top silk hat, the prize for bringing the first boat into Toledo one season. Living in the fo'c'sle was pretty bad on practically all of the Lakes schooners. Fresh straw was put in mattresses in the spring, and then neither it nor the blankets were cleaned until fall.

Many sailors were queer about their beliefs. He has seen men and sometimes the entire crew get off and nobody else knew why. Someone had seen or heard something. Many believed that seagulls had the souls of lost sailors and had strange powers. Sailors would not injure them. Fighting among sailors was quite common along the waterfront and "getting licked" was no disgrace, but running or "being yellow" was. Much of the discipline aboard ship was enforced by the brute strength of the officers, particularly the mate. Some boats carried a crew all year, and these were often "hometown boys," but most shipped a new crew each trip.

Late in the day, I went out to see Mr. Silas Hunter, seventy-five, who conducts a marine engineers school. He spent all his sailing days as a steamboat engineer, and then twenty-five years as a boiler inspector in the Cleveland district.

He is a peculiar old duck. I never felt so much like choking anyone before in a long time. It takes him ages to tell an incident, and when he gets to the point—there isn't any. He continually wanders off on all sorts of side trails. Mr. Harrison of the Lake Carriers said to ask him about his song, "The *Onoko,*" so I did. Hunter proceeded to tell how it wasn't much, but how all his friends thought it very wonderful. He said he'd written fourteen, but doesn't think he'll let anyone have any of them, as they don't amount to much, but still all who have heard them think they're fine.

Men and a woman sit or work on these canal boats photographed in Cleveland Harbor about 1870. (Courtesy Dossin Great Lakes Museum)

CLEVELAND, OHIO, SEPTEMBER 15, 1933

Captain C. D. Secord, manager of Ohio Tankers, Inc., began his sailing as a common sailor of the old schooners in the early 1870s. After a few seasons, however, he saw that the steamboats were taking over the best traffic and transferred to them. He soon became second mate, then mate, and finally master, and sailed the Lakes until his work required him to stay ashore. He recalled with evident pleasure the crews aboard sailing vessels singing chanteys when working the capstan, windlass, or when hauling on the halyards. He could recall only about a half dozen stanzas of "Leave 'er, bullies, leave 'er," which he said they used at the pumps, especially when emptying a vessel at the end of a trip before getting paid off. It enabled the men to express their feelings about the trip with no fear of reprisals by the officers.

Captain Secord said that he was mate for a number of seasons on steamboats owned by Eber Brock Ward of Detroit's company and used in carrying copper "pigs" [crude, oblong bars cast directly from the smelter] from Houghton and Hancock at the foot of the Keweenaw Peninsula in Lake Superior down to Detroit and Lake Erie ports. At times, they carried coal up to the smelters, but more often had package freight or went up light. They used only Negro deckhands and would ship about twenty big, husky men at Detroit on the upbound trip at about fifty cents a day, and they would eat, "shoot craps," and sleep most of the trip. Their only work was in preparing the hold for loading. Once loading began, they would stop only half hours for each meal, day and night, until the vessel was loaded with six hundred to eight hundred tons of copper pigs from the local smelters. That usually required from forty-eight to sixty hours.

The copper was brought aboard on hand trucks, which the Negroes pushed before them as they walked along in a loose circle between the storage yard and the boat. During the first few hours of loading, the men did much wisecracking and horsing around. Then, someone would start up a familiar song of the capstan chantey type, and they'd keep it going as long as any of them could think up new lines, or until someone began a new song. Sometimes they'd sing familiar marching songs such as "Marching through Georgia," but to these they'd take a step on every second beat. "You couldn't hurry them much."

During the second day of continuous loading, he said, the men wouldn't feel much like singing. So, the mate in charge would pick one who could play some instrument, preferably a banjo—they always seemed to have one—and place him over the main loading gangway and have him play some lively tunes. Then, some other player would take over. "A good rhythm would bring the copper aboard." The two mates "bossed the job" watch on and watch off, that is, four hours on duty and four hours off. They were responsible for keeping the truckers working and the load evenly distributed. Sometimes, the captain would also assist, particularly near the end of loading when the men might slow down and get careless.

Captain Secord recalled one trip when, for some reason, the captain wanted to get an early start, but as daylight began to appear, they still had about fifty tons to go and the Negroes were pretty well worked out. One, as he shuffled along the gangway where the mate was standing, said, "Mister Mate, we all needs some suds." The captain agreed and sent the second mate downtown to get a couple gallons of cheap whisky. The two mates then borrowed a tub and a tin dipper from the ship's cook. They also borrowed a package of hot pepper and mixed it into the whisky and then cut the mixture about two to one with water. "The tub was soon empty, but how the copper came aboard!" After they had finished loading, the cook gave the deckhands a hot meal and they all went forward and flopped with their clothes and shoes still on, "and we didn't see a damn one of them for two days.

"When the vessel was approaching the Soo Locks, a big Negro named Dick came up and said, 'Mister Mate, what was in dat tub we drink las' night?' An' I answered, 'Dick, you didn't have anything to drink last night, that was the night before, and what you drank is called the elixir of life.'

"Dick replied: 'Well, Mister Mate, dat may be de 'lixer o' life for white men, but it sure ain't no 'lixer for black men.'"

There was a letter here for me when I got back. The dean says he'd "appreciate" my being back to Ann Arbor to assist in enrolling next Friday morning. That cuts two days off.

CLEVELAND, OHIO, SEPTEMBER 16, 1933

Lafayette Stough was alone at home when I called. He is a slender, active, wiry man with thick gray hair, and apparently is in good physical health. His wife was buried two weeks earlier, and he seems to be quite lost. He found it difficult to keep his attention on any one subject very long.

He was born in 1844 and was sailing on the Lakes when the Civil War broke out. He immediately enlisted in the military service. After a brief training period, he was assigned to guard duty and mending tents at the Union prisoner-of-war camp on Johnson's Island in western Lake Erie. He said that the guards, armed with rifles, watched the compound from a high walk on the outside and near the top of a thick plank fence. They could never keep warm in winter or cool in summer, and he didn't like herding human beings within a fence, anyhow. After many months of trying, he finally got transferred to the Navy and was assigned to a gunboat on the Ohio River, where he still was when the war came to an end. After being discharged from the Navy, he returned to the Lakes, got a job on one of the Bradley Transportation Company's ore schooners out of Cleveland and, as common sailor, mate, and then master, continued sailing for Bradley until the old schooners became scarce. He then retired ashore.

CLEVELAND, OHIO, SEPTEMBER 17, 1933

Captain William R. Dunn said he began sailing out of Cleveland in 1875 when fifteen years old, and after many seasons in sail, changed to steamboats. "Life aboard the old schooners was a dog's life. In fact, no one now would make a dog live in the quarters we had, nor eat the food we ate. And often we had only snatches of sleep day after day during bad weather. But, by God, I'd do it again if I had the chance! A vessel under canvas is alive—you'd feel it, an' how we'd drive 'em! But them damn steamboats are just lifeless machines with no personality." He explained that work aboard the steam-powered vessels was much easier, more regular, usually had shorter hours, and the quarters cleaner and more comfortable than in the old schooners, "but a good spread of canvas gives a vessel an appeal that no steamboat ever had."

Lakes sailors, he explained, knew to take advantage of the prevailing winds. When coming down Lake Michigan from Chicago with a good west or northwest wind, they would carry sail until the lee bulwarks were full of water and the masts and spars were groaning with the strain. "No vessel wants others to pass them, and we'd carry everything until some canvas or some sticks [spars] blew out, and we'd have to slow down for repairs. Often we'd get a good slant [a wind over the side that did not require tacking] all the way down Lake Michigan to the Straits [of Mackinac]. A southwest wind would always veer to the west and northwest, and schooner captains would try to get far enough down the Lake to take advantage of a fair wind [one over the stern] through the Straits. Sometimes, the wind would veer all the way around to the northeast and we'd have to make a couple of legs to get through, but then we'd have a fair wind down Lake Huron."

Sometimes, when in northern Lake Michigan and particularly anxious to make good time, they would cut in on the east side of the shoals at the end of "the Shanks" [Waugoshance Point] and use the centerboard of the schooner for a lead line to measure the depth of the water. It was so shallow there, the centerboard would often stir up mud from the bottom. "You had to really know the area to do that and not run aground." Captain Dunn said he had been on schooners that logged better than twenty miles per hour the length of Lake Michigan, and added that the record time for a sailing vessel from Chicago to Buffalo was three days and sixteen hours, but he had forgotten its name.

Lorain, Vermilion, Huron, and Sandusky, Ohio, September 19, 1933

Much seeking and little finding today. Called on James B. Lyons, about seventy-five, this morning and didn't get away for two hours. He sailed all the seven seas and the five Lakes. He sailed on ocean ships for four years and then came to the Lakes and went on schooners, then steamboats, and then, in 1898, back on the schooner *Our Son*, which he sailed for a season. She was three-masted with a square sail forward and quite fast. At the time she was lost in upper Lake Michigan in September 1930, he was sailing a big freighter twenty-one miles away. They picked up an S.O.S. from the steamer *William Nelson* and started for the *Our Son*, full speed, through big seas and fifty- to sixty-mile-per-hour winds. They kept in radio communication with the *Nelson*, which first reported she couldn't get the men off the schooner. When Captain Lyons was about halfway there, the *Nelson* reported it had the men and Captain Lyons put back over to the western shore in the storm and continued on to Chicago.

He spent one season with a captain who would never shorten sail until something was about to happen. One time, after being windbound in Buffalo, about twenty schooners towed out of Buffalo harbor and his was about last, starting after the leaders were several miles out. The captain said he'd beat them all to the river, so they started beating up Lake Erie carrying all sails with the northwest wind increasing. Most of the others took in their topsails and reefed the main sails, but this captain left on everything and the schooner heeled over until the water came up on deck, halfway on the hatches, the lee sail about buried. Finally, she hauled over so far that the rudder would no longer take effect and they couldn't steer her and keep up in the wind. The captain then ordered the jibs and topsails taken in. They were so near rolling over that the men cut the sheets and let the jibs and topsails go, and then she slowly came up and hauled into the wind. The captain was "sore as hell" because they cut the sheets, but he was also

Lumber boats at Sandusky. (From *Picturesque America*)

somewhat scared, so they dropped the anchor, pumped out the hold, and rode out the gale the remainder of the night.

Mr. R. J. Blantern, about sixty-five, sailed on schooners and didn't like steamships. He said that boy stowaways were quite common on boats going to the upper Great Lakes. On one vessel where he was mate, he would take stowaways to the captain, who would say, "Well, son, hang your cap on the main truck [the top of the mainmast] and you can make yourself at home." Usually they'd try, but come down before reaching it. He remembers one boy, about eleven or twelve, who started up the 132-foot mast on the *Mont Blanc*. The captain saw that he "was game," and called for the boy to come down when he was only about halfway up, but the boy kept on going, and they all stood around breathless. The lad fastened his cap there and stayed up a while enjoying the show. When he came down, nothing on the boat was too good for him and he stayed as "boy" all season.

In Sandusky, I found Richard C. McKean, in his early sixties, who knew a lot of the superstitions I had heard and one that was new to me: putting silver under the mainmast step as it was being built to guarantee a profitable ship life.

McKean went with me to call on "Jerry" Nacy, late seventies, a former schooner sailor who retired as mate of the Marblehead Coast Guard Station after more than twenty years. He told of an incident in the 1880s when he was at the station and received a call from a schooner anchored off the peninsula a few miles west of the station. According to the story, the schooner cleared for Detroit with a captain, two sons, and a big Norwegian as crew.

When off Sandusky, the Norwegian drew a gun and shot the captain, who was at the wheel. The shot took his front teeth, some of his upper jaw and laid him out. The son who was mate came running aft and the Norwegian shot him a couple of times and put him unconscious, too. The second son, who was coming up from below, was shot in the arm and the back of the neck. Just then, the father began to come to and grappled with the Norwegian, which allowed the second son to get his father's gun, and he shot the Norwegian through the neck and flattened him on the deck. He then bound the unconscious Norwegian to the deck and with one limp arm sculled the yawl boat ashore and walked a mile to the Coast Guard station. They went out with a U.S. marshal and a doctor and sent word to a tug to go for the schooner. It brought them all in. The captain and his sons recovered, but the Norwegian died a month or so later in the county jail. Before he died, he told a friend that he had seen the captain draw $258 out of a Detroit bank before taking off and that he had considerable before that. He had planned to kill all three, launch the boat, take the money and disappear.

TOLEDO, OHIO, SEPTEMBER 21, 1933

Captain "Doc" R. B. Millard, day dispatcher for the Toledo office of the Great Lakes Towing Co., began his sailing career on schooners, but after a few seasons changed to tugs out of Toledo and on the Detroit and St. Clair Rivers. He has continued on them for over half a century.

He stated that in the early 1880s when he first began working on tugs,

This scene at Sandusky, Ohio, shows the variety of craft on the Great Lakes. At front left is a flat barge. At front center is a dredge, its shovel extending to the right. Next to that is a small harbor tug. It is just in front of the 134-foot *R. B. Hayes,* named for the U.S. president Rutherford B. Hayes. It was built as a side-wheel passenger excursion steamer at Sandusky in 1876 and ran out of that port to Fremont, Ohio, Cedar Point, and the islands in western Lake Erie. Before this photo was taken, its upper deck had been cut down and converted to carry freight. (Courtesy Dossin Great Lakes Museum)

there were plenty of sailing vessels to be towed the length of the rivers and in and out of Lake Erie harbors to keep them all profitably busy. By the end of the decade, the number and size of the tugs had increased and the number of sailing vessels had decreased as they lost more and more traffic to the newer and faster steamboats, and competition among the tugs became keener. Tug captains resorted to various methods to get tows before their competitors did. Competing lines watched each other day and night for any signs of inside information concerning approaching schooners, and would race each other for the tow. Some lines, knowing they were being watched, would at times send a tug out at top speed in the wrong direction to lure a watching tug away from a prospective tow and then, before the tricked tug could get back, they would send out another tug in the right direction.

At night, they would sometimes rig up some high running lights to stimulate those on a big steamboat to get past their watchful competitors, and in the daytime they would, when possible, secretly move out toward a tow screened from view by a passing steamboat.

Captain Millard said that he had a number of times heard tug captains boast of secretly chaining a competing tug, under cover of darkness, to a piling or to another tug to delay its getaway. They might also foul a competing tug's propeller with a length of tough hawser so that the tug could easily be outdistanced in the race for a tow.

In the 1890s, it became common practice for Detroit River tugs to cruise western Lake Erie as far down as Long Point, Ontario, looking for tows, and sometimes they would go all the way to the head of the Welland Canal or to Buffalo Harbor. On Lake Huron, they would frequently cruise as far up as Saginaw Bay and, if unsuccessful, go on to the mouth of the St. Mary's River or through the Straits of Mackinac into Lake Michigan.

On long pulls, the vessels being towed would usually spread some canvas, if the wind was right, and assist the tug. The tugs got paid only for taking the vessels through the rivers and Lake St. Clair between them. The rates, depending on the size of the vessels being towed, ranged from fifty dollars to one-hundred twenty-five dollars one way, he said.

Racing was almost universal among the Detroit River tugs, and the stakes were high. The larger tugs could tow up to eight and even ten schooners at a time, especially if the schooners carried some sail and assisted. Tugmen all were jealous of their reputation for speed and endurance, and for being skilled navigators, and they drove themselves to the limit. The larger tugs carried a captain, a mate, two engineers, two firemen, and a cook. The cook and the fireman not shoveling coal doubled as linesmen.

Frank Wigton, tugmaster with the Toledo office of the Great Lakes Towing Co., said he spent most of his time as a young boy on Great Lakes schooners and drew his first pay as a sailor in 1880 at the age of twelve. He continued on sailing vessels as common sailor, mate, and master until the old schooners became scarce, and he then changed to tugs. He can still recall vividly many of the big, fast schooners of the time and among them the *Annie M. Peterson*, the *Moonlight*, the *J. M. Hutchinson*, the *Erastus Corning*, the *Porter*, the *Saveland*, and the *Hunter Savage*.

The *Peterson*, he said, was reported to be the fastest schooner in the grain-carrying fleet. Her skipper-owner, Captain Peterson, named his vessel after his only daughter, and would carry only clean cargoes: grain, hard coal, and miscellaneous freight, but no ore or soft coal. The schooner was relatively narrow, with clipper lines, and a capacity of 1,200 tons. She carried an extra large spread of canvas on her three masts, and her entire rigging and decks were always kept in the best of condition, and even her hold was painted white. He added that her cabin was finished with only choice wood and was richly finished. Finally, she carried a broom lashed to the main truck most of the time as a challenge to any other schooner that would like a trial of speed.

The *Hunter Savage*, he recalled, wasn't in a class with the big grain carriers, "but she was a beauty and fast." She was built much like a yacht, with two tall masts. The forward mast was square rigged, including a topgallant sail, and the other carried an extra-large fore 'n' aft mainsail and topsail. Her skipper-owner also kept her in top condition and usually had her decorated with flags and a long pennant streaming from her main topmast. She, too, was a good sailor and would race anything.

"Some of them old schooners, before they were sold by their original owners and had their mainmasts removed and also their mizzen topmasts and the vessels cut down to barges, was about the prettiest sight a man could ever wish to see. When they'd heel over in a good breeze—well, there was never anything like them on the Lakes before, and there never will be again."

Wigton said experienced sailors would amuse themselves by telling the "boys" on their first trips all sorts of wild stories and give them ludicrous errands such as taking a lunch to the captain when he was asleep in his cabin in the middle of his night watch below. He recalled an occasion when he was master of a schooner going up Lake Huron and came on deck at the beginning of the second watch [4–8 a.m.] just as dawn was breaking. He looked up and was able to make out the "boy" sitting out on the lee topsail yard looking intently down at the water. "When I asked him what the hell he was doing, he answered that he was 'the shark lookout.'" On a similar occasion, he found the "boy" up on the foreyard, half frozen, but faithfully "standing whale lookout" so he could warn the wheelsman of the approach of any big ones in time to avoid a collision and the loss of the vessel. Wigton added that on one of his first trips up the Lakes they were being towed past the Fort Gratiot Light at Port Huron, Michigan. He was told that the tower there marked the place where George Washington was buried after he and his party were attacked, scalped, and killed by Indians.

He stated that as far as he could recall, every schooner he had ever sailed in, and most of the tugs, had horseshoes nailed up over the cabin door, prongs up of course, so that the good luck could not run out. Most schooners also had at least one coin under the foot of the mainmast to ensure a profitable career, and he recalled a widespread practice among sailors on sailboats of tossing small coins over the stern of the vessel as it left port to ensure a profitable season or trip.

Many schooner sailors, he added, believed that a slight list to port—the mate's side—on towing out of port at the beginning of a trip was a good omen, but a list to starboard—the captain's side—was a bad omen.

He added that chanteying on Lakes vessels was about over when he began sailing, but occasionally, when some old-timers were in the crew, they would sing while working at the capstan or halyards. Most captains however, thought chanteying made the work too slow, and would discourage if not prohibit it.

Wigton said there were "lots of old songs about Lakes vessels around" when he first began sailing, but he cannot recall any of them now.

I drove to a couple of places late in the afternoon, but found nobody home, so headed north for Ann Arbor and arrived about 8 p.m. The end of this summer's journeying. Lynn came running down the street shouting and climbed on. Then, in the driveway and out came Peter.

Now, a few hundred letters and finis.

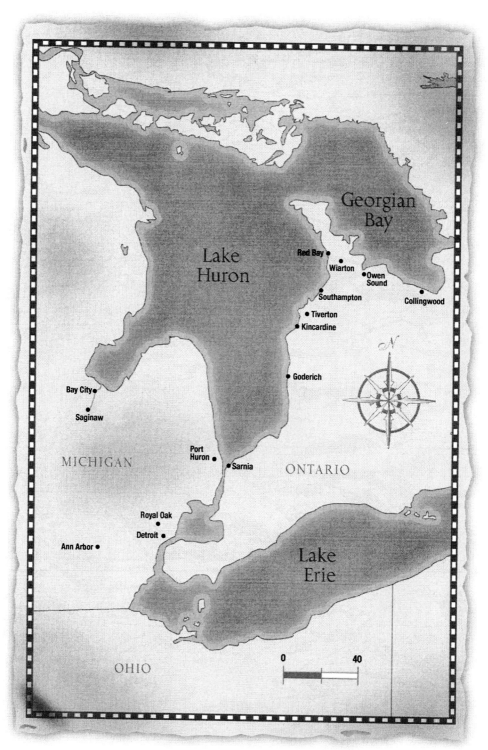

Map by F. S. Fluker.

CHAPTER 3

1934: Southern Lake Huron

> He sank beneath the deep blue sea,
> In life to rise no more,
> Where the wind and desolation sweep
> Lake Huron's rockbound shore.
> "The Ill-Fated *Persian*"

Springtime illness and a summertime class shortened the season for Walton in 1934. He had less than a month to interview people before he had to be back at the front of a classroom at the University of Michigan. He asked the university for $300 in research money, rather than the $500 he had requested the two previous summers. He conserved time by sticking close to home, mainly around the southern end of Lake Huron, revisiting sources he knew to be productive—and puzzling.

The longer Walton collected, the more sources a song acquired. In 1932, Captain W. A. Ashley of Milwaukee had credited authorship of "The Schooner *Bigler*" to a man named Cunningham of Port Colborne, Ontario. In 1933, another informant said that a man named Kelly had written the song. William Bangard of Picton, Ontario, said that a man named Clark wrote the song. William Head gave the full name as "Billy" Clark and added, "I once heard that he finally drank himself to death." When interviewed later that summer, Billy Clark himself—very much alive—claimed no such authorship. In 1934, Sylvester "Ves" Ray, of Port Huron, Michigan, said that his friend, William J. Small, had written "The *Bigler*." But Small said, no, it was "Singing Danny" Sullivan. Norman "Beachie" MacIvor, of the same neighborhood, said Jimmy Reid of Buffalo wrote the song.

Song authorship wasn't the only area in which Clark's history became muddled. Ray told how Clark had gotten into a brawl in Marquette, Michigan, was shot in the leg and crippled. "There's a song tells about it," Ray offered as proof. Later in 1934, John McCauley reported that Clark had been stabbed, not shot, and that it happened in Duluth, not Marquette, and that he had died from his injuries. Ray and McCauley might have both been recalling versions of "The Old Schooner *Africa*," for which Walton collected:

> We wallowed Lake Superior through,
> And then we reached Marquette
> Where Billy Clark, our singing friend,

By Charlie Turpin was shot.
The row was commenced by a sailor lad
And a man they called "The Moor."
But Clark to a hospital had to go,
And we left him there ashore.

This summer was to include a visit that, although its mention in his journal is slight, would begin a partnership. A. J. Fisher of Royal Oak, Michigan, had written to Walton after reading in the Oct. 8, 1933, *Detroit Free Press* about Walton's quest for marine lore. Fisher, a manufacturer of scale models and fittings, said that another man, Loudon Wilson, was "a commercial artist with an intense interest in the Great Lakes."

Walton visited on Sept. 7, 1934, and the two later agreed to collaborate on Walton's book. Each man had a vision. Walton's was to gather the songs of the Great Lakes sailors; Wilson's was to create an illustrated genealogy of the Great Lakes schooner. Wilson did a few sketches for Walton's song collection, including the one on the cover of this book, but neither man achieved his goal.

Sound technology was making waves in 1934, both on the air and in the news. The Detroit Symphony Orchestra chose Chicago's Century of Progress Exposition to become the nation's first broadcast symphony orchestra. Eleanor Roosevelt became known as the First Lady of Radio by using the airwaves to address the American public. Detroit auto manufacturers began offering cars with built-in radios. The advances in sound technology were not lost on Walton. On Aug. 3, 1934, he wrote to the Victor Talking-Machine Company in Camden, New Jersey, "I am writing to inquire if you have on hand or can build some sort of a portable sound-recording apparatus, preferably of suitcase size, that can be carried about in an automobile and used where there is no outside electric current available." RCA Victor wrote back about a conveniently portable model "contained in three carrying cases."

In another letter that day, Walton wrote to folklore pioneer John Lomax, noting that they had crossed each other's trails at Buffalo and the Erie Canal in 1933 and asking about reports that Lomax had made sound recordings of his informants. At the end of the summer, Walton returned to find Lomax's answer: "The sound recording machine I am using was bought for me by the Library of Congress, where all my records will eventually go, at a cost of about $450. It gets easily out of repair. In fact, we have had the machine largely built over on a new principle by the physics department of this university [the University of Texas]. Just now I am acting as Honorary Curator and Consultant in Folk Songs for the Library of Congress. We may soon be able to offer you the use of a machine in return for copies of your findings."

Walton would have a chance to work with the new machines, but it would be with another Lomax.

PORT HURON, MICHIGAN, AUGUST 21, 1934

Arrived today at noon from Mount Pleasant, Michigan [near Walton's birthplace of Rosebush]. Spent the afternoon and evening prospecting without very propitious results. And this is lonesome business!

William J. Small, of last year's acquaintance, didn't have much to add except a few names of prospects. He introduced me to an old shipbuilder who happened along, but there is no poetry in his makeup. Found Jim McCarty in a beer place. He is an Irishman of more than sixty autumns and has been on the Lakes all his years except a few at the beginning. He said there was lots of sailor singing both aboard and ashore when the schooners were around. A schooner would be making sail while towing up the rapids into Lake Huron and there could be heard chanteying almost any time of the day or night. Some of it "yo-ho-ho"-ing, but most of it halyard and windlass chanteys: "Paddy Doyle's Boots" was very common. A favorite anchor chantey was "Heave and Bust Her!"

Call the cook, the mate, the captain, too
    Heave and bust her!
Call 'em out, the whole damn crew
    Heave 'm up and bust her!

[This chantey describes how the crew would push the capstan around to pull up the anchor chain, drawing the boat up over the anchor where it could be broken free from the muddy bottom.]

Small said that "Singing Danny" Sullivan composed many songs about Lakes vessels. "He could stand up to a bar and after having a drink or two make up songs about any vessel you'd mention." Small said McCarty said Sullivan composed "The *Bigler*," "The *Persian*'s Crew," and many more. "Baldy," an ex-engineer who also drank my beer, had heard hundreds of songs during the 1880s when the schooner men were plentiful, but he "never knowed none."

I found Dan McDonald working on his houseboat at the foot of Broad Street. He is caulking and painting it for the winter. He is now in his late seventies and began sailing as a boy. There was no end of songs then, he said. "They've all gone away. I haven't sung or heard them in near forty years." He knows parts of "The *Bigler*" and recalls singing "When the Raging Seas Did Roar," as a chantey when making sail. Work was much easier when done to a song and they would use any song that had a good rhythm.

Sailors had to know all about weather then, as there were no government help in the early days. They sailed by dead reckoning and by checking the shore. He was with one captain who "shot the sun with a homemade horse's head [sextant] every day. He was religious and would not work at all on Sunday. The vessel entered a harbor at midnight Saturday and left Monday morning. If there was no harbor near, he would 'heave to.' However, he made just as good time as any skipper in the fleet."

He was in four wrecks and three burnings and spent three years in the Navy and six in the Merchant Marine. He got married and moved to a town in Illinois. He lived there three months and then "I couldn't stand it any longer and my wife wouldn't come back to the Lakes, so one day when downtown, I made all the property out to her, got myself an outfit and went home and told her I was going back on the Lakes and she could do as she pleased. She stayed and I came and I haven't been back since.

"Sailing was a damn slave's work, but a man once at it would always go back. Working on them freighters is not sailing; it's just a job. They have their courses all laid out like an automobile highway. They couldn't get lost if they wanted to. The real captain is back in some office. I never liked steamboating.

"It took several years to learn to sail. You had to know about weather. There were hundreds of weather signs that a sailor had to know: 'First the wind and then the rain, set your topsails out again.'"

There are many more boats on the Lakes this summer than last. While I was at Captain McDonald's residence, several ore carriers, about four package freighters, the *Tashmoo* and another passenger vessel, an Erie Canal oil tanker, two lumber carriers and one loaded high with pulpwood, and a half dozen fish tugs went by. The deep and slow whistle of the passing boats has a poetic character as heard from far off in the night.

PORT HURON, MICHIGAN, AUGUST 22, 1934

Much seeking and pumping today, but not many results worth shouting about. Looked up Captain Sylvester "Ves" Ray, eighty-four, this morning. I found him in his room in a garage at a home where he is taking care of the grounds. He is now pretty feeble minded and a little mixed up. He told me three times about getting his old-age pension. He couldn't recall any more songs than he gave me last July 11. He said there was a sailor named "Billy" Clark who was on several vessels with him and he could sing "hundreds of them old lake chanteys." Ray said Small composed "The *Bigler*," "The Red Iron Ore," "The Steamer *Alpena*," and many more. [These are the first five of eleven verses in Ray's version of "The Red Iron Ore."]

> Come listen young fellows who follow the Lakes,
> In iron ore vessels your living to make.
> I shipped in Chicago, bid adieu to the shore,
> Bound away to Escanaba for red iron ore.
>
> In the month of September, the seventeenth day,
> Two dollars and a quarter was all they would pay.
> And on that same day, the north branch did take
> The *E. C. Roberts* out into the lake.
>
> The wind from the sou'west sprang up a stiff breeze,
> And down through Lake Michigan the *Roberts* did sneeze,
> And away through Lake Michigan the *Roberts* did roar,
> And on Friday morning we passed through Death's Door.
>
> Across the mouth of Green Bay this packet did ride
> With the dark and deep water rolling over her side.
> We rounded Sand Point, and our anchors let go,
> We furled all our canvas, and then went below.

Next morning we hove in alongside the *Exile,*
And the *Roberts* made fast to an iron ore pile.
They let down their chutes, and like thunder did roar
As they emptied their pockets of red iron ore.

Ray said that on a trip to Marquette, Michigan, after ore they got in a brawl and Clark was shot in the leg and crippled. "There's a song tells about it." On some vessels, there was singing about every evening during the dogwatch. They often had some musical instruments aboard and sang anything they could think of, but mostly sailor songs.

Ray said they would tell all sorts of "damn lies" to the new hands: wild Indians from Manitoulin Island would come out to passing vessels, overpower the crew, tomahawk them, and sink the vessel. Spearfish on Lake Superior would drill their bottom planking and sink vessels. Schools of whitefish were often so big that a vessel would get held fast in them. They would leave the "boy" on lookout for them.

Called next on Captain Andrew Bonnah, who is older than seventy and aging very fast. Mr. Bonnah is seriously ill and not expected to live. He is quite worried and preoccupied. He was in tugs when wood was used as fuel. They picked it up at wood docks all along the river and took it to the harbor. Captains had to plan their trips and fuel so as not to run short. Bonnah sailed the tug *Fisher* for several seasons. He said it was two hundred feet long and had a forty-two-foot beam and "had every goddamn thing in her a tug could have. She was the best damn tug ever on these Lakes. Goddamn her, nothing could stop her. When I signaled the engineer to go ahead, by God, she went." She was "sold to the French government and taken across the Atlantic to France. I took her down to salt water and showed them Frenchmen how to handle her and then came back. By God, there was nothing could touch her on the Lakes."

He thinks the world's all going to mush now. Sailing isn't what it used to be. "It used to take real sailors to handle them boats, but now with all their government aids, any damn mechanic can do it. And ashore, you can't trust anybody, anymore."

Captain Andy wasn't in the mood for my stuff.

Port Huron and St. Clair, Michigan, August 23, 1934

Found Captain A. L. Grisdale at home. He was born at Port Robinson, Ontario, on the Welland Canal and spent all his life on tugs, first on the Welland and then on the Detroit and St. Clair Rivers, and then the Soo and all about the Lakes. He never heard any songs about tugs. He says tugmen were usually pretty close to land and didn't congregate much. There was some great racing.

The tug *Nyland* of Port Colborne, Ontario, put an American vessel on the beach at Buffalo, and the American owners got a judgment against her. Later, when the *Nyland* was in Buffalo, she was seized and a U.S. marshal put aboard. She was taken up the creek and tied up. After a few days, the tug captain started giving the marshal beer, and one evening when no one was aboard suggested they go to a nearby saloon for a drink. The tug captain had earlier paid the saloonkeeper to close up when they saw him coming with the marshal, and the saloonkeeper did. The captain and the marshal then went on a block to find another saloon with the same results and then to a third still farther away. There, they drank and were joined by some other men who insisted on treating—with as much delay as possible. Finally, the captain and the marshal started back to the tug. They met a woman and the captain said, "Did you see that dame give me the high sign? You go on to the tug and I'll be along later." So, the captain started back after the woman and, as soon as he was out of sight, he cut over toward the outer harbor and got aboard the *Nyland* at the appointed place and raced back to Canadian waters.

Back in St. Clair, I found William F. "Major" Leach, eighty-four, at his home. He said his brother Charles was now in very bad health and was in Detroit with his son. We went to the home of the other brother, George, and visited a while. He, too, is in bad health—high blood pressure. A damsel came and joined us shortly after we began to talk with "I hope I'm not butting in, . . ." and stayed as long as we did. One can't very well throw women out.

William and I drove downtown for some beer. He took up engineering after learning sailboats and still has an engineer's license. He told me about a mate sending green sailors to the engine room after the key to the keelson or a bucket of compass grease and how they'd load them up with the most cumbersome things they could carry. The crew would also have new men on the lookout for "dark light," pirates, whales, and other things of the kind.

Got back to Port Huron after the rooming places were closed, so I pulled into the driveway of a school building and rolled up in the backseat of the car. About 1 a.m. when I'd just gotten to sleep, three men came ducking around behind the building and had a quick conversation nearby and then hurried off across the street and between two houses. Shortly after, a cop came along on the trail and found me. With an "A-ha, I have you now!" expression, he proceeded to convince himself that I was three bad men. About 4 a.m., I was awakened by two cops banging on the car window and flashing a light in and it required about half an hour to convince them that I was harmless. Before they came, the neighborhood cats had put on a concert. I decided to give up on the sleeping and went downtown for some eats, but could find no place open, so drove out on the river side of Pine Grove Park and watched boats and early-morning fishermen a while. An 'ell of a night.

Goderich, Ontario, August 25, 1934

Found Norman "Beachie" MacIvor, sixty, down at the dock and had a couple of hours with him. He was on schooners in the 1890s and as long as they lasted. He said there was considerable singing about, especially in the sailor holdouts ashore and in fo'c'sles whenever a couple of vessels were tied up together or hove-to in a canal or someplace for shelter. Crews got together and each man had to sing a song or tell a story in his turn or be sort of a dud.

Two river hogs stand aboard floating logs near the bow of the Canadian tug *Frank G. Macauley* on a sunny day at Kincardine, Ontario, around 1900. In the background are the steamers *Bayfield I* (left) and *Protector*. The wooden *Macauley,* nearly 68 feet long, was built at Saugeen, Ontario, in 1898. (Courtesy Dossin Great Lakes Museum)

MacIvor recited "The *Bigler*" entire—essentially as I have it, and started on "The *E. C. Roberts*," but got stuck, so I gave an extra typed copy to him. He also wanted "The *Persian*'s Crew," and I promised to send him a copy. He gave me a couple verses of "The Steamer *Asia*" and promised to get the remainder and send it to me. He recalled one stanza of a halyard chantey, "Ho-Ho-Me-Riley-Oh" and gave me some of "The *Jennie P. King*" and "The Steamer *Wyoming*," which I already have. MacIvor said his father sailed in the *King* for a number of seasons. He recognized parts of "Hooray for a Race down the Lakes" ["The Schooner *Moonlight* "]. He said that on some schooners, there was always chanteying when making sail and similar work. Jimmy Reid of Buffalo composed "The *Bigler*" and "The *E. C. Roberts*" and many more, he said. He said he spent some seasons living in Buffalo saloons, singing songs for food and drink. [He recalled at least parts of "The Buffalo Whore"]:

> My first trip down old Lake Erie,
> With some sailors to explore;
> Then I met Rosy O'Flannagan,
> Best of all the Buffalo whores.

She says, "Boy, I think I know you,
Let me sit upon your knee,
How'd you like to do some lovin'?
A dollar and a half will be my fee."

Some were singing, some were dancing,
Some were drunk upon the floor;
But I was over in a corner
A'making love to the Buffalo whore.

She was slick as oil on water,
I didn't know what she was about
'Til I missed my watch and wallet,
Then I popped her on the snout.

Out came the whores and sons-of-bitches,
They came at me by the score;
You'd have laughed to split your britches
To see me flying out that door!

He has heard a number of stories about Paul Bunyan on old vessels. Paul scooped the Lakes out to float his great lumber vessels, which carried deckloads so tall that one couldn't see over. They were towed through the St. Clair River by his blue ox. He often kidnapped boys off smaller vessels to put in his crews. He also poled great rafts of logs from Lake Superior and Georgian Bay down to the Lower Lakes.

John Redfern "Red" MacDonald, a red-faced, stocky and somewhat scarred Scotsman of about sixty years, has had a two-volume career so far, spending all his seasons on the Lakes as a child, sailor, and fisherman. MacDonald had spent most of the night before lifting his fish nets, which were set off a cape thirty-six miles to the northward [around Douglas Point]. When I arrived at the pier about the middle of the forenoon, Red was bargaining with a trucker who made the daily shore run buying fish. "I had to use the engine, and it took twenty-eight gallons of gas an', by God, I got only twenty-five pounds of fish, and he cheated me out of half of them."

MacDonald began sailing as a youngster with his father and has been on water every season since. He knows most of the old lakesmen I could mention from Chicago to Kingston and far more vessels than I've ever heard of.

His father, John "Minister" MacDonald, was a schooner captain of the old school who acquired his nickname, according to Red, from his strong language. His mother, Red added, went along many seasons as cook, but she was better at the wheel and much of the other work about ship than most of the regular crew. She took along Red and younger members of the family who were not old enough

With the fishermen on Lake Huron. (From *Picturesque Canada*)

to be left ashore. Red stated that at the age of about six he could go aloft and climb all about the rigging, and a few years later "when on an easy course," he used to stand on a big box and take his "trick at the wheel." Most of the time his father carried lumber and sawmill products from Georgian Bay, Manitoulin Island, and the North Channel ports down to Sarnia, Tonawanda, and sometimes on down the Welland Canal and Lake Ontario.

Red stated that his father liked singing and favored sailors who could. He recalled an occasion when their vessel was tied up at Port Huron "and an old Irish sailor named Paddy LaRoe came onboard and asked the Old Man for a job. We had a full crew and the Old Man knew from an earlier trip that Paddy wasn't much of a sailor so he told him 'no.' Paddy went ashore and pretty soon came back aboard and said he had no money and asked to go along for just this one trip. The Old Man turned on him and roared, 'No!' and told him to get the hell off the ship before he kicked him off. Paddy went ashore and stood around for a while and when he saw the Old Man within hearing distance, he sang:

There stands Captain MacDonald, boys,
    And him you all do know,
He'll ship all the bums upon the Lakes
    But he won't ship Paddy LaRoe.

There's MacDougal, MacConnell, MacIvor, MacKay,
    And any who will go;

MacPhearson, MacKinnon, MacLeod and more,
　　But he won't ship Paddy LaRoe.

"The Old Man hunched his shoulders and said, 'All right, get your stuff and come aboard.'"

Judged by his own accounts, Red has long had an insatiable appetite for strong drink and, according to his and his friends' statements, it has brought him trouble with the police in many of the ports about the Lakes. In Milwaukee, the police followed him onboard ship, but he climbed aloft and fell off a yardarm and gashed his scalp. "The officers left me in the charge of the mate, who sewed me up." In Chicago, he "cleaned out a damn hole" and spent a week in jail. In Cleveland, his ship had to depart without him, and also in Detroit. His shipmates paid a fine for him in Sarnia and brought him aboard his father's schooner. While the vessel was towing up through the rapids into Lake Huron, Red woke up and, discovering that he had left his bottle somewhere, he promptly jumped overboard and swam to Port Edward on the Canadian side. "When told that I was overboard, the Old Man just said, 'Let the damn fool go,' and picked me up on the next trip." In Port Huron, he said, he got a head start on the police and swam out to the channel markers in the river and then over to the Canadian side. In Sarnia, in another brush with the law, he swam to the American side of the river. On still another occasion, he pushed a Sarnia cop overboard and had to dive in himself and help the cop ashore as the policeman couldn't swim. "I used to be a pretty good swimmer, but now I'm afraid to even take a bath."

He can't sing at all, so he says, but he has a head full of odds and ends that ought to be written down and saved, both Lakes and ocean. Recited "The Stately *Southerner*," parts of "The *Flying Cloud*," "The *Lady Leroy*," "The *Cumberland*'s Crew." He had had a couple of "bracers" and I couldn't stop him long enough at times to get the words down. He said he didn't know the tunes. "I guess any tune will do."

He recited a couple stanzas of "The Steamer *Asia*," the same as I got from MacIvor, one stanza of "The *Fayette Brown*," a railroad parody on "Watch her, catch her, jump up on her juberju," and a couple of other stray stanzas and then gave me "The Schooner *Kolfage*" entire.

MacDonald had to leave to see about his crew for tonight's fishing trip.

His fishing boat, the *Margaret MacDonald*, was named for his sister, and he said, "It's bad for a boat if the person it's named for dies." After a pause he added, "It's also bad to change a boat's name." It has an inboard gasoline engine and carries a tall mast, which distinguishes it from others in the harbor. He much prefers running under sail and uses his engine relatively little.

Goderich just got legal beer yesterday, and the place was jammed with all the low-downs of that part of the province, two-thirds of them seemingly drunk. [The Ontario Temperance Act of 1916 had banned the sale of liquor or beer, but had subsequently been relaxed with laws allowing the sale of full-strength beer for home use and 4.4 percent alcohol for beer or ale in hotels and taverns. The Ontario Liberal Government announced the legalization of full-strength beer by the glass in 1934, creating celebrations like this one throughout the province.] Red also was well on. He and a half dozen other sailor-fishermen friends and a couple hundred more thirsty customers were having a hilarious time. Red introduced me as "Waltham, the man who repairs watches" and somebody wanted me to do something with his. [This was a play on Walton's last name. The Waltham Watch Company in Waltham, Massachusetts, pioneered the production of watches on an assembly line.]

For two hours I listened to fragments of more Lakes songs than I had heard in a month before, and an equal number of arguments about various vessels, sailors, trips, and episodes, and practically always several men were talking at the same time. There was little or no opportunity to make any notes. Red hauled over another Scotsman, Malcolm Graham, who knew a song, "Scrubber Murphy." He started to sing it in spite of the hubbub of a hundred or more half-drunken natives all shouting and talking at once. I got down a couple of stanzas, and then he decided he wanted $50,000 for it and wouldn't give me any more. He said his wife was home sick—had been for two years—and he had five kids and was out of a job and had to have $50,000. "You see, I shouldn't be in here at all. I'll get hell when I go home unless I have $50,000."

Will look him up tomorrow. He may be cheaper then.

Goderich, Sunday, August 26, 1934

Went over to Red MacDonald's and his mother said he'd been drinking and was out in the country somewhere. "Poor Reddie, he just can't leave liquor alone, and when he takes one drink, he never stops until everything is gone. Oh, my. Oh, my. I'm so sorry liquor has come back."

At 7 p.m., no Malcolm Graham, and still not at 8, so I walked over to his home again and found him out beside his house, pretty sick. Said "they" went out to a bootlegger last night and now he had a terrible headache and stomach and chills. He just couldn't think of any words to anything. He said he'd write out "Scrubber Murphy" and send it to me.

[Graham evidently did. The song tells of Captain Henry Murphy, who put cleanliness above all else. This is how it starts.]

> Scrubber Murphy was the captain of the steamer called *Mohawk;*
> And Scrubber is the scrubber about whom all sailors talk:
> From painting and from scrubbing, he's the scrubber's title got,
> Given to him by the sailors of the gallant ship *Mohawk.*
>
> It was the spring of nineteen five Old Scrubber took command,
> And the orders that he first gave us was, "By your suds stand!
> Into your suds dip your brooms and at her, lads, you go,
> For I'm bound to have the *Mohawk* scrubbed before I go below."
>
> The crew, all being well-drilled men and knowing what to do,
> Into the suds dipped their brooms and scrubbed the bulwarks through.

The *Hattie Hutt,* as seen off the rail of the *Lyman Davis* on Lake Huron in 1912. This was one of the photos that Aran Westell loaned to Walton. (Courtesy Ivan H. Walton Collection, Bentley Historical Library, University of Michigan)

"On to her deck," Old Scrubber cried, and without more ado
Those brave lads scrubbed the upper works while streams of water flew.

For ten long hours they scrubbed her down before the scrub was o'er,
Then "Rory," says he, "go scrape the mast and then we'll scrape some more."
Brave Rory for the mast did dash and never did let up
Till Scrubber cried, "Come, my lad, and scrub the brindle pup!"

KINCARDINE, ONTARIO, AUGUST 27, 1934

Red's fish boat was tied up at the pier, and that evening I saw him on the street headed for the Bedford House. In the hope that he might recall some of the songs he had already started or mentioned, I arranged to go out with him in his fish boat the next morning to examine his nets.

When I arrived at our appointed time, Red had already gone out. His brother, who operated an amusement park nearby, said Red was up all night and went out, he thought, about 4 a.m., but would be back before noon. A fresh wind was blowing from the west, and some white-topped seas were coming in the harbor mouth. Late in the forenoon I returned, but no Red. The wind had freshened and veered to the northwest, and big seas were rolling entirely over the north breakwater. When I asked his brother where Red was, he said he wasn't in yet. "Isn't it dangerous to be out there in a fish boat now?"

"Oh, yes, some, but don't worry about Red. He'll be holed up somewhere, and will be along later."

Called at the lighthouse and found Aran Westell, about forty-five, lightkeeper, harbor master, former sailor on the *Lyman Davis,* and land sailor. He had a number of negatives of schooner pictures, which he loaned me to take to a local photographer and to have a copy made of the picture I have of the *Davis* under full sail, as he had none and very much wanted one. Westell told me the Graham brothers owned and sailed the *Davis* for five or ten years. I found Alex Graham cleaning out an old "sugar house" in anticipation of using it for storage. There is no poetry in his soul. "We didn't make nothing on the *Davis.* She was too big and too small. We had to carry seven men to handle her and she couldn't carry cargo enough to make money. She was a good sailor, though. Nothing ever beat her on the Lakes. No, sir, she could outsail anything. The *Hunter Savage* was built just to beat her but couldn't do it. The *Hunter Savage* turned over one trip in a squall and drowned the owner's whole family. We doubled our money on the *Davis,* though. Sold her down to Lake Ontario about ten years ago for $7,000. I hear they burned her at Toronto this spring. That was a hell of a thing to do."

Kincardine, Ontario, August 28, 1934

At the Lee Studio, got prints of the negatives I'd borrowed from Westell: the *Bertha Barnes, Maxwell, Hattie Hutt, John Ketterhouse, Isabella J. Boyce, George A. Marsh, Sephie,* and deck scenes of the *Lyman Davis.* Some are the last of the Great Lakes schooners. They were all lakers in 1912 and 1913.

In the evening, Westell and I went out to the home of Collin Graham. He is about sixty-five and started on fish boats that carried only sails. He was then in steamboats for nine years and then with his brother in schooners. They had the *Burt Barnes* for about twenty years and then sold her "down below"—Lake Ontario—and bought the *Davis* for $3,250. They sailed her for six years and sold her, also to Lake Ontario, for $5,700, about twelve years ago. They practically always carried a crew from Kincardine, and so didn't come into contact with much Lakes lore. He told of Paul Bunyan towing a great raft of logs down the Lakes with a canoe. Paul also had a sailboat in which he transported much of his timber, and it was so big it couldn't make the bend in the rivers unless he lifted the stern around the land.

Tiverton, Southampton, and Red Bay, Ontario, August 29, 1934

I found John McCauley busy with his pipe and newspaper in his backyard. He is eighty-four but looks seventy. He began on Lakes schooners in 1862 "and I'd be sailing now if there was any jobs." He went down to salt water one fall at the close

Looking up the harbor at Owen Sound on Georgian Bay, with a vessel under construction to the right. (From *Picturesque Canada*)

of the season, intending to return in spring, but sailed the ocean for three years. "Yes, you could hear them shellbacks sing halfway across the ocean when putting on heavy canvas." Lakes schoonermen were largely "salties" and used mostly the same chanteys. He went into steamboating in the 1880s. He said it was hard work, but a gentleman's job in comparison with that on sailboats. He said a sailor named Billy Clark made up a lot of songs and would sing them in saloons at Buffalo, Detroit, Chicago, and other places for drinks. "But he came to a terrible end, he did. Was stabbed to death in a saloon brawl in Duluth." McCauley said he never could sing and never knew any songs, but would make a noise with the others when pulling. McCauley knew a few lines of "The *Fayette Brown*" and "The *E. C. Roberts*" and seemed to recognize all schooners about which I have some fragments. He also had a few lines about the weather:

> Sun in the west, as clear as a bell.
> Westerly winds as sure as hell.
> Rain before wind, stand by to take in,
> Wind before rain, haul 'em up again.

Port McNichol, Midland, Ontario, September 1, 1934

I spent about three hours with Captain John McConnell aboard the Canadian Pacific Railway boat the *Assiniboia* at her dock at Port McNichol. He began his lake sailing on schooners largely out of Buffalo and Chicago. He said there was much singing on old vessels out of both places, especially while making sail or being towed out of the harbor. He said he never paid much attention to it except that the chanteys did make pulling easier. On one vessel he was in there were a couple of Irishmen in the crew all season who always sang while going out the creek at Buffalo and all the dogs along the banks would bark and howl "and there seemed to be thousands of them." He said, "[T]hey were good singers, and could be heard all over town." Schooner sailors were a hard and tough but happy lot. They generally made enough on their last trips late in fall to winter them and so blew their summer's pay as they got it, usually in saloons. Practically all old schooners had a horseshoe nailed to the foremast and another over the cabin door for good luck. "There are enough horseshoes on the bottom of the Lakes to shoe the whole British cavalry."

He says his present mate won't pass anybody on a stairway or companionway because it means bad luck. Many sailors are that way. One time in Chicago, he picked up a black kitten on the pier and took it aboard to feed it and some of the crew made a big fuss and got off. That night, a little fire started in the cabin and they declared that bringing the cat aboard caused it.

Canadian ports always present the first captain to bring in a boat in spring with a silk topper, or a check for its equivalent. That custom has been followed as long as he can remember. Members of his crew at time initiate new members by having them do various things such as "stand the spark watch," which consists of carrying a bucket of water and a broom or mop about on the upper deck to put out all sparks that fall on it from the smokestack. They would have them outfitted for all night with extra coats and oilskins. Captain McConnell said he had to put a stop to the prank of sending a new man to get the key to the keelson and then loading him up with all the gear he could carry. Captain McConnell was afraid some boy might get injured. He says the favorite trick now is to send some nosy passenger to him with a basket of crackers or similar food to ask him for the key to the beaver cage so he can feed the pets.

I'm not certain that I noted down a trick that I was told about a few days ago. Should the Old Man be particularly crabby, the greenhorn would be told that it was his duty to entertain the captain, to go aft to his cabin and walk right in and awaken him if he was asleep and then sit down and talk to him. "He'll probably be a little sharp with you, but you just sit right there and talk to him, no matter what he says." Anything was apt to result.

Captain Kinnie, sixty-five, was getting a tug ready to do something. He had been on steamboats and tugs all his life, mostly in Georgian Bay, and didn't know much about the world. He has a daughter "married to a Yankee" and she lives "in some state near Detroit" but didn't know what its name was.

Back down from the tug dock, a sawmill was cutting into planks some old pine logs that had been used as a boom and were soaking in the bay until that morning. When a half dozen were cut into two-inch planks, they were loaded on the tug to be taken out to be used in the cofferdam being built around the beached *Midland City*. [A cofferdam is a watertight enclosure that is pumped dry so that work can be done below the water line.] About a week ago, the vessel had hit a shoal and was run on the beach about four miles from the bay while on an excursion run with a hundred or more passengers. I asked to go along. Captain Kinnie said his tug, *Lilly,* was thirty-five years old and leaking and overloaded and also a rainstorm was making, but if I wanted to go, all right. I thought I could swim as far as he could, so I went along. We found the *Midland* with her bow up out of the water so that a man could walk under it, and her stern all under. The cofferdam was about half built. They are working twenty-four hours a day trying to get her off before any storm hits. The *Lilly* came back with all aboard who went out on her. I noticed a horseshoe nailed to the stern post.

COLLINGWOOD AND GODERICH, ONTARIO, SEPTEMBER 3, 1934

In the afternoon, I drove to Goderich hoping to find that my sailor friends were sober enough to be of more use than on my last visit here. Felt somewhat weary so, after arriving, about 7 p.m. I went to a movie: Will Rogers in *Handy Andy.* I stayed through the feature twice. Not so bad.

On the way back to the rooming house, I was stopped when a man took my arm as I was going past a tobacco store. Behold, it was Red MacDonald, soused to his adenoids. He said he had a song he was going to sing me, but he couldn't think what it was. His tongue was pretty thick, anyway. He insisted that I go with him to get a drink. I got away from him only by going into a corner store and out the side door. I heard he hasn't been sober for a week. He says he's going out to lift his nets early in the morning. He may be more sober by the time he gets back. I will hope so.

GODERICH, COLLINGWOOD, AND BAYFIELD, ONTARIO, SEPTEMBER 5, 1934

I located Louis MacLeod in Bayfield, Ontario, and while we were talking, Red MacDonald and a man named MacKay drove up in an old Model T Ford coupe, both gloriously drunk. MacKay was driving or, as he said, "wheeling," and when their craft was opposite the house it turned in, but missed the driveway and stalled at a dangerous angle on the side of a shallow ditch. On the low side, Red spotted us through his open window and called out, "Sailor, heave us a line! Our ballast has shifted and, damn 'er, she's on!" He fumbled with the door a while and then it suddenly burst open and Red, obviously full of beer, rolled out. He got himself right end up and, without brushing himself off, staggered up to us and said, "Dr. Waltham, maybe you can repair watches, but can you steer a boat? That bastard MacKay I've got wheeling ain't no sailor. He was off his course all the way here; and, damn 'er, you've got to get 'er off an' wheel 'er back." Then he added, "I've got a good song for you," but he couldn't even recall the subject of it. After much trying, he started off on "The *Flying Cloud,*" but soon bogged down. He then discovered a nearby clump of shrubbery and while so occupied, I drove away.

PORT HURON, MICHIGAN, SEPTEMBER 6, 1934

I found Mr. William J. Small on his porch swing, talking with Sylvester "Ves" Ray. Ray had been over before and Slim McCauley had written out Ray's song, which

Collingwood Harbor. (From *Picturesque Canada*)

The schooner *Helen MacLeod II*, part of the fishing fleet at Bayfield, Ontario, in 1939. The 36-foot vessel, one of the type referred to as a "Huron boat," was built with cypress and white oak planking in 1936. (Courtesy Dossin Great Lakes Museum)

he had mentioned and given me the last stanza of when I saw him last. Also "The Girls of Liverpool" or part of it, and a fragment of another. He told of sailors making up songs on different old vessels he had sailed on. He said they mostly sang when working the windlass. "It made the work not half as bad." A good chanteyman would give it to the Old Man, but they'd never let on." Mr. Small said that when he was in the Coast Guard at Sand Beach [Harbor Beach, Michigan], "dozens of schooners would come in there to wait out a blow and when heaving in anchors you'd hear some of the best singing in the world. It never entered my head to get them songs down."

In the early evening, I called at the Lynn Bros. Reporting Agency and then at Mrs. Dan Lynn's home. She showed me her husband's *Shupe* scrapbook. He was awarded a congressional gold medal for attempting the rescue of the *Shupe*'s crew and has a scrapbook of newspaper clippings, letters, etc., about the event. Among them was the song, "The Cruel Waters of Lake Huron," which I copied out.

Port Huron and Royal Oak, Michigan, September 7, 1934

I called at the home of Loudon Wilson, but he was in Detroit where he works. Mrs. Wilson showed me some of his paintings and told of his interest in the Lakes and his materials and information, so I decided to wait about the city until he returned. That evening, I spent two hours at his home examining his photos, newspaper cuts, etc., and paintings and sketches of Lakes schooners and in visiting

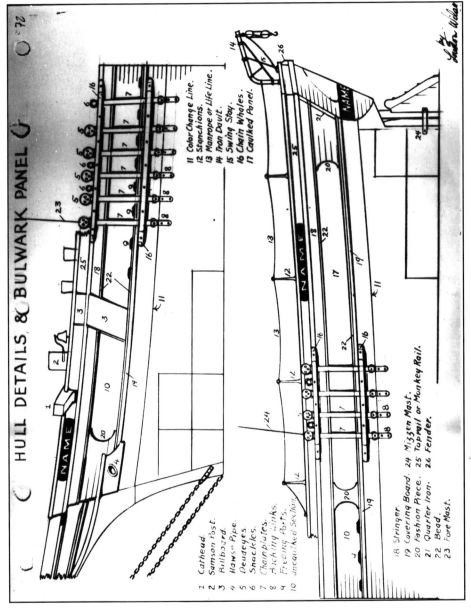

Loudon Wilson's sketch of a vessel's hull and bulwark details, one of hundreds of pieces of his artwork about Great Lakes vessels. (Courtesy the Historical Collections of the Great Lakes)

and talking about my work. He has a pretty good collection. He also has a collection of C. H. J. Snyder's "Schooner Days" series from the Toronto *Evening Telegram*. Wilson knows a number of old sailors. He wants a copy of "The *Bigler's* Crew."

DETROIT, MICHIGAN, SEPTEMBER 12, 1934

Found Captain Henry A. Pocock, seventy, at his home this morning. He began sailing on a Lakes tug about 1880. He was on the tug *Erie Belle* when her boiler blew up while trying to pull the schooner *Carter* off the beach at Kincardine, Ontario, in 1883. He then sailed on schooners for many years. He said he didn't recall any of the songs or chanteys, although "I've heard aplenty of them and liked them, and by God, some of those sailors were damn good singers. Some of those damn bums could make up songs about anything." He told of being on a Canadian tug in the 1880s and going up among islands near Tobermory [at the head of the Bruce Peninsula between Lake Huron and Georgian Bay] where a schooner was on the bottom. They found the American tug *Winslow* there in violation of Canadian navigation laws, which permitted only Canadian wreckers in Canadian waters. Captain Pocock had a customs official aboard, and when they arrived, the American tug was ready to run for it. The customs officer told the captain of the *Winslow* he was "under arrest in the name of Her Majesty, the Queen." The American captain replied, "You and her majesty can go to hell. Get out of the way," and he started full speed ahead. Pocock said, "We were in the passageway between the islands and had to give way or get sunk. He went past us and headed across the lake for the Michigan side, and we gave chase. One of our deckhands, who later turned out to be a former sailor on the *Winslow,* volunteered to help our fireman and he soon smothered the fire, and the *Winslow* pulled away from us and hoisted a broom on her foremast as she did. I didn't want to catch him anyway. I've been shipmates with him many times." The customs officer confiscated the *Winslow's* lines, pumps, and other materials left aboard the schooner. Some time later, the *Winslow* put in to Amherstburg, Ontario, for fuel and tied up to the dock and a constable came down to take possession of the tug. Before he could get aboard, the *Winslow's* captain ordered her lines cut and pulled away, telling the constable he could have the lines.

Captain Pocock once was in command of the Detroit-Windsor ferry with one hundred fifty passengers out on the river when a storm struck with an eighty-three-mile-per-hour wind. The rain was so heavy one could see nothing and there was so much wind one could not head into it, so he turned stern-to and reversed engines, but the wind still blew them upstream. Captain Pocock said the engineer "showed the white feather" and lost his nerve. "We finally got in safe when the rain slacked."

Captain Pocock said he once sailed with a captain who wouldn't enter the pilothouse except through the port-side door, no matter what the weather conditions were. He knew others who insisted that their cabin bed be on the port side or that their heads be toward the port side.

Looking up the Thames in Chatham, Ontario, near Lake St. Clair. (From *Picturesque Canada*)

On the trip before the *Erie Belle* went to Kincardine and blew her boiler, two Negro firemen got off because they saw rats going ashore on lines. A friend also got off because he dreamed his dead mother told him to. On the Kincardine trip, six members of the crew were killed. "Now, how do you explain that?"

Competition among tugs got very keen. They would not cut the rates, but did many other things, like going all the way up to the Straits of Mackinac for tows and taking them down for only the river tow bill. Some schooner captains insisted on a five-, ten- or twenty-dollar "rebate" from the tug captain before they would give him their line, and then the tug captain would make it up at the fuel dock by getting a bill for more wood than he actually took aboard. It would take an average of twenty-four hours to tow up the river. They could go down much faster.

On a trip down from Escanaba, Michigan, in a schooner with a load of ore, a tug picked them up just north of the Straits of Mackinac to take them through the St. Clair and Detroit Rivers [more than 250 miles away]. Coming down Lake Huron, a fresh fair wind came up and they made all sail. Their captain told the tug to let go, but it wouldn't. "We could make better time than the tug, and we sailed past her and finally towed the tug stern first until he let go."

DETROIT, MICHIGAN, SEPTEMBER 14, 1934

Near the corner of Atwater and Beaubien, I found the old "Patomic," the place of "Billy the Bum" Boushaw. I learned that it was one of the schooner sailors' main holdouts. It is now a dilapidated old hotel and beer saloon. A former schoonerman and, I judge, "high flier," Tom Daily, eighty-nine, was in. He is quite deaf and has one cocked eye and wears a derby hat. A beer and a look at the schooner pictures that I had along started him off. He said that the building in the old days was one of the liveliest in Detroit. It often had more than a hundred sailors staying there and "many girls. Right in this room I've seen some terrible fights, and out on the street in front. No one would interfere and the best man won. Sing? You're goddamn right, and Jesus Christ, how them fellows could sing! Why, Jesus Christ, some fellow would start out on a song after a couple of drinks and they'd all join in on the chorus and damn near raise the ceiling. Anyone who couldn't sing a good song or speak a piece or sometimes dance a jig had to buy the drinks. There was some of the best goddamn singing I've ever heard."

"What did they sing?"

"Oh, God, anything, and one fellow, 'Johnny the Whistler,' could whistle through his nose and his fingers, like this." He demonstrated. "Any goddamn time you'd say, 'and Patty the Piper,' he had a little tin whistle and, Jesus Christ, how he could play it!"

"Do you remember any of the songs?"

"God, yes, all the songs there were: 'Nelly Gray,' 'Where's My Wandering Boy Tonight?' and, and—well, all the damn sailor songs there was."

"The *Bigler*'s Crew?"

"Oh, Jesus Christ, yes. 'Watch her, catch her, jump on her juberju.' Jesus Christ, I can hear 'em yet. And that one about carrying iron ore from Escanaba, and—why, goddamn it, if they wanted to, there was fellows what would make 'em up right there."

I couldn't get any more details from him. He said he had to go, straightened his derby, danced a jig—somewhat stiffly—and departed.

Ralph Chene, a dark-complexioned man of French lineage with heavy graying hair, noticeably overweight, friendly, and talkative, is proprietor of, and makes his home at Chene Hall at Monroe and Chene Streets. It is a meeting place for various local organizations of people of French descent. He said he was born on the Detroit riverfront and spent his boyhood in the late 1880s and 1890s as a "river rat" on wood, sand, and gravel scows on the Detroit River and Lake St. Clair.

There were at the time, he explained, "dozens and dozens" of flat-bottomed, shallow-draft, two-masted scows about, and they did a good business supplying fuel and building material for the river towns and passing traffic on the river. They were practically all individually owned and sailed by Frenchmen who spoke a mixture of French and English, were frequent visitors to shore beer halls, and did much singing as they moved leisurely up and down the river threading their way among the larger vessels.

They usually carried a "capitan," a cook, generally the captain's wife who doubled as "crew," and a third member, a deckhand called the mate, or a boy who soon learned to help with about everything that had to be done. Most of these craft drew from one to four feet of water, and, with the crew poling, could ascend several miles up the rivers that empty into Lake St. Clair to the wood docks all along their banks. After loading beech, maple, oak, walnut, or anything else that was to be transported, they would float downstream to Lake St. Clair. They would then hoist their canvas and sail to the big wood docks along the Detroit River that made a business of supplying fuel to the inhabitants of the border cities and also to wood-burning tugs and steamers. Sometimes, the smaller scows would tie up to a passing steamer and transfer their cargo of cordwood while the steamer was under way.

They loaded sand and gravel, which they generally obtained free from the many sandbars in the area, and for years they supplied this important building material to cities on both sides of the river.

The wood-carrying scows lost out when steamers, tugs, and inhabitants found coal a more efficient and economical fuel than cordwood. The sand and gravel scows lost their business to the big gravel scows that brought in a superior grade of gravel that the old scows could not supply, and on a bigger and cheaper scale. As a result, the old two-winged river scows that were much in evidence in the early schooner period were more and more left tied up along the river to rot.

There was, Mr. Chene explained, always much bantering among the crews of the different scows, and there was also much racing, even though all were square at both ends and very slow. They were mostly open-decked and couldn't take much of a sea without filling and foundering. As a result, some were lost with the people aboard when caught in a severe blow, particularly on Lake St. Clair, which is shallow and doesn't require much of a breeze to become dangerously rough.

On some scows that had three or more men aboard, they would sing old voyageur paddle songs when hoisting sail or pumping. He added that French fishermen in the area would also sing these paddle songs to accompany their rowing to or from their fishing grounds. He was not able to repeat any voyageur songs, even though he used to enjoy listening to them "by the hour." He is presently making his livelihood as an interior decorator, but looks back with nostalgia to "the old life on the river" and not infrequently entertains gatherings of his friends by singing songs about it that he learned in his boyhood years. He knows and sings "The Scow *Julie Plante*," which he said narrates the loss of a scow on Lake St. Clair, and another about "the Scow *Brenton*," and one about "The Scow *Flying Cloud*," and another about a scowman, "Cross-Eyed Riley." He also sings one called "The Scow *Nettie Fly*," which he states was composed "many years ago."

> Oh, sailors, come gather and list to my ditty,
> To picture aright this hero I'll try—
> He seldom was sober, and more is the pity,
> He's Captain Poulan of the scow *Nettie Fly*.
>
> He sailed from Chene Street, the wind blew a gale,
> An' down Detroit River the *Nettie Fly* flew;

Says Captain Poulan, "She can carry her sail,"
Took a pull at his bottle and sized up his crew.

But all he could see was his mate, the brave fellow,
Who stood by the mainm'st with bottle in hand;
His legs they were shaky, his face it was mellow
As he thought of the boodle he'd make on the sand.

The captain looked sad, but with stern resolution
Seized hold of his bottle and took a long pull—
"By the stars and the stripes of our beloved Constitution,
If the captain ain't drunk and the mate is half full."

She was headin' sou'west with the wind on her quarter,
An' her sharp eagle eye oft peered through the gloom.
He then hauled her up seven points and a quarter,
An' shot into the Rouge not a moment too soon.

A heavy squall struck, and her lee rail went under;
An' out went her mains'l, into ribbons it flew.
While out flashed the light'nin', and loud rolled the thunder,
The captain took a drink, and the mate took one, too.

She righted at last through their manly endeavors,
An' they took in their fores'l, and stood for the bank;
They swore they would stick to each other forever,
An' pulled out their bottles and together they drank.

Says the captain to Jack, "You had better go forward
An' take in your stays'l and let go your hank,
For I've skinned my nose, my shins, and my forehead,
An' my legs are all tangled with this centerboard crank!"

In three days, they loaded an' were homeward bound;
They sailed up the river with a favorin' breeze—
They came up the river just like a scared hound,
An' the owner made money and was very much pleased.

The captain explained how they nearly went under,
How the scow and their lives they thought they would lose;
An' the last time I saw them they were in a saloon,
An' the last that I heard they were still on the booze!

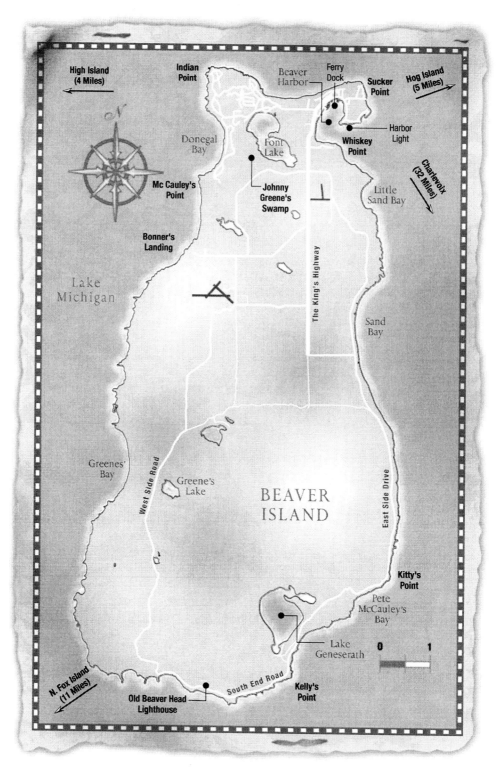

Map by F. S. Fluker

CHAPTER 4

1938: Beaver Island, Milwaukee, Lake Erie, Lake Ontario

> She towed us out and left us outside the river light
> Lake Erie for to wander and the blusterin' winds to fight.
> The wind being fresh and fair, we paddled our own canoe,
> Her nose points o'er the dummy, we're hell-bent for Buffalo.
> "THE TIMBER DROGHER *BIGLER*"

Walton had spent the 1935–36 academic year in doctoral studies at the University of Chicago and was bedridden for a while with pneumonia. He returned to the field in 1938, more concerned than ever that the trail was going cold and determined to bring back the sounds of the Great Lakes sailors. His teacher was Alan Lomax, field-recording pioneer. A fish house on Beaver Island became their classroom. Lomax furnished the gear; Walton invited the informants.

Lynn, then thirteen, accompanied his father on his second trip in 1938 to Beaver Island and recalled almost sixty-five years later, "When I went with him to northern Michigan, what he had with him was this big, gigantic machine. Heavy, heavy, heavy."

Lynn also remembered, "The car that [Dominick] Gallagher had was a big old Buick—black. He was going to take Dad and me to a place where there was going to be a big gathering of people. A black cat ran across the street in front of us and he was going to go all the way around the island the other way, but Dad talked him out of it."

Lomax had a very busy year in 1938. He collected in Illinois, Indiana, Wisconsin, more than a dozen cities in Michigan's Upper and Lower Peninsulas, Akron, Cincinnati, and Hamilton, Ohio, as well as Gloucester, New Jersey. Also that year, Lomax recorded several important singers at the Library of Congress, including Leadbelly, Woody Guthrie, Judge Learned Hand, Blame Stubblefield, and Jelly Roll Morton. The Morton recordings became one of jazz's most important collections and the basis for Lomax's 1950 book, *Mister Jelly Roll*. Beaver Island was just a side trip for Lomax.

But for Walton, Beaver Island was once again pivotal. After he and Lomax parted, Walton went to borrow a machine from the university. Traveling with graduate student Imis Bouton for the rest of the summer, Walton next tried to record his singers. They battled electrical shorts, bad needles, and the differences between U.S. and Canadian electric currents.

Just as the ability to record came within Walton's grasp, the last people who recalled the sounds of the Great Lakes under sail were slipping away. A few summers before, William Clark had been rumored dead. Now, he was really dead.

Guy L. "Irish Mac" McCracken, battling to save "The Anchorage" from foreclosure in 1932, had died in jail after his arrest for heaving a rock through the front window of a bank where he had lost some money.

William Small was gone, too. And Thomas Hylant, and William Summerville. There was to be no easing up. Walton had to work faster than ever.

Charlevoix, Michigan, July 15, 1938

Left Pentwater, Michigan, about 10 a.m., Thursday the 14th for points north: Ludington, Manistee, Traverse City. Arrived at Traverse City in the Cherry Festival jam. The billboard program said a "Cherry Queen" was to be crowned later in the day, but didn't say with what. The boys and girls walked up one street and down the same one, and tried to talk and enjoy themselves above the blaring of a half-dozen loudspeakers. Nature has been very generous with Grand Traverse area hills, bays, and bountiful orchards. Cherries sold for thirty cents a box on the streets.

Captain Manus J. Bonner was born on Beaver Island in northern Lake Michigan in 1858 of recently arrived Irish immigrant parents. He said he used to go on summer trips on the Lakes at the age of six with his schooner captain father and, before he was nine, he would go aloft with the experienced sailors and help handle the top rigging. In his early twenties, he became master of a family-owned schooner engaged in the lumber trade to Chicago. His life since then has been intimately connected with Great Lakes sailing, mostly in the lumber trade, but also in carrying ore, grain, and coal on all five Great Lakes.

He stated that there were "hundreds of sailboats on the Lakes in the 1870s and 1880s," and many of them were "beautiful three- and four-masted vessels that could carry from six to nine hundred tons of cargo." They loaded ore and grain and usually coal into the hold by chutes but unloaded by buckets that were elevated by horse power. The horses got to know the routine so well that they would work by the hour without a driver. A sailor soon got to know about every vessel he met and could recognize them at a distance. He also could recognize landmarks in the daytime and lights at night the length of the Lakes, and seldom got lost, even in storms. Most sailing was done by dead reckoning, which was checked by landmarks whenever possible. "Fogs were the worst conditions we had to contend with, as they blotted out landmarks and also greatly increased the danger of collisions," Captain Bonner said. He recalled meeting the steamer *Manitou* once in a thick fog on Lake Michigan. They passed so close that they almost touched. He named many vessels that disappeared in fogs, presumably as a result of collisions.

Hanging on a living room wall of his home was an enlarged picture of the schooner *Rouse Simmons*, the Lake Michigan "Christmas Tree Ship," which was lost off Two Rivers Point, Wisconsin, in a late-November gale and snowstorm [in

The *Rouse Simmons* loading tanbark at Iron Ore Bay at the southwest end of Beaver Island about 1900 in this photo furnished by Captain Manus J. Bonner. (Courtesy Ivan H. Walton Collection, Bentley Historical Library, University of Michigan)

1912]. In the photograph, the *Simmons* was anchored off the southwest corner of Beaver Island loading tanbark. Her sails were up but hanging limp in readiness for a hurried getaway should an on-shore breeze develop. In the foreground were a dozen or more men and boys and several horse-drawn wagons. The vessel, Captain Bonner continued, was in good condition when lost. She had been rebuilt two years earlier, and in the season before, Captain Bonner had ridden out a seventy-mile-an-hour gale in her which "riddled her canvas, and we fought twenty- and thirty-foot seas from off the Beavers to a few miles south of Grand Haven [about one hundred eighty miles] without foundering."

Before the *Simmons*'s fatal trip, Captain Bonner said, he had sold a half interest in her to Captain Herman Schuenemann of Chicago, and an eighth interest to a Chicago merchant in the Christmas tree business. Captain Schuenemann assumed command and Captain Bonner went along as mate. They loaded a full cargo of small evergreens, both in the hold and on the deck, along the north shore of Lake Michigan. As the weather was getting very cold, Captain Schuenemann was afraid of getting frozen in and missing the early December market and, even though the bad weather was threatening, he determined to pull out as soon as they could make ready. Captain Bonner said that he had a strong

The *Rouse Simmons*, fully rigged and with a triangular raffee. (Courtesy Ivan H. Walton Collection, Bentley Historical Library, University of Michigan)

hunch that he shouldn't make the trip to Chicago and didn't, even though Captain Schuenemann insisted that he should.

The *Simmons*, Captain Bonner learned later, was sighted by a car ferry on the afternoon of the day she set out and "was under easy canvas before thickening weather from the northwest." Early that evening, a local Coast Guard sighted her off Kewaunee, Wisconsin, flying a distress signal in a rising blizzard. The Kewaunee Coast Guard informed the Manitowoc, Wisconsin, station. A crew in a powerboat from there went out, sighted the *Simmons* in an opening in the storm, but at once lost her in the snow and darkness. That was the last the vessel and those aboard were ever seen. Some Christmas trees drifted ashore, and two years later Captain Schuenemann's purse was found, and for some time local fishermen brought up Christmas trees in their nets.

With the help of his wife, Captain Bonner recalled a poem about the loss of the car ferry *Pere Marquette 18*. Mrs. Bonner's only brother, Captain Peter Kilty, was master and went down with the vessel and about twenty-five others aboard. As the car ferry approached the Wisconsin shore, the wheelsman became increasingly aware that the vessel wasn't steering as it should and reported the situation to the captain. A hurried investigation showed that the after compartment had filled and the vessel was in danger of sinking. Seventeen loaded railroad freight cars were allowed to run off over the stern into the Lake. The reduced load allowed the stern to rise and she was proceeding slowly on her course with the car ferry *17* standing by to take off the crew if necessary, when suddenly the stricken vessel went down stern first, trapping all the crewmen on the car deck.

Captain Bonner recalled that in his early sailing years, sailors did much singing at their work and in gathering places ashore. He said that he was never much of a singer, but was able to recall some lines of the chanteys "Rio Grande," "Blow, My Bully Boys, Blow," and "Shenandoah." He added that some sailors would sing many more, especially when a full crew was at the capstan on a long haul. He added that usually when men were working at the halyards they did so as the mate called out, "Heave-ho," and the like. He dictated a version of "The Sailor's Alphabet," and parts of "The Red Iron Ore" and "The *Bigler.*" He also recalled some lines of a song about an Irish sailor, "The Rambler from Clare."

Captain Bonner grew very eloquent in denouncing the "damned English" for their treatment of Ireland, and could find nothing good that they had ever done.

He is full of Beaver Island episodes and said it used to be called a place of tame Indians and wild Irishmen. His brother Pat, Francie Roddy, and John Green are still there. Several of the older men I met there before have died, however. He suggested I leave my car in Charlevoix because of the cost of taking it over on the ferry, and get his nephew to drive me if I need a taxi. Am staying at a tourist house overlooking the bay. And so, the end of the first day.

Beaver Island, Michigan, July 16, 1938

Didn't bring my car as I figured taxi fare would be much more within my budget than the six-dollar charge. It seems to cost more to bring a car over here than across the big Lake. Captain Bonner assured me all the people I'd want to see were within three or four miles of the village. After lunch, I started out down the King's Highway to call on Francie Roddy and Pat Bonner. I found Pat's place about five miles down the line and the road pretty well torn up by a log truck that travels up and down it at about forty miles per hour loaded with logs for a sawmill at the harbor. I stopped at Francie's on the way and found him under a tree in his yard directing a young man how to cut hay. Francie had received my letter and was expecting me. Is in pretty bad health.

"Didn't you sail with your father?"

"Yes, I sailed with me father for years."

"Wasn't he quite a singer?"

"Singer! He knew more old songs—and good ones, too—than any man I ever see'd. He could just hear a song once't and he'd know it. He'd sing all through his watch at the wheel."

"And ashore?"

"Sure, wherever he was. When he had a drink or two, he could sing anything. I don't mind his songs; that was over thirty years ago."

Then we got to songs Francie knew, and he explained folks didn't sing anymore and "you forget 'em when you don't sing 'em."

I mentioned the "Lily of the Lake," which he'd attempted when I was here before, and after a number of attempts, he got out a tangled version of it. This "Lily" seems to have bloomed on Lake Champlain. He tried many more, but no harvest. He showed me an old capstan he has off the schooner *Milwaukee Belle* that went on the shoals off the island. He also has the cabin top as a floor for a shop.

BEAVER ISLAND, MICHIGAN, JULY 18

Rented a car from the proprietors of the hotel in the evening and drove out to visit Mr. Green, but again found nobody home. So, I went on out to the Bonner home and eventually got Pat and his brother Dan remembering episodes and bits of old songs so fast I couldn't even keep up with them, especially when both were talking at the same time. Pat had told me earlier in the evening that he couldn't recall any more songs than he'd given me before, but I've discovered that statement doesn't mean anything. I showed him and Dan some pictures I have along and recited "The *Bigler*" and bits of others to them and that did it! I should have some kind of a recording machine, but couldn't locate any before leaving Ann Arbor.

Pat loaned me his copy of a song he composed a number of years ago, "The Steamer *Clifton*." I already have it, but took it again, as though I'd never heard of it and during the evening copied it off line by line when I could slow them down enough. There were several other songs that they'd learned in boyhood. There was part of "The Lady and the Sailor," "The Cruel Merchant," a stanza of "The *Lady Leroy*," "The Little Au Pleine" in part, "Yankee Brown," about a local fisherman and his famous boat, *Mattie*, "The *Cumberland*'s Crew," "The Yankee Man-of-War, "The *Flying Cloud*." They mentioned bits of a dozen or so more by the time I caught up with them and then they had gotten away beyond recapture. They were largely Irish songs of a mournful love theme and humorous episodes. One should have about a month here. "Yankee Brown," as the brothers recalled it:

> My boys, if you will listen now, I'll sing you a little song,
> It's about a man you know well whose tales are always strong.
> He is a well-known fisherman who lives here in our town,
> He's a very noted lawyer, and his name is Yankee Brown.
>
> Oh, sing titty high, high titty um,
> With a whack ful-lor-il-lie.
>
> He was born way down in York State in a family of sixteen,
> And his boyhood deeds would fill a book, the greatest ever seen.
> He farmed and lumbered half the state, but found it too confined,
> So he came to Beaver Island in the year of seventy-nine.

When here he took up fishing and he followed up his trade,
And several times he's told me that his fortune he had made.
He says he's acres by the thousand and pond nets by the score,
And twenty thousand dollars in a bank in Baltimore.

His boat he calls the *Mattie*, and the truth to you I'll tell,
Several times he has rebuilt her and he can sail her well.
For once when beating down the lake he had to come about,
He heeled her in the seas so far she scooped up thirty trout.

He swore when he was fishing once down on Hog Island Sound,
That alone he caught a whitefish that weighed a hundred pounds.
At first we didn't believe him, then he began to swear,
He said he'd bring his young son out and prove the story there.

Oh, when he went to Charlevoix, to preach the Gospel there,
He swore that he was Antichrist, and for them to prepare!
His feats they are most numerous, and the truth now I must tell:
The old Nick never will be at rest till he gets the Yankee in hell!

There are episodes to no end and character songs. Pat and Dan mentioned ten or more people about the island who know various songs. Francie Roddy's father, who died some years ago, seems to have been the king of them all and the source of a large percentage of the songs still floating about. He could sing songs by the hour. He was a big man, more than two hundred forty pounds, and would sing down by the fish dock. He could be heard plainly across the harbor at lighthouse point, "and he had a grand voice."

BEAVER ISLAND, MICHIGAN, JULY 19, 1938

It rained in the morning, so I spent it writing and examining some of my plunder. Then, about 11 a.m., I started out. I called in at the post office for William Boyle. I heard he had written a book about the Mormon occupation of the island. He said he had his manuscript in the Charlevoix Bank for safekeeping. I didn't learn much about it. He seems to suspect I want to steal some of his material. He said he didn't publish it this year because of the Depression, but planned to next year. I think I'll have to have another talk with him tomorrow, after he's had time to quiet his nerves.

I explained what I am looking for, and he then recommended that I look up or visit the secretary of an organization that is doing about the same thing all over the state and would probably have a lot of material. I asked what organization it was, and he said it was called "The Michigan Folklore Group." I told him I felt complimented on his knowing so much about an organization I had founded. He said he'd read about it in a Grand Rapids newspaper. He said he would like to become a member, and I told him that he had, by that wish, fulfilled all the requirements and was in. He said he was planning to be on the lookout for Indian lore.

I went out to the home of Mr. Green again, but found him out in his hay field, so decided to return in the evening. In my "borrowed" car, I went east about one and a half miles to call on "Big Owen" Gallagher, who is supposed to know a song once popular among the local sailors: "The *Middlesex Flora*." His daughter, about fifty, said he was sick in bed and not able to talk. I told her what I wanted and about that time heard someone talking from an adjoining room. Daughter Gallagher disappeared in that direction and soon came back and explained that her mother heard us and said she knew some songs, but added that her mother was very old and had gone entirely blind and her mind wandered. I said I'd like to talk with her if she were able, so the daughter helped her out to a chair and she began rattling something off at once. Her daughter explained to her that I had to write the song down and, sure I couldn't understand her, acted as interpreter. The song turned out to be "The Bold *Princess Royal*" and she went through it without a hitch. She must be nearly ninety and weighs probably sixty pounds. She was born in Ireland and came here as a girl. She said she knew others, but her daughter took her back to bed.

A heavy rain came up and, as that would end Mr. Green's haymaking for the day, I went back over there and found him entertaining his six-month-old grandson. After various preliminaries, including the pictures I brought along, a cigar, his own experience on Lakes vessels, the superiority of the old vessels and times to the new, and to sailors gathering in waterfront saloons and singing, he gave me "The *Middlesex Flora*." He sang it line by line so I could copy it down. I doubt that my time notations will be intelligible in a week. He then went through "The Bold *Princess Royal*" with some variations from Mrs. Gallagher, which I noted, then checked his "The *Flying Cloud*" against mine and to keep him coming copied down from his singing "When First I Went to Sea," a good air.

Beaver Island and Charlevoix, Michigan, July 20, 1938

Found Dominick Gallagher. He is a tall, slender, gray-haired, witty Irishman. His wife, the sister of Francie Roddy, died last year. He explained that the song "The Gallagher Boys" was about a real accident that happened when he was six and he recalls it clearer than some recent incidents. Two Gallagher boys and Tommy Boyle went out to the mainland for equipment to use in a camp they were stocking on the south end of the island. Dominick's father was with them when they went over and was coming back with them, "but Captain Roddy, then sailing the *Our Son*, was in port and he and my father were old friends and he persuaded my father not to go back that day, as his barometer was falling and he said a blow would soon be upon them. He also wanted my father's company. The others insisted on returning that day and started out and were lost. Their boat came ashore down at Seven Mile Point on the island, still right-side up with a camp stove and two sets of double harnesses in it. There was much talk about the island at the time and many were sure of foul play. The night before the boys left here to go over, they were all three in a saloon and Tommy Boyle had a fistfight with the Gallaghers, but the next morning they had a drink together and decided to be friends again. While on the mainland, they had some words again and did some drinking. There are those that think they had a fight on the way over and the Gallagher boys put him overboard and left him and that only one of them was actually lost. For a number of years afterward, different people from the island reported seeing the other Gallagher boy. He had been living in Chicago a while before this and married, but he and his wife never got along.

"Once a few years afterward, my father and I were out in our fish boat and had made a good catch and were out off Sand Bay where a dozen or more Chicago schooners were anchored, waiting out a blow. The captain of one schooner hailed us and we rowed over and he wanted some fish, so the old man threw him up about a dozen and then we went aboard. The old man wanted some lumber to build a new boat, as our old one was about worn out. The captain, of course, couldn't sell him someone else's lumber, but as the old man wouldn't take any pay for the fish, the captain picked out a few choice pine boards and put them over for him. I was up forward where the crew was bringing in the big anchor with the capstan and one of the men who kept his cap down low looked very familiar to me. After they had gone around a number of times, he began asking me about people on the island, and mentioned a Mrs. Gillespie, who was an aunt of the Gallagher brothers and also some other relatives and he said he knew every stick of timber about the bay. While I was answering his questions as he came around each time, my father called me. While we were rowing back, I told my father about the man and I told him how he looked, a mark below one of his eyes, and a squint in one eye and his height. My father said the deckhand fit exactly this one Gallagher boy. The schooner was by that time before a fair wind down the Lake."

In another story, Dominick told of a sailor who was having some tribulations making his way along shore off the harbor a ways when he saw a man come aboard his starboard bow and start toward him. It so startled him that he dropped the wheel and scrambled up the port side and hid behind the mainmast and looked aft in time to see the man walk right on off the stern into the Lake. He wasn't familiar with ghosts and was pretty scared of this one.

Came back to Charlevoix on the 2 p.m. Arrived in Charlevoix about 5:30 p.m.

Charlevoix to Pentwater, July 21, 1938

Planned to go across Lake Michigan to Sturgeon Bay from Frankfort, but found no ferries that would take a car across until tomorrow night, so decided to come on to see my family at Pentwater and go across on the p.m. ferry tomorrow.

Milwaukee, Wisconsin, July 22, 1938

Repacked this morning and Mildred and Lynn took me to Ludington, Michigan, and I came across to Milwaukee on the *City of Saginaw,* a pretty fine "car barn." On our southwest course across, the Michigan sand dunes remained visible for about one and a half hours: three noticeable peaks about where I judged Pentwater to be and farther south the silver dunes without any vegetation showed up well in contrast to the dark shoreline. Then, the land receded into a haze and the sky and

Milwaukee River at Milwaukee. (From *Picturesque America*)

water shut in a narrow world with us in the center until the Wisconsin shore was raised. I think I would find a sailor's life quite to my liking.

We passed a small boat, about a thirty-foot steamer or diesel in mid-Lake, getting well dusted in heavy seas. We met one car ferry and saw four freighters. Arrived at the Milwaukee pier about 6 a.m. and at the slip about ten minutes later. Came through one bridge with about a foot of water on one side and probably three on the other and never touched.

Came to the Hotel Antlers, recommended by the steward as economical and pretty good. A heavy rain blew up just as I got inside. Unpacked, lunch, a letter to [assistant to the president at the University of Michigan Frank Egleston] Robbins, asking to borrow a sound recording machine from the university if one can be found loose around there. Want to take it and go back to Beaver Island.

Milwaukee, Wisconsin, July 23, 1938

Read over my former Milwaukee notes, looked up addresses, etc., and then called at the offices of Joys Brothers, long-established ship chandlers, for some information and suggestions. Talked with present manager, Mr. Eastlake Joys. His father, John Joys, died about two years ago. Uncle Carl Joys is now living with his daughter, Mrs. Florence J. McCulloch. Said he knows a lot about the material. I phoned out and explained my purpose and arranged to see ex-sailor, ship broker, etc., Carl. I went out à la streetcars, buses, and hoof and found him. He began by saying he knew none of it. I mentioned the painting of schooners in the Joys Brothers office, and that interested him. I then showed him the pictures I have along, and he thawed some more and that led him into the history of the *Wells Burt,* shown in one of my prints, and that into early sailor life, to waterfront saloon life to sailor songs. I repeated some of "The *Bigler*'s Crew," and he took it up. I then showed him my copy and he added a couple of stanzas, one referring to "Dave and Mose," the Buffalo, New York, clothes peddlers who catered to sailors. He added that Dave and Mose sent out boys in rowboats to meet vessels entering Buffalo's harbor and gave the sailors sheets of paper with Lake songs and their own advertising printed on them. He said he had seen bundles of them in Buffalo. I must make a more thorough search when I get over there later this summer. Joys said Dave and Mose would print any songs that sailors would give them.

I asked about the prevalence of ocean songs on the Lakes, and he answered that native sailors scrapped with salt-water men and preferred songs about their own vessels. He added that when he first began sailing in the late 1870s and 1880s, sailors would sing when working the capstan or on a line. He couldn't recall any of the songs, as he said they were never alike any two times. He mentioned a song about Milwaukee's crack schooner fleet, and about some races, but couldn't recall them. He said he hadn't thought about any of those old songs for years.

Milwaukee, Wisconsin, July 27, 1938

Captain Herman Oertling first sailed on Lakes schooners at age twelve in 1876 with his father. He retired only two years ago on his daughter's insistence. He has on one of his house walls a painting of the brig *Dival,* in which he sailed with his father and later commanded himself. He also sailed the schooner *Walter Vail* and several others before changing to steamships. At the time of his retirement, he had completed twenty years of sailing iron-ore freighters for the Cleveland Cliffs Iron Co., but added that he still liked the old windjammers. Life on them was freer, more varied, less regular and at times much more strenuous than on the big freighters.

He recited some lines of "The Timber Drogher *Bigler,*" "The *E. C. Roberts,*" and "The Scow *Julie Plante,*" and added that although he never was much of a singer, he used to know quite a number of songs. "Sailors got up songs about most of the old schooners." Also, there was much singing of chanteys on the old sailboats, especially if the men were feeling good. "It helped much on the long, hard hauls such as setting the heavy courses [big, heavy sails just above the deck]. The men would be wondering what the chanteyman would come up with next, and it kept their minds off what they were doing. And it also gave them a good rhythm to work to.

"Sailors ain't much like they used to be," he continued. "They used to spend all their money as fast as they got it, and never thought of laying any up. It all went in saloons on liquor and women. Now all that's changed—all of it. Down in Buffalo along Canal Street—I tell you, that was a bad place. Many a man has gone in there with his pockets full of money and was never seen again. That's all been cleaned up, and the same in Chicago and other places."

He explained that deepening the connecting channels, especially in the St. Mary's and Detroit and St. Clair Rivers, favored the deeper draft steamboats, and in the 1890s they got all the best traffic and practically drove the sailing vessels off the whole chain of Lakes. "And this deepening of the St. Lawrence is going to do the same thing for our present ships. That'll be the worst thing that ever hit the Lakes, if it comes. It'll ruin Buffalo and all our Lake ports. Them foreigners 'll come in here and take our exports right from under our noses, and then what 'll we do? Sailors' wages will be reduced from a hundred dollars a month to around twenty or less that foreign ships pay now. Yes sir, it'll ruin the Lakes!"

Pentwater, Michigan, August 7, 1938

I found Captain Christopher Fowler, about sixty-five, aboard the U.S. Engineering tug *Manitowoc* in the local channel, where it had come for a pile driver to take to Muskegon, Michigan. He had been away at his former home of Montague, Michigan, over the weekend, and didn't get back until 10 p.m. and was not very talkative. He said his wife had died two years ago, and he was now making his home aboard the tug. He had made only one trip on a sailing vessel as a boy, and had to pump water out of the vessel all the way from Muskegon to Chicago and quit when they got there. He has been on steamboats ever since. Fowler said Guy McCracken of Sturgeon Bay, who made several models, died a couple of years ago. He had lost a few dollars in a local bank that failed there and one day when pretty well filled with liquor, he appeared in front of the bank and heaved a big black stone through the plate glass front. All the people in front, thinking it a bomb, dashed out of the nearest exits. The police took McCracken to the jail and locked him up. He died there during the night.

Fowler planned to start back to Muskegon about 6 o'clock Monday morning where they are doing some work on the harbor breakwater.

[Walton did not make any entries in his journal for the next two weeks.]

Pentwater, Michigan, August 22, 1938

Captain Corey did practically all of his forty and more years of sailing on Lakes Michigan and Superior in the lumber trade to Chicago. He said he was born in western New York State and came with his family to Wisconsin when he was still a boy, and only a few years later he came across Lake Michigan to work in the lumber mills. He has made his home mostly in Pentwater since.

He stated that there were five big lumber mills on the Pentwater lake in the early 1870s and that the village was a very lively place. Many times he has counted twenty to thirty "lumber hooker" vessels in the harbor. Most of them were two-masters and carried a captain, mate, cook, and four men forward. The crew stowed the lumber aboard under the direction of the captain or mate, and the vessel would tow out when fully loaded, day or night, and would generally head for

Milwaukee and then along the shore to Chicago. If weather conditions were favorable, they could cross Lake Michigan overnight and make Chicago late the next day. They practically always had much company on the way and vessels would race each other to the unloading docks.

The Chicago River was almost always full of sailing vessels, mostly lumber hookers, he said. There were also some big three- and four-masted schooners in the grain trade to the Lower Lakes, and some big side-wheel steamers that carried passengers and freight.

The lumber vessels would frequently have to wait one or two days to get an unloading dock. Local "dock wallopers" did the unloading. The crew would be paid off as soon as the vessel was tied up, but they could eat and sleep aboard if they wished until the vessel was ready to tow out for another trip when "their time began again." Most sailors, however, would go to the riverfront saloons and entertainment places and come back to the vessel broke for another trip.

On the trip to Chicago, sailors were always too tired and sleepy to do any singing, but on the trip back, especially in the evening dogwatches when all were on deck, they were always singing or telling big lies about what they had done. That was about the only way they had of entertaining themselves.

BEAVER ISLAND, MICHIGAN, AUGUST 25, 1938

Left Pentwater about 5:45 a.m. The inside of the car was filled to the ceiling almost. Just room for the dog and kittens, a canoe on the top and a bicycle on the front, and Lynn and I in the front seat. We arrived in Charlevoix at 8:30 a.m. I left the car in the garage and grabbed a couple of sandwiches on the way to the dock a few minutes before the *Mary Margaret* left for Beaver Island. Alan Lomax of the folksong section of the Library of Congress met us at the dock and came across with his sound-recording outfit. He said he had spent the day before at the lumberjack festival at Edenville, Michigan. He said there was an ex-showman in charge who was much more interested in a show than in the lumbermen. Lomax didn't get anything there. He spent the two days before that in Mount Pleasant, Michigan, mostly with William McBride to whom I had referred him. Lomax got many recordings from him.

On arrival at the island, Lomax's car refused to function, and we lost about three hours. We took Lomax around the harbor to the fish house of Andy Gallagher and found him. He was all for getting drunk and celebrating something, so Lomax and I bought a case of beer while Lynn slept in the hotel room. I found Dominick Gallagher and we drove out to see John Green and Pat Bonner about coming to the village in the evening to make recordings. Both promised to come in. Dominick talked religion on the way back. He said he was a good Catholic for forty years, but finally decided religion was all a graft and priests the worst offenders, concerned with keeping the people ignorant, and he quit. A priest used to come talk with him, but doesn't anymore.

After eats in the evening, we went to Andy Gallagher's fish house, where Lomax had the recording equipment set up, and soon Andy's whole family and

Beaver Island fiddler Pat Bonner at the King Strang Hotel in the 1950s. (Courtesy Beaver Island Historical Society)

friends came in and Dan and Pat Bonner and family and his "Strad" fiddle and a number of other natives. The case of beer had been emptied in the afternoon, it seems, and Andy was strong for liquor—for someone else to get it—but no one did for a couple of hours as the recording was going along fine. Andy, with much pomp and ceremony, sang in a high pitch, "Don't Judge a Man by the Cut of His Clothes," a "wonderful" song, and every time anybody came in he wanted it played over. Dominick sang "Roll Her to the Wall," and was in the middle of it when some women came in, but he kept on to the end. He then sang a number of others and told a couple of stories that Lomax recorded. One was about a Protestant missionary lecturing to Irishmen here when the jibboom of the mail boat came crashing through the side of the building. Another was about an Indian on the island who cut his own leg off with an axe after he had been pinned down in the dead of winter by a falling tree.

Dan Bonner sang "Yankee Brown," and Pat sang his song, "The *Clifton*," and fiddled a half dozen Irish jigs. After much coaxing, Andy then sang about an Irish peddler, but refused to sing one "that me own mother learned me. No sir, it'll cost anyone $500 to get that song. I'm the only one in the whole of Americay who knows it."

The evening seems to have been a big occasion for all present, even though outdoors it was raining. We all sat about on fish boxes with nets, reels, etc., for background, and a strong aroma of fish in the air. Light was furnished by a couple of gasoline lamps.

John Green didn't come. Dominick said there was considerable rivalry between him and Andy, "although John's a much better singer and knows more songs." He was pretty sure John wouldn't come to Andy's place to sing.

Beaver Island, Michigan, August 26, 1938

In the evening Lomax, Dominick Gallagher, Lynn, and I and some beer drove out to John Green's and found him quite talkative. We set up the recording machine and didn't take it down until about 1 a.m. Most of the time, John was either singing, listening to reproductions of his songs, or talking about them. We made about twenty-five recordings and got the names of about thirty-five to forty titles of others he knows. They range from Child ballads to ocean songs to American outlaw songs. [Harvard ballad scholar Francis James Child is described in Laurie Sommers's introduction.] Lomax will send me the list at Oswego. Green said he thought he knew about a hundred songs. Knows little about the origin of his songs or where or when he learned them. His voice is pretty bad, but he remembers the songs and once started can go through with them. One can't but marvel at his memory for songs. This recording machine is so far ahead of handwriting that there's just no comparison. The flow of the song is in no way interrupted and the melody is recorded complete.

Lomax promised me complete control of all recordings made from "my" informants for two years or more if I wish it. Can get duplicates in a year—he hopes, or copies by special arrangement anytime after October.

Beaver Island, Michigan, August 27, 1938

After a visit with Dominick Gallagher, drove out to Green's again and, with the help of some beer, John again "opened up." He talked songs—Lomax, he, and I— until noon. Green said his people were from Arranmore Island, County Donegal, Ireland. They were mostly fishermen and seafaring people. They had heard of Beaver Island and came. His grandfather had been a "great singer" who remembered a song after hearing it but once. Green mentioned his singing all night, with the help of a jug of liquor. Green said his father owned Lakes sailing vessels and he began sailing as a boy about ten and continued until about twenty-five when he began fishing and working in the lumber woods. He worked in the woods out of Big Bay de Noc in Michigan's Upper Peninsula. He did much singing in both occupations.

He sailed mostly on Lake Michigan, and there was much singing about the vessels. There were no instruments. One individual and then another sang as he thought of songs. They sang at the wheel and whenever a group was together on deck. Francie Roddy's father, with whom he sailed, "was a great singin' man." Green had often heard him sing all through his watch. Peter O'Donnell, an uncle, was also a singer whom he said had composed "The Red Iron Ore." There were many singers in the lumber camps. Friends there would scarcely allow Green to leave when he came back to the island to help his father fish. About that time, he got a chance to buy his present farm of one hundred acres for $1,500 and much timber on it. He cut and shipped out most of it. He had never farmed before, but had been at it mostly since. He sailed on the vessels taking his lumber out. He said there was much singing about the island twenty to thirty years ago during winter parties. He said that if I wanted any particular song I should write him and he'd send it if he knew it. We talked all forenoon out in his "shop."

Didn't get to see Charley Anthony Gallagher or to have Francie Roddy sing. Both Dominick and John said his health was all "shot," and his memory, too.

Between lunch and time for the *Mary Margaret* to leave, I gave Lomax names of informants from Charlevoix up around the Straits and down the west shore to Waukegan, Illinois. He's not interested in Chicago now.

The Charlevoix boat was about an hour late in leaving the island. There was considerable rolling on the way back. Lomax is staying on at the island. He plans to stay with Green as long as the material keeps coming. Arrived in Charlevoix about 6:30, eats, repacked auto, and drove to Mount Pleasant arriving about 1 a.m. and left for Ann Arbor the next noon [Sunday] and arrived about 6 p.m.

Ann Arbor and Port Huron, Michigan, August 31, 1938

Planned to leave on a trip around Lower Lakes yesterday, but could not get sound-recording machine until today. Practiced operating it last evening. It is not much different from Lomax's. Got packed and off shortly after noon. In Detroit, purchased ten blank recording discs and cutting needle, then drove over to home of my student helper, Imis Bouton, and about 7:30 started out for Port Huron. In

The clubhouse at "the Flats" on Lake St. Clair. (From *Picturesque Canada*)

Mount Clemens, our car overheated and the smoke rolling off the top of the engine attracted a considerable audience.

PORT HURON, MICHIGAN, SEPTEMBER 1, 1938

I went visiting among my former acquaintances and located three whom agreed to sing for recordings. Captain William Small, about whom I centered former visits to Port Huron, died about two years ago. We found Dan McDonald living in his house on Quay Street. I explained my purpose, and he offered use of his house and went with me to ask Captain James Putnam.

In the afternoon, Bouton and I set up the sound-records in Mr. McDonald's home, and after getting Captain Putnam, began making recordings. We had considerable trouble with a loud hum and other noises, but finally reduced the noises enough to proceed. Putnam, seventy-nine, sang "The *Julie Plante*":

> On wan dark night on de Lac St. Clair, de win' she blow, blow, blow,
> An' de crew of de wood scow *Julie Plante* got scar' an' run below.
> For de win' she blow like hurricane, by-'n'-by she blow some more,
> An' de scow bus' up jus' off Grosse Pointe, ten acre from de shore.
>
> De captain walk on de fron' deck, he walk on de hin' deck, too—
> He call de crew from up de hol', an' he call de cook also.
> De cook, she's name was Rosie, she kom from Montreal,
> Was chambermaid on lumber barge on de beeg Lachine Canal.

De win' she blow from nor'-eas'-wes', de sout' win' she blow too,
W'en Rosie cry, "Oh, Capitaine, Capitaine, w'at I shall do?"
De captain den t'row out de hank, but still de scow she dreef;
De crew he can't pass on de shore becos' he los' hees skeef.

De night was dark like wan black cat, de wave run high an' fas',
W'en de captain take hees poor Rosie an' lash her to de mas'
An' den he take de life preserve an' jomp off in de lake
Say'n, "Au revoir, ma Rosie dear, I go drown for your sake."

Nex' mornin' veree earlee, 'bout half pas' two-t'ree-four,
De captain, scow, an' poor Rosie was corpses on de shore.
For de win' she blow like hurricane, an' den she blow some more,
An' de scow bus' up jus' off Grosse Pointe, ten acre from de shore.

Now, all good wood-scow sailormen, take warnin' by dat storm,
An' go maree some nice French girl, an' leev on wan beeg farm—
De win' may blow like hurricane, an' s'pose she blow some more—
You can't get drown on Lac St. Clair so long you stay on shore.

Putnam then recited a poem in French patois about some fishermen on the Detroit River and another poem about Peter White. [This song and the poem, about Marquette, Michigan, civic leader and investor Peter White, are in a book by William Henry Drummond.] Following this, Mr. McDonald sang "The Red Iron Ore."

Captain Alex "Pat" Gallarneau, now seventy-nine, sang a song about the *Oliver Cromwell* and part of "The *Bigler*." Dan McDonald then sang "The *Bigler*" entire with the help of the version I had typed off. Next, Gallarneau sang a song about "The Wabash Cannonball" and another, "Mike Maloney's Arrival in New York." He also sang without being recorded "The Fatal Wedding," "The Baggage Coach Ahead," and a couple later ones.

Tom McLaughlan, eighty-two, in the morning promised to sing what he could of "The *Africa*," but about noon had a heart attack and couldn't. He said the song told of the loss of the schooner in Georgian Bay. McDonald and Gallarneau mentioned a number of other Lakes songs. Mr. McDonald said a man named "Red" O'Brien of Oswego, New York, wrote dozens of songs about the Lakes including "The Red Iron Ore." He was shipmate with him a number of times. McDonald and Gallarneau said that many of the amusement songs, such as "The *Bigler*," were used in place of work chanteys and made good pulling songs. They also mentioned "Paddy Doyle's Boots," "Away, Rio," "Rolling Home," "The *Dreadnaught*," and "The *Cumberland*'s Crew."

I was just reminded since I got here that all of Ontario has a twenty-five-cycle electric current instead of the American sixty-cycle current and that the sound-recording machine I have will not operate on a twenty-five-cycle current. I tried all over town to get a converter or the necessary additions to attach to a storage battery, but without success. It looks like no recording in Ontario.

PORT HURON, MICHIGAN, SEPTEMBER. 2, 1938

Tried out some of last night's records and found them so bad—loud hum—that we decided to have the machine checked over for shorts or whatnot. I also wanted to get a converter to take into Ontario so that our sound-recorder can be used on the twenty-five-cycle current. Nothing of the kind in Port Huron or Sarnia, so we drove back to Detroit. Found nobody at the Metropolitan Sound Co. on Woodward Avenue who knew anything about what was needed, so phoned half a dozen places and finally found a radio engineering shop out E. Jefferson Avenue. He found a "short" in the microphone cord connection for four dollars and informed us that the motor in the machine would have to be re-wired to permit its use on twenty-five-cycle current. So, minus four dollars and a short, we drove back to Port Huron. In the evening, we set up again at Mr. McDonald's and made a new record of Captain Gallarneau's "*Oliver Cromwell*" and "Wabash Cannonball." Then we got Alfred Osborne, eighty-seven, an early sailor and later plasterer, and he sang for recording "The *Lady Leroy*," "The Shantyman's Life," "The Boston Burglar," "a Dutch song" from the ocean, and a couple of short ones. Ruined one record when the cutting needle didn't cut. Got repacked and away to the rooming place about midnight.

BRIGHTON TO PICTON, ONTARIO, SEPTEMBER 8, 1938

Located "Bobby" Dale, eighty-eight, at his farm home a mile south of Brighton. He is a five-foot Englishman with a memory as clear as an eighteen-year-old's. He said he ran away to sail on the Lakes when he was twelve, and has sailed in all the Lake ports and in all kinds of vessels. The old schoonermen, according to him, were the real sailors. Any land jack can sail in a steamboat. I showed him some schooner pictures and he recognized about half of them at once. When I mentioned "The *Bigler*," "The Red Iron Ore," and "The *Maggie Hunter*," he recited a number of stanzas of each. He said he had heard songs about the *Moonlight*, "Sally Riley-O," and many others.

Came on to Picton about noon. After lunch, found Captain Nelson Hudgins at his gas and soft-drink station. He is not in very good health. Bad heart. He went over "The *Maggie Hunter*" with me. It seems to be the only song he knows. He changed the order of some of the stanzas from what I have. He said the day she was lost was a bad one. Some vessels going into the harbor at Oswego met the *Hunter* towing out and told Captain Nixon that it was not fit for a vessel out there but he replied, "She'll go to Toronto or to hell." He kept on and was lost not far above the harbor.

Mr. William Head, eighty-two, was at his home, looking about the same as he did four years ago. He remembered my work. He said he sailed in the schooner *John Bigler* in 1881, the year before he was married, and that "The *Bigler's* Crew" was current then. Men sang it in the fo'c'sle and in shore saloons. She was carrying timber from Lake Superior to Tonawanda, New York, and was full canal size, bluff forward, with two masts and a big spread of canvas, but very hard to steer—a "man killer"—and the chorus referred to this. He said she pushed the whole Lake before her as she traveled. The "juberju" [mentioned in the song] he thought meant simply the rigging. He had heard it was composed by a man named Clark who hailed from Buffalo. He said Clark would make up songs about each vessel he sailed and then when his money was gone would sing or trade them for more drinks in shore saloons. Clark also wrote "The *Jennie P. King*," he said.

Aboard one vessel he was in was a man named Al Kelley from Nova Scotia who knew all the sailor songs he ever heard of and sang them continuously and made up some. He remembers that a song about "The *City of Boston*," an ocean clipper, was a particularly beautiful one.

PICTON, ONTARIO, SEPTEMBER 9, 1938

After several calls at his home, I finally caught up with Henry McConnell, a wiry, high-strung, medium-sized man who is still going strong. He was in a makeshift garage in back of his house, well covered with grease and dirt from his automobile, which he was "overhauling." On the mention of sailing on the Great Lakes, he brightened up and dropped his tools, and after hurriedly wiping his hands, insisted that we go into the house and sit down.

He said that he began sailing on Lakes windjammers in 1879 when he was twelve years old, and continued until there were no more to sail in. He never liked working on steamboats. Early in the present century, he "took up farmin' an' about everything else around here."

He recalled that there were many old "salties" in the Lakes vessels when he first went sailing, and when several of them were aboard they would always sing chanteys at their work. He said he always liked to be shipmates with ocean men as they were good sailors and most of them had some good songs. "I learned a good one once from an Irish sailor from Dublin about an American captain in some war who outsailed the best of the British fleet and made his escape from the whole of them. And I remember another man who sang some songs about some sailors and their vessel being lost up in the Arctic Ocean on a whaling trip. [These might have been "The Stately *Southerner*," with its account of John Paul Jones's exploits, and "The Greenland Fisheries."]

He also recalled fragments of a song called "The Seamen's Union":

We are a band of seamen, a jolly, jolly crew,
As ever sailed the ocean, or wore the jackets blue.
We plow the deep dark waters, without a thought or fear,
We sing and sport in every port, and drive away dull care.

We are a band of seamen, with a password and a sigh;
The shamrock, rose, and thistle around our banner twine.
The maple leaf is our embrace, Victoria is our queen;

Not her's the blame, our union's name, the Orange and the Green.

Here's a health to every captain who ships a union crew,
Here's a health to the girls with flowing curls that like the boys in blue.

He continued that he never paid much attention to the nationalities of the vessels they sailed in. "I guess I shipped in many more American than Canadian vessels, and the 'salties' who came here from all over, it made no difference to them where the vessel came from. They knew ship talk and could get along on any vessel." He continued that the men from the oceans, and even some from the Lakes ports, went by all sorts of nicknames. No one seemed to know their real names, and many of them had been all over the world, but had no home, no family, nor even any money. They spent it as fast as they made it, or faster. In the spring at the opening of navigation on the Lakes, the men who spent the winter in port boardinghouses were always in debt and wouldn't be "in the clear" until the middle of summer. If any of them lost their lives by accident or otherwise, they would nearly always be buried at public expense in whatever port they happened to be brought to, or were in, and their families would never know anything about it. "I often wondered what that would be like—their people not knowing, and still expectin' to hear from them or, perhaps, see them."

He told of some Lakes episodes including several concerning a big Irish sailor named "Con" Shay who "was built like a damned gorilla, and as strong," with whom he had been shipmates a number of times. It seems that "Con" made quite a name for himself for drinking and fighting and for playing practical jokes. He would often pass himself off as master of a vessel when in a saloon and "hire" some greenhorns and send them aboard some big vessel, telling them to pay no attention to what a crazy man aboard did or said, as he often thought he was captain or mate. He once got a big supply of goods out of a ship chandler by playing the part of a captain.

After a four-hour session, McConnell's son reminded him that he was supposed to be out at his oil well. At the door as I was leaving, he extended his hand in a good-bye, and then, after a pause, he remarked, "I understand that all the sailing vessels are gone off the oceans, too. I always hoped to get in a few trips on one of them big square-riggers."

Oswego, New York, September 11, 1938

John S. Parsons was reading a newspaper in his ship chandler's office on the Oswego riverfront when I made my return visit, and several other ex-sailor frequenters of his establishment were doing the same. He was not overjoyed at my intrusion, even though he took me for a customer, but he at once warmed up when I explained my purpose. He and his "guests" talked more of the Great Lakes, sailing vessels, and sailors than I had heard at any one time or place before.

He said he made many trips up the Lakes with his schooner-captain father during summer vacations while he was in high school, and then afterwards he sailed on windjammers a half dozen seasons before getting a full-time job with Daniel Lyons and Son, Oswego ship chandlers. In 1890, he purchased the business and has operated it in the same location on Water Street and the Oswego riverfront until the present. One of the men in the store said that Mr. Parsons knew more about Lake Ontario vessels and many others than any other man living, and he added that one of the last schooners on the Lakes, the *John S. Parsons*, was named for him.

He has a considerable store of all sorts of marine supplies on hand, but said, "Business has never been as good as when the old schooners sailed the Lakes." He seems to be a mine of information, and talked freely about Great Lakes sailing vessels and their careers, and sailor life aboard them. He recognized many of the song fragments I have assembled, gave additional lines to some, and information about the vessels concerned. He also wrote out half a dozen new songs, dictated others, and made corrections on several I had obtained elsewhere.

He recalled that during the 1880s there were over sixty sailing vessels registered in Oswego, and when they were lying in the river during the winter season their masts and spars made the river look like a forest. There was also much rivalry in the spring among the owners, each trying to beat the others in fitting out for the season. He added that there was quite a lively waterfront life here, especially in the early season when the ocean sailors came in from the St. Lawrence and from New York to ship on Oswego vessels.

He was much interested in the material I had assembled since my first visit. He also dictated parts of a number of chanteys he recalled from his sailing days about half a century earlier. [John S. Parsons died in 1940, and his wife gave his collection of ship models, drawings, paintings, and photographs of Lakes vessels to the Oswego County Historical Collections.]

OSWEGO, NEW YORK, SEPTEMBER 13, 1938

I spent most of the afternoon with Ben Peckham in his chicken-coop workshop. He is seventy-three and has a bad heart and spends his time whittling out vessel models. He began sailing in the late 1870s and continued for about twenty-five years. His father and three brothers all sailed on schooners. He said his father, Thomas, knew hundreds of songs and composed a large number himself. George Peckham said his father would make up a song about some event while he was walking away from it, "and damn good ones, too." Ben's brother George said he learned most of the songs he knows from his father. He said his father wrote down all the songs he liked and those he composed in a big notebook, and a short time before he died, he loaned it to a cousin, a Mr. Cloud of Pittsburgh, and never got it back. "If I only had that book now, I'd be setting on Easy Street. It would be worth a pile of money."

Ben Peckham told of one time when he was in a Chicago saloon and a group of men were singing and drinking, and "a well-dressed man, who had been singing a lot, said he knew every damn sailor song there was. I knowed he didn't, for I had one in my pocket the Old Man had sent along in a letter, so I says, 'I don't believe you!' just like that, an' I says it right to his face. He jes' looked over to the table where me and me friends was a'settin', and went right on talkin' as if we wasn't there at all, but me pardner, he speaks right up an' he says, 'Hey, Mister, didn't ya hear what me friend here says?' An' the man says right back, 'That feller don't look to me as though he knowed anything.' Well, that made me mad, an' I was about to go over an' spoil his good looks when me pardner says, 'Would ya like to lay a bet on it?' The man took him up and put some bills on the bar, but we didn't have no money, so me pardner says, 'How 'bout drinks for the house?' an' he says, 'It's all right with me.' Then, I gets up and sings me father's song about 'The Wreck of the Schooner *Antelope*,'" what was lost on Lake Michigan. I jes' made up a tune—an' when I finished he said, 'By God, I don't know that one—drinks for the house!' An' would ya know it, some of the men there at the bar damn near cried when I sang that song.

"I mind a feller singin' there that, by God, had the sweetest voice that ever came out of a man's mouth. He was old, musta been sixty or seventy, an' had on jes' plain sailor clothes, but he had tears runnin' down the cheeks of every damn one of us. The bartender gave him all the free drinks he wanted. Some of them sailors was the best goddamn singers that I ever heard in all me life, an' none of yer damn crooning and silly jazz songs. Them was real songs. I knowed some of the men and vessels they was about."

Peckham gave me in a half-singing, half-talking way the words of "The Schooner *Oriole*," "The Schooner *M. J. Cummings*," "The Propeller Old *Bay State*," and "The Tug *Alanson Sumner*," all composed by his father, and parts of some others. He also recited some stanzas of the chanteys "Reuben Ranzo" and "Away, Rio," and added that "I used to lead them in chanteys when me friends made canvas, an' brought in the anchor—jes' any damn words that would rhyme. We usually had a mouth organ, banjo, or accordion aboard, an', by God, we had some good music. If ya couldn't sing or play something or dance a jig when in a bar, ya had to buy the drinks."

He then sang and hummed a number of sentimental Irish songs, some he said were Scotch, some others, and two from the lumber woods. He said he "must o' knowed a hundred or more" when he was sailing and "learned 'em all" from his father and other sailors. He dramatized the actions of his songs as he sang and pretty well lived the stories in them. He took each song to be a true account of an actual happening.

BUFFALO, NEW YORK, SEPTEMBER 15, 1938

Learned that Captain William Clark, who gave me some fragments in August 1933, and seemed to have possibilities, was killed in an auto accident two years ago. Captain Thomas Hylant, another promising informant I met that month, died about the same time.

Found Captain Duncan McLeod, about seventy, at his home on Amber Street in the southeast section of the city. An old shipmate of his, Peter MacPhail of Sarnia, told me with much certainty that he was a singer and knew many Lakes

The *William F. Barnum* of Buffalo, New York, in its home harbor. Grain elevators stand across the Niagara River, at right. (Courtesy Dossin Great Lakes Museum)

songs, and especially one about the steamer *Idaho*. Captain McLeod, however, insisted that he never was much of a singer, knew only "The *Bigler*" and "The Red Iron Ore," and didn't recall ever having sung any song about the steamer *Idaho*. He seemed to be anxious to help, but couldn't recall any songs at all. He has made a number of vessel models and is now making one of the ocean clipper *Flying Cloud*. He said his brother R. R. McLeod was master of the car ferry *Bessemer 2* when she was lost on Lake Erie with all aboard, and his brother J. C. McLeod was mate. The vessel left Conneaut, Ohio, in threatening weather, but nothing unusual. While in mid-lake, a blizzard struck, blanketing both shores and lashing the Lake. The steamer evidently tried to make its destination, as the whistle was plainly heard there, and later back at Port Stanley. When the storm subsided, she could not be found and never has been to the present time. She carried a load of railroad cars loaded with structural steel and had no stern gate to protect her in high seas. She had a crew of thirty-two and one passenger. The day after the disaster, a yawl boat was found about fifteen miles northeast of Conneaut with nine bodies, all frozen stiff. The mate's body was found frozen in some ice in the Niagara River the following spring, and the captain's body was found half buried in the sand at Long Point the following September 10, months after the disaster. The porter who missed the steamer and stayed in Conneaut that trip was the only regular member of the crew saved. Most of the men came from Conneaut. Captain McLeod said he was in Buffalo at the time and, when he heard of the loss, went immediately to Conneaut and for several days searched the Lake for bodies or wreckage, but found neither. He said someone had written a song about the loss, but it was a pretty poor one.

Captain McLeod said he did his first sailing on schooners and that it was much harder than working on steamboats, but he liked it much better. "There were real sailors then, men could do anything aboard a vessel that had to be done. Now, most of the men we get as sailors don't know one end of a vessel from the other.

And when they dress up to go ashore, my God, you'd think by the looks of them that they owned the vessel."

On the old vessels there was strict discipline. The captain was always addressed as "sir" and the mate as "mister," and no sailor went aft of the mainmast unless to take the wheel or to do some work. They always went and returned along the leeward side of the vessel. They would never go to windward of an officer. Most sailors would not associate with steamboat men, and many boardinghouses that catered to sailors would not admit steamboat men. They were not admitted to the Seamen's Union until the old schooners had pretty well disappeared.

Sailors were and still are quite superstitious. They followed their hunches. Should a vessel have a streak of bad luck, the crew would usually hold some individual sailor in the crew as being a "Jonah," especially if it were known that any in the group had been in difficulty. Whistling was seldom permitted, as it brought headwinds. But in a calm, whistling might bring up a wind. Captain McLeod still does not like to hear whistling aboard a vessel.

Buffalo's waterfront boardinghouse district was probably the largest on the Lakes. It centered about Canal Street at the foot of Main, and also along Conneaut and Ohio Streets. One could always meet trouble there if he wanted it, but otherwise the region was as safe as any other part of the city. Canal Street was about solid saloons. The larger ones all had their side rooms for dancing and for the free-and-easy shows. They had professional entertainers who put on dramatic skits, sang, and danced, but who would always give the floor to anyone who wanted to try his hand. Sailors often tried it, and some were good. Entertainers catered to the sailors and sang their songs.

The shows were free, that is, a man paid nothing to get in. There were always plenty of girls around. They would dance with anyone, but after a few minutes, they always wanted drinks and before a man got out, his money was mostly gone. The second stories also catered to sailors. Many tales got around about men getting dropped out of the back doors of these places into the canal by the house bouncers, but Captain McLeod never knew of a case. The best-known sailor hangout in Buffalo in the 1890s was Bonney's Concert Hall on Canal Street. It had a long bar, probably sixty or seventy feet long, with a dozen bartenders and more waitresses and twenty-five or thirty girls about.

Later in the afternoon, we drove back to Shearer's restaurant and exchanged experiences with Mrs. Shearer a while and then she piloted me to the edge of Tonawanda to call on a Mrs. Broadbeck, former cook and operator of canal boats. She made her last trip in 1915, taking a load of lumber to Syracuse. Her relatives lived aboard their three boats the year around. They made their winter home wherever they happened to take their last load. They carried six horses and two mules, four pulling and four riding in six-hour shifts. The vessels also carried two drivers, two wheelsmen, a deckhand, and themselves.

Men on the towpath sang a lot, especially late at night, to keep awake. They mostly sang songs popular at the time.

Ship canal and coal docks at Buffalo. (From *Picturesque America*)

Buffalo, New York, September 17, 1938

Am at the "Homestead" rooming establishment, formerly a sort of YMCA place for sailors, located near the foot of Main. Didn't find anybody with any new information, so went to the Anchor tavern, another twenty-five-cent rooming place and saloon on lower Main Street, and located Jimmy Riley, about eighty, who has spent most of his life in Buffalo. He knew the chorus of "The *Bigler*," some lines of "The Red Iron Ore," and the chorus of "The Raging Canal," but nothing else of that nature.

The best known "sporting houses" here were operated by "Cat-Eyed" Annie on Canal, Big Carrie Austin, and Carrie Sanders. The last two acted as their own bouncers. These and others all had a dozen or two girls attached.

The saloons sold schooners of beer for five cents and whiskey for five cents and ten cents and gave a free lunch with it. It was the girls' job to get the sailors' money and they worked on commission. Things were orderly most of the time, but occasionally some men "started things" and then it was "plenty rough."

The old canal passed along the back doors of the establishments on the Lake side of the street, and the crews of the canal boats came in numbers, often in bare feet and trousers rolled up to their knees. They were pretty heavy drinkers. Sailors liked to poke fun at them by singing of great storms that the canal boats had to weather. Mates from vessels that wanted to ship crews would come to the boardinghouse-saloon-whorehouse place and sing out that they wanted some men, vessel men, steamboat men, or any others and the men who wanted "sites" would go along. When the vessel tied up at her destination, the men were at once paid off and they went to the sailor boardinghouse-saloon district in the port they were in.

In the spring, large numbers of "Liverpool men"—ocean sailors—appeared about the places on Canal and stayed until shipping out. They usually made slighting remarks about sailing on the Lakes until they had made a trip or two. They found they had difficulty steering and usually didn't stay long. Some worked their way up on the canal, but most came by railroad.

The old life on Canal Street is now entirely gone. The sailors left and now hundreds of Italians live there. The name of the street even is changed to Dante Place.

Akron and Cleveland, Ohio, September 19, 1938

Not a very early start today, but arrived in Akron about noon and after lunch found home of Captain Pearl R. Nye, singer and former Ohio canal man. His niece said he was in the city hospital, and had been for several weeks. Went there and found him after some waiting, of course. He is quite short and thick, but interesting and full of Ohio canal songs and incidents. We talked in a hallway for about an hour. He is troubled with dropsy. He said most all of his material was at his room, but he had with him a song, "An Old Canal Skipper," which he loaned me to copy. He said he made recordings of about sixty songs for Lomax's Library of Congress collection and gave them manuscripts for a couple hundred more. He said he made up songs to popular tunes of the day. He expects to be out of the hospital Thursday noon and added that if I'd return then, he'd make any recordings I wanted.

Came on to Cleveland, lunched, and located a room. Too late to make any calls, so went to a movie, *Boys Town,* with Spencer Tracy in the lead.

Cleveland, Ohio, September 21, 1938

Post office—no mail. Went to the library and started Imis examining some "Great Lakes clippings" files and local histories. Had lady in charge of a Works Progress Administration indexing project go through their now incomplete index for Lakes material, but we found none.

Called at the office of Joseph Kendrick in Rockefeller Building and learned that he's out of the city and not expected back until Monday. Captain F. A. Bailey in the same building was in, but had nothing new to supply except a couple of names. Captain William Summerville died two years ago. My batting average so far today is about zero. Dodged rains all morning, but got caught in a downpour in front of a theater where Ignace Jan Paderewski's *Moonlight Sonata* was playing and went in. A pretty good show, about half of it being Paderewski's music.

Later in the afternoon, I walked down along the east bank of the river north of Superior Street. I talked with a couple of bridge tenders who had been about the river a half century or more. One was a former sailor and policeman and had several other occupations. He said that the sailor boardinghouse district in the early 1890s, as far back as he knew, was centered about the end of the Main Street bridge. "No rough life like Canal Street in Buffalo," he said. "People here wouldn't stand for it."

At Hansher's marine supply store, found Louis, about sixty, and three other men who have spent their whole lives near there. They said the Merchant's Hotel, operated by Dave McCarthy at the west end of the Main Street bridge, was one of the best known during the schooner period and patronized largely by sailors. It was a saloon and a hotel. In the later 1890s, Henry Rye's saloon on River Street, now Ninth, was also popular with sailors. The proprietor had a pet donkey that stayed in the barroom and would beg for beer and if given enough would get real intoxicated. Brother Jones, a one-armed sailor-preacher had a "floating bethel" which he usually kept tied up on the east end of the river near a chandler's, and held services aboard early Sunday and often between times.

Cleveland and Akron, Ohio; Ann Arbor, Michigan, September 22, 1938

Found Pearl R. Nye in his overstuffed third-floor back room, having a few hours earlier been discharged from the city hospital. He was about five feet, six inches tall and weighed probably two-hundred fifty pounds. He informed me that he was born in 1872 on his father's canal boat on the route from Cleveland to Lake Erie to Portsmouth on the Ohio River, and lived on canal boats until about 1913. Then, the railroads took all the local freight and they could no longer get anything to carry. "Hundreds of boats had earlier operated the length of the canal carrying farm products, mostly grain, to Cleveland for shipment east, and to Portsmouth for shipment down the Ohio and Mississippi Rivers." In the busy season, each boat employed two teams of horses or mules, two drivers, two steerers, and a cook. Each shift worked six hours on and six hours off around the clock.

In slack times, they used only one team, and tied up at night wherever they happened to be, frequently alongside close friends, and they would spend half the night on one boat singing and otherwise entertaining themselves. They always had some musical instruments aboard, "and we had some grand times." He said that there was much rivalry for cargoes and some feuds and fighting among various boat crews. Each boat could carry from twenty-five to thirty tons of cargo, depending on the depth of the water over the sills of the shallowest locks. The owner's family lived in the after cabin, the crew stayed up forward, and the horses rode in the center of the boat.

Nye stated that he never sailed on any Great Lakes vessels, but when his boat was tied up and unloading cargo in the Cleveland harbor, he got acquainted with many lakesmen. "We got along all right, but of course, there was some fighting when the men had had too much to drink."

He stated that his whole family [of eighteen] were singers; he himself had "made up" probably 300 songs mostly about canal life, to the various tunes he heard in other boats as well as in theaters along the canal. Some of them "caught on" and were frequently sung by the crews of other boats. He explained that he used to pass the time when steering by composing songs. He also mentioned that

Ivan Walton sometimes attempted the songs he collected. (Courtesy Lynn and Sue Walton)

as a young man he had composed the song "A Trip on the Canal," which was changed to fit the Erie Canal and said to be ninety years old. He has many songs pasted together to form a scroll about twenty-five feet long. He added that he also had a collection of several hundred pictures of early life along the old Ohio Canal. A local schoolteacher, he added, was assisting him in writing a book on the old Ohio Canal.

We drove back to Cleveland in a rain, arriving about 7:30 in the evening. Found Mr. Walter Patterson, about seventy, at Hutter's restaurant-hotel-saloon and he suggested that we might find an ex-sailor/singer named Barney at Webber's saloon later in the evening. After eats, we went down there and found him, a bit "high." He sang with super flourishes "The Red Iron Ore," about two stanzas and the chorus, the same amount of "The *Bigler*," an original version of "The *Julie Plante*," and his "Turkey in the Straw" in what he said was French. That seemed to be his whole repertoire.

He turned out to be Harvey Bonnah, formerly of Algonac, Michigan, and a cousin of Andy Bonnah of Port Huron [July 6, 1933]. He showed me his master's papers, his "union book," and other evidence of much sailing experience on Lakes and oceans. He is now about sixty and on the bottom. He does chores at saloons, sleeps in flophouses or anyplace he can find, and spends what little money he gets for whiskey. There seems to be scores of others in his circumstances about Cleveland and still more in Buffalo.

We got packed up again about 10 p.m. and set out on the home stretch of our summer's trip. We both had to be in Ann Arbor on the 23rd, Imis to enroll and I to help on the enrollment committee. We stopped a few times along the route for gasoline and lunches and finally arrived in Ann Arbor about 2:30 a.m.

The people who Ivan Walton met and the songs he collected in the 1930s sustained him through his retirement from the University of Michigan until his death in 1968 in Arizona. His family says he never stopped working on refining and organizing his collection.

Yet, Walton never completed his book of songs. A friend speculated that Walton could not close the covers on the book because the people he met provided so much color and context that the songs could not be separated from them. Essentially, the whole thing was just too big.

Fortunately, Walton's notes, recordings, and a few photographs were saved by his wife, Mildred, his son, Lynn, and Lynn's wife, Sue. They shipped the material back to the University of Michigan, where it is today, preserved and catalogued at the Michigan Historical Collections in the Bentley Library. Walton's meticulous record keeping, the foresight of his family, and the stewardship of the people at the library saved the collection.

In 2002, Wayne State University Press published *Windjammers: Songs of the Great Lakes Sailors*, which is, as faithfully as I could edit it, Walton's intended volume of song, musical scores, artwork and, in a wrinkle he did not foresee, some of his field recordings. This book is meant to supplement that one with the personalities and travails of the informants who kept the age of sail alive long enough for Walton to capture it.

GLOSSARY

aft: Toward the rear of the vessel.

bone in her teeth: A vessel moving fast enough to throw up white water at its bow was said to have a bone in its teeth.

bow: Forward end of the vessel.

bowline (bo'lin): Line used to haul the leading edge of a sail forward; a mooring line from the front of the boat to the pier.

bowsprit: Spar extending forward and up from the bow to secure foremast stays and head sails.

bulwarks: Sides of a ship that extend above the top deck.

canaller: Vessel built to the maximum width that could fit through a canal system, often having sheer sides and a blunt bow and stern; also a worker who assisted vessels on their passage through the canal.

capstan: A winding mechanism with a vertical axle. It is set in the deck and rotated by men pushing on capstan bars that radiate from it like spokes in a wheel.

cathead: Heavy timber extending over a vessel's bow to which the anchor is hoisted.

centerboard: A retractable keel.

chandler: A seller of specific goods. A ship's chandler would sell nautical goods, but there are chandlers in other businesses as well. The chandler's place of business is called a chandlery.

corposant: An electrical discharge during a storm, usually at a point, such as the end of a mast or spar. Its root words mean "holy body." These discharges were also called St. Elmo's fire. St. Elmo was the patron saint of sailors.

davit: One of the crane arms supporting the vessel's small work or lifeboats.

dogwatch: A customary four-hour watch cut into two two-hour segments of 4–6 p.m. and 6–8 p.m. used to let men move or dodge from one schedule to another. "Dogwatch" appears to be a corruption of "dodgewatch."

drogher: Derogatory name for a slow and clumsy vessel, often used in the Great Lakes lumber trade.

drudge: A dredge.

dummy: A navigation buoy without a bell.

ensign: Flag showing a vessel's nationality.

forecastle (fo'c'sle): Originally a forward raised structure above the maindeck, it came to refer to a space forward and below deck where the crew slept.

fore-'n'-after: A vessel with a fore-and-aft rig, that is, with two sails set along the line of the keel.

gaff: Spar that spreads the top edge of a sail.

green water: When spray and foam come aboard, the water is white. When green water comes aboard, look out!

gunwhale (gunnel): The highest trim along the sides of a vessel.

halyard or halliard: Line used to hoist a yard or sail.

hooker: A small vessel that was moved in the harbor by repeatedly being drawn up over its anchor—its hook—which was taken out in a small boat and dropped for the next maneuver.

jibboom: A spar extending forward beyond the bowsprit of a ship from which a headsail or jib is set.

kedge: A small anchor set out a distance from a boat. Kedging is the act of moving the boat by pulling on the anchor line.

lanyard (lan'ard): A light line, usually used to lace equipment to rigging.

lee: The side of the ship that is away from the wind; on the side of something that shelters the vessel from the wind. The opposite of windward.

mainsail: Literally, the main sail.

masthead: Top of a mast.

packet: Vessel making regularly scheduled trips carrying passengers, mail, and express freight.

pier: A platform extending over the water from shore, supported by piles.

quarterdeck: The after-part of the deck from which officers issue commands.

raffee: A triangular sail set above the uppermost yard of a topsail schooner.

reef: To reduce a sail's area by making the reef points fast to a boom or yard, thus eliminating part of the sail from the wind.

salties: Sailors or vessels who have sailed on salt water.

scow: A flat-bottomed boat used to transport bulky material such as sand, stone, or gravel.

scull: To propel a boat forward by pushing an oar side-to-side at the stern of the boat.

sheet: Line used to control the position of a sail. A sheet is boarded, or the sail is sheeted home, when it is hauled around nearly parallel with the keel to enable a vessel to sail close to the wind. "Give her sheet" means let the sheet pay out so that the sails will be at right angles to a following wind.

shroud: A stationary line, usually used in multiples, to hold a mast upright. This is part of a vessel's standing rigging.

Skillagalee: Corruption of Isle aux Galets, French for "island of pebbles," in northern Lake Michigan.

spar: Any pole, including mast, yard, or boom.

spile: A post or piling.

starboard: The right side of the vessel as the observer is facing forward.

stay: Standing rigging that supports a mast.

staysail: A fore-and-aft sail hoisted on a stay.

stern: The aft end of the vessel.

steward: Crew member who oversees the supplying, storage, and provision of food and drink.

stokehole: Compartment in which the furnaces of a vessel are stoked or fired.

sundog: Bright spots or fragmentary rainbows appearing to the left or right or on both sides of the sun. It is a diffraction caused by ice crystals. Also called a dog or a weathergaw. The moon can also have dogs.

tonnage: Dead weight is a vessel's actual carrying capacity. Gross tonnage is the internal capacity measures in units of 100 cubic feet. Net tonnage is the actual area available for freight and passengers. Net tonnage is gross tonnage less the space taken up by boilers, engines, chain lockers, quarters, and other unavailable areas.

topsail: The sail set above and sometimes on the gaff in a fore-and-aft rigged ship.

vang: Tackle running from the end of the gaff boom to the deck.

windlass: A horizontal bar or barrel used for hoisting or hauling.

windward (wind'ard): Toward the direction from which the wind is blowing but outside the vessel.

wing and wing: Sails set to extend over both sides of the vessel.

Wobble Shanks: A corruption of Waugoshance Point in northeast Lake Michigan.

BIBLIOGRAPHY

Barrett, J. Lee. *Speedboat Kings: 25 Years of International Speedboating.* Detroit: Arnold-Powers, 1939.

Beck, Earl Clifton. *Songs of the Michigan Lumberjacks.* Ann Arbor: University of Michigan Press, 1941.

Bronner, Simon J. *American Folklore Studies: An Intellectual History.* Lawrence: University of Kansas Press, 1986.

Bunce, Oliver Bell, and William Cullen Bryant, eds. *Picturesque America; or, The Land We Live In.* 2 vols. New York: D. Appleton, 1872–74.

Child, Francis James, ed. *The English and Scottish Popular Ballads, 1882–98.* 5 vols. New York: Folklore Press in association with Pageant Book Company, 1957–65.

Dean, Michael Cassius [M. C.]. *The Flying Cloud, and One Hundred and Fifty Other Old Time Songs and Ballads of Outdoor Men, Sailors, Lumber Jacks, Soldiers, Men of the Great Lakes, Railroadmen, Miners, etc.* Virginia, MN: Quickprint, 1922. Reprint. Norwood, PA: Norwood Editions, 1973.

Evening Telegram, Toronto, June 30, 1934.

Filene, Benjamin. *Romancing the Folk, Public Memory & American Roots Music.* Chapel Hill: University of North Carolina Press, 2000.

Havighurst, Walter. *The Long Ships Passing: The Story of the Great Lakes.* New York: MacMillan, 1942.

Hendrix, Glen A. "Songs of Beaver Island." *Journal of Beaver Island History* 2 (1980): 59–111.

Hirsch, Jerrold. "Modernity, Nostalgia, and Southern Folklore Studies: The Case of John Lomax." *Journal of American Folklore* 105/416 (spring 1992): 183–207.

Karamanski, Theodore. *Schooner Passage.* Detroit: Wayne State University Press in association with the Chicago Maritime Society, 2000.

Leary, James P. "Fieldwork Forgotten, or Alan Lomax Goes North." *Midwestern Folklore* 26/2 (fall 2001): 5–20.

Library of Congress, American Folklife Center. *The Ethnographic Experience: Sidney Robertson Cowell in Northern California.* In California Gold, Northern California Folk Music in the Thirties. Collected by Sidney Robertson Cowell. http://memory.loc.gov/ammem/afccchtml/cowsonek.html.

Lomax, Alan. Excerpt from the Archive of American Folk-Song, Report of the Assistant in Charge. *Annual Report from the Librarian of Congress, 1939.* Washington, DC: U.S. GPO. 218–25.

———. *Saga of a Folksong Hunter: A Twenty-Year Odyssey with Cylinder, Disc and Tape.*

http://www.alan-lomax.com/about_saga.html

Lomax, John A., and Alan Lomax. *Cowboy Songs and Other Frontier Ballads.* New York: Sturgis and Walton, 1910.

McEwen, George M. "Ivan H. Walton: A Pioneer Michigan Folklorist." *Michigan Academician* 2/3 (winter 1970): 73–77.

Mansfield, J. B. *History of the Great Lakes.* Vol. 2. Chicago: J. H. Beers, 1899.

Munro-Grant, George, ed. *Picturesque Canada: The Country as It Was and Is.* 2 vols. Toronto: Belden, 1882.

Poremba, David Lee, ed. *Detroit in Its World Setting.* Detroit: Wayne State University Press, 2001.

Rickaby, Franz. *Ballads and Songs of the Shanty-Boy.* Cambridge, MA: Harvard University Press, 1926.

Sommers, Laurie Kay. *Beaver Island House Party.* East Lansing: Michigan State University Press, 1996.

Telescope. Detroit: Great Lakes Maritime Institute. January–April 2002. p. 5.

Titus, Harold. *Michigan Log Marks.* East Lansing: Michigan State College, 1941.

Wilgus, D. K. *Anglo-American Folksong Scholarship since 1898.* New Brunswick, NJ: Rutgers University Press, 1959.

Zumwalt, Rosemary Lévy. *American Folklore Scholarship: A Dialogue of Dissent.* Bloomington: Indiana University Press, 1988.

A CHRONOLOGY OF IVAN H. WALTON'S WRITING

1935. "Sailor Lore of the Great Lakes." *Michigan History* 19 (autumn): 355–69.

1939. "Michigan Sailor Lore." *Michigan Guide: Federal Writers' Project.* Washington, DC.

1941. "Great Lakes History, 1615–1815." *Michigan History* 25/3–4 (autumn): 276–300.

1941. "Marine Lore." *Michigan: A Guide to the Wolverine State*, 113–35. American Guide Series compiled by workers of the Writer's Program of the Work Projects Administration, sponsored by the Michigan State Administrative Board. [Walton's chapter was the only bylined chapter in this 682-page book.] New York: Oxford University Press.

1942. *Patterns and Perspectives: Essays for College Use.* Ed. with W. Earl Britton, Carl E. Burklund, and William H. Egly. New York: F. S. Crofts, 1942.

1943. "Developments on the Great Lakes, 1815–1943." *Michigan History* 27 (1943): 72–142.

1949. "Ballads of Disasters on the Great Lakes." *New York Folklore Quarterly* (autumn).

1950. "From Michigan's Lumber Camps." Review of *Lore of the Lumber Camps* by E. C. Beck. *Southern Folklore Quarterly*, March 18.

1951. "Songs of the Great Lakes Sailors." *Journal of International Folk Music Council* 3:93–96.

1952. "Folk Singing on Beaver Island." *Midwest Folklore* 2/4: 243–50.

1955. "Eugene O'Neill and the Folklore and Folkways of the Sea." Reprint from *Western Folklore* 14/3: 153–69.

1955. "Indian Place Names in Michigan." *Midwest Folklore* 5/1.

1955. "Nights on Lake Superior." Poem. *Inland Seas* 11/1 (spring): 24–25.

1955. "Origin of Names on the Great Lakes." *Names* 3/4: 239–46.

1958. *Selected Bibliographies of American Folklore in the University of Michigan Libraries.* Ann Arbor. Revised ed., 1960.

1976. "Songs of the Great Lakes." Texts only. *Folklore of Canada.* Ed. Edith Fowke. Toronto: McClelland and Stewart. 196–212.

2002. *Windjammers: Songs of the Great Lakes Sailors.* With Joe Grimm. Detroit: Wayne State University Press.

UNPUBLISHED MANUSCRIPTS

"Songs of the Great Lakes Sailors"
"On Ballad Scholarship"
"Types of Great Lakes Sailor Lore"

Walton Papers and Sound Recordings. Michigan Historical Collections, Bentley Historical Library, University of Michigan, Ann Arbor.

INDEX OF NAMES

indicates informants interviewed by Ivan H. Walton

SUBJECT INDEX

customs officials, 196
Cuyahoga River, Ohio, 164

D. D. Calvin rafting yards, 138–39
Daniel Lyons and Son, Oswego, New York, 224
David Dows (schooner), 105, 152
Death's Door, Wisconsin, 180
Delaware (schooner), 134
Democratic national convention, 34
Detroit, Michigan, 196–200; Burton Library, 27, 29; hiring, 116, 167; passenger destination, 24, 119; in song, 37, 81, 120; saloons, 120, 190
Detroit and Cleveland Navigation Company, 119
Detroit Free Press, 178
Detroit Historical Museum, 76
Detroit River: channels, 214; fuel, 152, 199; racing, 173; scows, 198; in song, 229; in story, 37; tugs, 35, 67, 104–5, 108, 114, 151, 173, 181, 197
Detroit Symphony Orchestra, 178
Dival (brig), 213
dogwatch, 52, 124, 181, 215
Dossin Great Lakes Museum, 76
Douglas Point, Ontario, 184
Duluth, Minnesota, 21, 33, 37, 112, 117, 120, 130, 163, 177, 190

E. C. Roberts (schooner), 104, 107, 116, 137
East Jordan, Michigan, 65
Eastland (passenger steamer), 27, 88
Edenville, Michigan, 215
Elm (schooner), 140
Empire, Michigan, 50
Erastus Corning (schooner), 173
Erie, Pennsylvania, 122, 160, 178, 183
Erieau, Ontario, 122–23
Erie Belle (tug), 196–97
Erie Canal, 45, 92, 137, 147–49, 157, 231
Escanaba (Sand Point), Michigan: iron ore, 70–72, 131, 159, 197–98; lumber, 22, 58, 59; in song, 30, 33, 116, 137, 180
Exile (schooner), 181
Ex-Servicemen's League, 95

Fair Haven, Michigan, 122
Fair Haven, New York, 131
Fairport, Ohio, 160
False Presque Isle, Michigan, 82, 143
Fayette Brown (schooner), 28, 104, 152, 161
Fisher (tug), 181
fishing: boats, 21, 22, 88–89, 180, 104;

commercial, 20, 55, 72, 184–89; illegal, 80, 88; recreational, 42–43; tall tales, 37, 181, 208–9
Flying Cloud (schooner), 32, 226
Fort Gratiot, Michigan, 82, 174
Frankfort, Michigan, 49–50, 211
Frank G. Macauley (tug), 183
Franklin, Pennsylvania, 158
Fremont, Ohio, 172
fruit trade, 17–18

G. J. Boyce (schooner), 77
Garden Island, Michigan, 57
Garden Island, Ontario, 138–39
George A. Marsh (schooner), 71, 189
George C. Finney (schooner), 142
Georgian Bay, Ontario, 39, 64, 72, 106, 138, 139, 184, 185, 190, 191, 196, 220
Gilbert Mollison (schooner), 142, 144, 147
Glad Tidings (gospel ship), 48–49, 59, 68
Goderich, Ontario, 182–88, 192
Golden Dollar Bar, Detroit, Michigan, 120
Golden Fleece (schooner), 104–5, 124
Grand Haven, Michigan, 26–34, 80, 205
Grand Haven Daily Tribune, 27
Grand Marais, Michigan, 137
Grand Rapids, Michigan, 63
Grand Traverse area, Michigan, 204
Grand Trunk, 80
Great Lakes Towing Company, Toledo, Ohio, 160, 171, 173
Green Bay, Wisconsin, 72, 77, 180
greenhorn tales: carrying articles, 182, 191; compass grease, 182; dark light, 182; disturbing the captain, 174, 191, 223; George Washington's grave, 174; Indian attacks, 181; key to the keelson, 182, 191; pirates, 182; serpents, 157; shark lookout, 174; spark watch, 191; spearfish, 181; whitefish schools, 181; whale lookout, 174, 182
Griffin (schooner), 63
Grosse Pointe, Michigan, 219–20
Grosvenor Library, Buffalo, New York, 155, 157

Hamilton, Ohio, 203
Hamilton, Ontario, 134
Hancock, Michigan, 116, 167
Harbor Beach, Michigan (Sand Beach), 194
Harbor Springs, Michigan, 66
Harmsworth Regatta, 141
Hastings (schooner), 142
Hattie Hutt (schooner), 188, 189

Manitoulin Island, 181, 185
Manitowoc (tug), 214
Manitowoc, Wisconsin, 61, 74, 77–79, 159
Manitowoc Shipbuilding Co., 78
Maple Leaf (schooner), 34, 82
Marco Polo (schooner), 29
Margaret MacDonald (fishing boat), 186
Marine City, Michigan, 119
marine hospitals: Chicago, 16, 36, 90, 91–92,
    96–97; Cleveland, 91; Marinette,
    Wisconsin, 72, 73; Marquette, Michigan,
    98, 131, 137, 177, 181, 220
Marine Hospital Service (Public Health and
    Marine Hospital Service or Public Health
    Service), 90
Mary Ludwig (schooner), 99
Mary Margaret (ferry), 215, 218
Marysville, Michigan, 116
Mason Lumber Company, Muskegon,
    Michigan, 123
Mattie (fishing boat), 208–9
Maxwell (schooner), 189
Mechanic (schooner), 79
Menominee, Michigan, 72–73
Mennonites, 112
Merchant Marine, 179
Metropolitan Sound Co., Detroit, Michigan,
    221
Michigan (side-wheel steamer), 160
Michigan Folklore Group, 2, 209
Michigan State University Museum, 2
Midland, Ontario, 190–92
Midland City (side-wheel steamer), 191–92
Milwaukee (railcar ferry), 80, 88
Milwaukee, Wisconsin, 24, 80–86, 99, 211–14,
    215; in song, 116, 137, 177
Milwaukee Belle (schooner), 208
Milwaukee Rescue Mission, 86
Milwaukee River, 212
Milwaukee Tug Boat Line, 80, 81
Minnie Battle (tug), 143
mirages, 98, 156
Misery Bay, Pennsylvania, 160
Mississippi River, 230
Missouri (steamship), 29, 39, 83
Mohawk (steamer), 187
Monsoon (schooner), 48
Moonlight (schooner), 80, 105, 143
Montague, Michigan, 40, 147, 214
Mont Blanc (schooner), 171
Montcalm (schooner), 161
Monticello (schooner), 161
Montmorency (schooner), 161

Montpelier (schooner), 161
Montreal, Quebec, 21, 108, 136, 139, 219
Mormons, 55, 209
Mount Clemens, Michigan, 219
Mount Pleasant, Michigan, vii, 178, 215, 218
Mud Lake, 116
Mueller (lumber barge), 76
Muskegon, Michigan, 33–40, 83; lumber, 53,
    99, 125; strike, 23
Muskegon Chronicle, 34
Muskegon Lake, 36, 37
Muskegon Observer, 35

navigation: barometer, 24, 134, 163, 210; buoys,
    116, 120; charts, 120; compass, 76, 152,
    153; dead reckoning, 47, 131, 179, 204;
    dummy (buoy without a bell), 82;
    foghorns, 26, 50, 103; lack of navigation
    aids, 131, 140; landmarks, 204; lights, 103;
    radios, 50, 120; range finders, 103, 120;
    sextant, 179
Nellie Reddington (schooner), 95
Newaygo County, Michigan, 68
Newberry, Michigan, 64
Newberry Library, Chicago, 95
New York City, 21, 45, 78, 91, 112, 148,
    155, 224
Niagara (tug), 161–62
Niagara River, 226
North American (steamboat), 24
North Channel, 185
Northport, Michigan, 51
Nyland (tug), 181–82

Oak Leaf (schooner), 72
Oakville, Ontario, 126
Ohio (tug), 160
Ohio Canal, 231
Ohio River, 168, 230
Ohio Tankers, Inc., 166
Oliver Cromwell (schooner converted to barge),
    109
Oliver Mowatt (schooner), 151
Ossian Bedell (passenger ferry), 55, 63–64
Oswego, New York, 131, 142–47, 217, 220, 221,
    223–25
Oswego County Historical Collections, 224
Oswego Palladium-Times, 147
Our Son (schooner), 37, 38, 169, 210; last
    commercial sailing vessel, 31, 75–76;
    sinking of, 2, 13, 34, 63
Outer Island Light, Lake Superior, 98

Sheboygan, Wisconsin, 79
Sheldon's Point, New York, 147
Shipmasters' Association, 82, 107, 165
Silver Dollar Bar, Detroit, Michigan, 120
Singapore (schooner), 140
Sister Bay, Wisconsin, 97
Skillagallee. *See* Ile aux Galets
Sleeping Bear, Michigan, 50, 65
socialists, 57, 77, 95
Soo Locks, 119, 167
South American (steamship), 23–24
Southampton, Ontario, 189
South Fox Island, Michigan, 106
South Haven, Michigan, 1, 16–21, 36
Star Hotel, Tonawanda, New York, 154
Steamboat Inspection Service, 38, 95
stowaways, 171
Straits of Mackinac, Michigan, 27, 46, 68–69, 79, 81–83, 86, 95, 118, 119, 125, 138, 173, 197, 218
Stram's Hotel, Ludington, Michigan, 43
Stuart H. Dunn (schooner-barge), 149
Sturgeon Bay, Wisconsin, 35, 72–77, 211, 214
Sturgeon Bay Advocate, 21
Susan Ward (side-wheel steamer), 110
Suttons Bay, Michigan, 49–51
Swallow (packet schooner), 40
Sweepstakes (tug), 82
Sweetheart (schooner), 135
Syracuse, New York, 146, 227

Tashmoo (passenger steamer), 111, 180
Thames, Ontario, 197
Thomas Brown (schooner), 156
Three Bells (schooner), 25
Thunder Bay, Michigan, 82, 118, 143
Tiverton, Ontario, 189
Tobermory, Ontario, 196
Toledo, Ohio, 93, 111, 165, 171–74
Tonawanda, New York, 154–55, 185, 222, 227
top hat, 165, 191
Toronto, Ontario, 102, 127–30, 133, 138, 141, 189, 221
Toronto Evening Telegram, 128, 141, 196
Toronto University, 127
Traverse City, Michigan, 49, 51–53, 58, 204
tugboats: competition, 35, 114, 151, 172–73; rates, 151, 173, 197; seizures, 181–82, 196; strike, 69
Twin Points, Wisconsin, 97
Two Rivers, Wisconsin, 79, 204

Undine (schooner), 134

unions, 28, 55, 70, 106, 132, 152, 227; halls, 16, 38, 41, 85, 90–94; in song, 222–23
U.S. Department of Health and Human Services, 90
U.S. Lifesaving Service, 38, 163
U.S. Lighthouse Service, 38, 66, 67
U.S. Navy, 66, 71, 124, 168, 179
U.S. Shipping Board, 121
U.S. Treasury Department, 90
United States Air Services, vii
University of Chicago, 2, 203
University of Illinois, 2
University of Michigan, vii, 3, 14, 80, 177, 203
University of Michigan Fisheries Research Camp, 46
University of Texas, 178

variety shows, 83, 92, 108, 125, 126, 154–55, 227
Vermilion, Ohio, 169–71
Vernon (schooner), 61, 63
Victor Talking Machine Company, 178
Virginia (steamship), 39

W. S. Ireland (steamship), 122
wages: amount, 28, 159, 165, 180, 214; Lakes vs. ocean, 29, 32, 33, 49, 159
Wahr's, Ann Arbor, Michigan, 29, 32, 67
Walter Vail (schooner), 213
Ward steamship line, 7
Waugoschance Point (Wobble Shanks), Michigan, 53, 64, 68, 81, 118, 169
Waukegan, Illinois, 89, 97–98, 218
Washington Park, Chicago, 95
weather signs: clearing, 134, 190; clouds, 61, 105, 134, 163; feeling it in the bones, 105; frost, 62; gulls, 62, 105, 119, 134; Milky Way (milkmaids' path), 62, 119, 134; new moon, 28, 62, 135; Northern Lights, 62, 134; pigs carrying straw, 62; pig smelling the weather, 145; pointing up or down, 62, 119; rain, 119, 180, 190; rainbows, 61, 118; ring, 105, 118, 134; rising and setting, 118, 144; shooting stars, 119; smoke, 61; stars, 134, 163; sundogs, 61, 105, 118, 163; sunrise, 163; sunset, 134, 163; wet moon, 35; wind, 35, 119, 134, 180, 190
Welland Canal, 97, 132, 135, 137–38, 140, 173, 181, 185
Wellington, Ontario, 133
Wells Burt (schooner), 78, 80
Whitefish Bay, Michigan, 86
Whitefish Point, Michigan, 88, 163

INDEX OF SONG TITLES